COMPANION PIECE

Women Celebrate the Humans, Aliens and Tin Dogs of DOCTOR WHO

Edited by L.M. Myles and Liz Barr

Published by Mad Norwegian Press (www.madnorwegian.com).
Edited by L.M. Myles and Liz Barr. Editor-in-Chief: Lars Pearson.
Cover art by Katy Shuttleworth. Design: Christa Dickson and Adam Holt.
ISBN: 9781935234197. Printed in Illinois. First Printing: February 2015.

Also available from Mad Norwegian Press...

The Geek Girl Chronicles
*Chicks Dig Time Lords: A Celebration of Doctor Who by the Women
Who Love It,* edited by Lynne M. Thomas and Tara O'Shea
(Hugo Award winner, 2011)

*Chicks Dig Gaming: A Celebration of All Things Gaming by the Women
Who Love It,* edited by Jennifer Brozek, Robert Smith? and Lars Pearson

*Whedonistas: A Celebration of the Worlds of Joss Whedon by the Women
Who Love Them,* edited by Lynne M. Thomas and Deborah Stanish

*Chicks Dig Comics: A Celebration of Comic Books by the Women
Who Love Them,* edited by Lynne M. Thomas and Sigrid Ellis

Chicks Unravel Time: Women Journey Through Every Season of Doctor Who,
edited by Deborah Stanish and L.M. Myles

Other Reference Guides/ Essay Books/ Critique Books
Space Helmet for a Cow: The Mad, True Story of Doctor Who
(Vol. 1, 1963-1989) by Paul Kirkley

*Queers Dig Time Lords: A Celebration of Doctor Who by the LGBTQ Fans
Who Love It,* edited by Sigrid Ellis and Michael Damian Thomas

Ahistory: An Unauthorized History of the Doctor Who Universe
[3rd Edition available] by Lance Parkin and Lars Pearson

*Running Through Corridors: Rob and Toby's Marathon Watch
of Doctor Who* (Vol. 1: The 60s) by Robert Shearman and Toby Hadoke

*Wanting to Believe: A Critical Guide to The X-Files, Millennium
and The Lone Gunmen* by Robert Shearman

Dusted: The Unauthorized Guide to Buffy the Vampire Slayer and
Redeemed: The Unauthorized Guide to Angel
by Lars Pearson, Christa Dickson and Lawrence Miles (ebooks only)

The About Time Series by Tat Wood and Lawrence Miles
About Time 1: The Unauthorized Guide to Doctor Who (Seasons 1 to 3)
About Time 2: The Unauthorized Guide to Doctor Who (Seasons 4 to 6)
About Time 3: The Unauthorized Guide to Doctor Who (Seasons 7 to 11)
[2nd Edition available]
About Time 4: The Unauthorized Guide to Doctor Who (Seasons 12 to 17)
About Time 5: The Unauthorized Guide to Doctor Who (Seasons 18 to 21)
About Time 6: The Unauthorized Guide to Doctor Who
(Seasons 22 to 26, the TV Movie)
About Time 7: The Unauthorized Guide to Doctor Who
(Series 1 to 2)

Companion Piece
Table of Contents

Editors' Introduction

The premise of *Doctor Who* is simple and brilliant: an enigmatic man travels the universe in a Police Box that can go anywhere in space and time. It's a story that's been going strong for over five decades and one that's been through countless permutations, yet the core of it remains the same. What that brief summing up fails to mention, however, is another central concept that's remained more or less the same since 1963: the Doctor travels the universe with his companions.

In comparison to the Doctor, the companions of *Doctor Who* have often been overlooked, and worse. They tend to be young, female and human, and – because they lack the Doctor's brilliance, his education and his vast centuries of experience – are too often dismissed as being not as good as, or not as interesting as, the mysterious Time Lord. They are criticized for screaming, the number of times ankles are twisted is vastly exaggerated, and how many times has a new companion been introduced with some variation of the words, "Finally, the Doctor meets his equal"?

The Doctor, so far, has always been male, while the primary companion is almost always female, leading to an easy accusation of sexism and dismissal of the companion's worth, since one character is the extraordinary alien scientist and the other tends to be an ordinary human. But this is too simplistic. It ignores that the companion is the character who grows and develops, while the Doctor remains more or less the same; it ignores that the companion is the viewpoint character that all the audience, male and female, are being asked to identify with; it ignores that *Doctor Who* offers an extraordinary breadth of leading female characters, each one sufficiently developed to have attracted their own share supporters and detractors.

In our fascination with the Doctor, sometimes we forget that it's the companions who step into the vast strangeness of a universe they're not quite ready for; who discover courage and strength they never knew they had; who change and rise, or fall, as they're tempered by their adventures. In *Companion Piece*, we aim to celebrate and critique these characters. We want to show the depth and meaning the companions have for fans, and how they can at times disappoint, but also delight.

Companion Piece
The Impossible Girls

Deborah Stanish is a Philadelphia-area writer and editor. She came to *Doctor Who* in 2005 and has spent countless hours trying to catch up on the 40-plus years she missed. She is the co-editor of the Hugo-nominated *Chicks Unravel Time: Women Journey Through Every Season of Doctor Who* with L.M. Myles and *Whedonistas: A Celebration of the Worlds of Joss Whedon by the Women Who Love Them* with Lynne M. Thomas. Her essays have been published in *Chicks Dig Time Lords, Time, Unincorporated* Volumes II and III, *Outside In: 160 New Perspectives on 160 Classic Doctor Who Stories by 160 Writers* and *Apex Magazine*. She is a regular columnist for *Enlightenment*, the official 'zine of the Doctor Who Information Network, and the moderator of *Verity!* Podcast, where six women from around the globe debate and discuss *Doctor Who*. When not wrangling kids, podcasters or deadlines, she blathers about *Doctor Who*, spies and whatever else has captured her fancy that week at deborahstanish.blogspot.com.

It always starts with a girl. Adventure, mystery, unintentional death... at the heart, there is always some brave, headstrong, sometimes foolish but always marvelous, girl. (Unless the girl is Jamie McCrimmon, but that's a whole different essay.) She is our gateway and guide, our egress into a world filled with unexplainable. We rely on her to be our eyes and, over the course of time, she becomes our heart. She isn't just the Doctor's companion, she is ours.

Doctor Who is complex, both in practice and theory. In the beginning, the edict was to educate and to inform, to take viewers by the hand and lead them down the dual paths of history and science, the knowledge seeping into their subconscious as they were being were being distracted by adventure and hijinks. As the show evolves, the adventure and hijinks break free from the path's border and overrun the story until it becomes the story itself. But there is still a girl, rushing headlong after the Doctor, calling back to us to follow, follow, follow.

This idea of a gateway character is so essential to the story that Russell T Davies made it the first building block in reconstructing *Doctor Who* for the new millennium. We spend the first five and half minutes of the first episode of the rebooted series being introduced to, and becoming intrigued by, "our" companion. Rose Tyler is so central to the new series

8

that her name is the title of the first episode.

But Rose isn't unique. She follows a grand tradition of companions grabbing our hands and pulling us into this new world. In 1963, at the very beginning, Susan Foreman – brilliant, a bit fey and completely endearing – straddles the awkward line between alien and contemporary teen, making her an identity figure for both young and old. In 1996, Grace Holloway asks all the questions that an audience for whom *Doctor Who* was, perhaps, both unknown and foreign would ask. These companions, all firsts in their own way, are critical components to the story and, as gateway characters go, slid neatly into their place and time.

The now iconic image of 76 Totter's Lane, banked in swirling fog, gives little hint to the wonders that will follow, but the first companion team of Barbara, Ian, Susan and the Doctor would have been immediately identifiable to the 1960s audience. The Doctor is the mad scientist, the crotchety grandfather, the mad relative in the attic; Barbara and Ian, the dedicated and concerned teachers bring a sense of authority to the show, one that instantly puts adults at ease. Their compassion and caring are both responsible and comforting. Susan, on the other hand, is something of an unknown quantity. She is a confusing mix of brilliance, hesitance and inquisitiveness. Susan isn't human, but more than that, she is a teenager and, in the early 1960s there is no creature more alien.

From the moment we first see her, fingers skating over the melody of contemporary pop music pouring from the transistor radio pressed to her ear, she is the very embodiment of the Youthquake that was sweeping London: young, hip and full of curiosity. The show aimed squarely for the family demographic and Susan serves a dual purpose: she captures the attention and imagination of younger family members who would have seen a reflection of what was happening in their world and, for adults, she is a gateway not only into the world of *Doctor Who*, but also into the mystifying world of contemporary teens. She is the Youthquake, but with the rough edges smoothed over. She is rebellious, but not too rebellious. And, really, a teenager self-identifying as alien? It explains so much. Parents of teens watching Susan's performance in *The Edge of Destruction* would have sympathized. Possession by the TARDIS and raging teenage hormones aren't all that different on the surface.

Susan should have been the ideal companion. But as she trips through time, she is hindered by two distinct disadvantages: the tendency of the writers to make her the companion in jeopardy, and her proximity to Barbara, who, as the show progressed, arguably became the companion prime for the first Doctor's era. As Barbara's character development and storyline deepens, Susan's role diminishes. While it is difficult to argue against the sheer brilliance that is Barbara Wright, it's not hard to feel a little sad for Susan, who was an idea that was never given the chance to develop as fully as she could have. As a template, however, she is important to the structure of the show, and one that would be used time and again over the next 50 years.

Three "generations" in the TARDIS was an ideal storytelling construct, with each strata having the opportunity to play both the role as teacher and explorer. This construct was considered so important after Susan's departure that another young companion, Vicki, is brought on board to fill the surrogate granddaughter role. Having a teen in the TARDIS not only acted as an identification character, but also served the purpose of fleshing out the Doctor's characterization, whether he's the grandfather/mentor or the giddy co-conspirator. The fact that both of these teen characters end up leaving the TARDIS, in the midst of war, for a boy, is problematic but the star-crossed lover trope is hard to shake and would have seemed appropriate at the time.

Grace Holloway, while not abandoned for love, does have the distinction of being the first companion to share an on-screen snog with the Doctor. While this sent tremors through the Whoniverse, it is only one of the many ways in which Grace opens the door to a new type of story, inviting us along for the ride. The success, or failure, of the TV Movie is a debate for the ages, but there is no doubt this was a new jumping off point and for that, according to a 26-year precedent (except for Jamie, of course), you needed a girl.

You can almost hear the exclamation points behind the adjectives describing Grace. She's modern! A doctor! A humanitarian! American! Yes, the living-in-sin, opera-loving-cardiologist-in-a-ball-gown who manages to kill the Doctor to the strains of Puccini was shaped to be a companion that American audiences would love. More than that, she has the unenviable task of introducing the resurrected bones of a British cultural institution to a new audience which would, fingers crossed, love it enough to provide the lightning strike of funds and ratings to bring it back from the dead.

Grace, unlike Susan, has to ask the questions, has to demand explanations, has to force the Doctor to drip exposition all over the screen and she does so with a sense of disbelief and wonder that feels entirely natural. For American audiences, Grace is a familiar character. Her "disillusioned career girl" story has been told over and over again in television movies and dramas. Tropes, after all, can be effective storytelling shortcuts, especially in a story that tries, desperately, to cram a generation's worth of backstory into 89 minutes. Without Grace, the audience would have been lost. This is a story that was serving far too many masters (pun intended), but Grace manages to shine.

Once she and, by default, the viewer buys into the story, she proves herself to be an able companion. Grace assists the Doctor in defeating the Master in sequences worthy of any superhero movie. This is *Doctor Who* for a new age and by gosh, we're going to throw some good-old American action scenes in to prove it! In a twist that will become a trope post-2005, it is actually Grace that saves the world from destruction and sacrifices herself to save the Doctor. The tone and scenery may have changed from the days of old, but the feeling of being involved in something bigger than yourself; that, at the very heart of it, the Doctor is important and what he does even more so, shines through all the flat accents and Hollywood flash.

And Grace is, so very much, us. Her gradual acceptance is organic. She leads us to a place where we're rooting for this mad bastard even though we are equal parts fascinated and terrified. And, at the end, when faced with a choice to accompany the Doctor or stay and try to rebuild her life, she chooses to stay. Running is always the easiest option and Grace, the plucky American, will stand her ground and see things through. Her role is finished, she's done her job and now it is up to the Doctor to carry on. Her obligation to us is finished as well. She has led us to the Doctor, introduced him and shown us how important he is, what we do with him is our decision. Well, ours and Universal's, but corporate shenanigans are a different sort of evil and far more difficult to defeat.

In 2003, the decision of what to do with the Doctor is once more asked and answered. *Doctor Who* will again be resurrected, but for this iteration the series looks backwards, shedding the trappings of Hollywood and becoming almost aggressively British. And Rose Tyler, so very grounded in London, has the distinction of not only being the companion to introduce us to this new series, she becomes the focus of the story itself. After *The Parting of the Ways*, viewers gasped and frantically reviewed recorded episodes trying to tease out the hints of Bad Wolf that we had all but ignored during the previous 12 episodes. Even more important than the reintroduction of a season-long arc, Rose's life and her family provide fodder throughout her time on the TARDIS in a way that we had never seen before. This is a companion with roots and a production team that aren't afraid to exploit them.

While the series pays homage to its history, choosing to honor rather than ignore, some significant changes are made, once again pulling the property forward in time. Received Pronunciation is chucked out the window; both the Doctor and Rose wrap their dialogue in working-class accents. The Doctor, in his leather jacket and boots, is rough around the edges, and Rose flirts with the chav tropes that dog kids from the council estates. This *Doctor Who* is gritty and real and adds a bit of sexual tension – hetero, homo and omni – to the mix.

It's a breath of fresh air that is counting on a girl to carry it off. Just as Susan was immediately recognizable to her contemporaries in 1963, Rose is that girl waiting at the bus stop, an every-girl, rocking a Punkyfish hoodie, working in shop, hanging with her boy and arguing with her mum. We know her, we *are* her. Even if she is younger/older/blonder than we are, she feeds into the near-universal longing of "wanting something more" that sizzles beneath our skins.

Rose also has the dubious privilege of kicking off the thread that runs through nearly all of the new series: the Companion as the Mystery. They may be traveling through time and space saving worlds and conquering evil, but the central mystery is always closer to home, or the center console, in Rose's case. All new series companions are tangled in a mystery, bookended by the Bad Wolf of Series One and The Impossible Girl of Series Seven. While the concept is now a bit worn around the edges it was, in 2005-2006, fresh and exciting. Here was a story with depth and arc and resonance!

Most importantly, Rose helps us through our first modern regeneration. For brand new fans that aren't steeped in the mythos of Time Lords, watching the Doctor morph into a new character is staggering. Very quickly, the new series had become a phenomenon and it is Rose's presence that stabilized the ground under the feet of a newly devoted fanbase. Just as Patrick Troughton's brilliant performance as the second Doctor helped fans transition to the whole concept of shifting faces and personalities for the title character, Rose eases the way for David Tennant to do the same thing, helping to ensure the series' continued success.

While some fans feel that her continued presence, both on screen and in the writer's memories, ended up being a deterrent to the story, it is impossible to deny her impact on the success of the new series. It is a testament to her importance that she and the tenth Doctor returned for the fiftieth anniversary episode. She set the tone for the "new" companion: independent, flirty and fiercely loyal, but who wasn't afraid of the messy entanglements of a life on Earth. She wasn't perfect and we loved her for that.

It is a heavy responsibility we put on the companion's shoulders. We look to them to be all things to both the Doctor and to the viewers, but no companions carried the burden more so than the very first ones. As *Doctor Who* morphed from an education served up at tea time to a cultural institution beloved worldwide these girls... no, *women*: Susan, Grace and Rose led us through the TARDIS doors with a come-hither smile. And someday, after the series rests a bit and some bright new thing shakes off the dust and breathes new life back into its bones, a new companion will extend the same invitation and we will accept. How could we not? It's the invitation to the adventure of a lifetime.

Companion Piece

That Nitro-9 You're Not Carrying: Violence and the Companion

Seanan McGuire started watching *Doctor Who* at the ripe old age of three, and holds it largely responsible for her lifelong passion for the genre. She wanted to grow up to be a Time Lady, but considers growing up to be a novelist a pretty good second place. Seanan has been nominated for some awards, and has won some awards, and has written quite a few books, which makes her very happy. She lives on the West Coast of North America with two abnormally large blue cats, a staggering number of horror movies and an even more staggering number of books. Her first Doctor was number three, but it was number seven who really stole her heart. She drinks too much soda to be strictly healthy, and doesn't sleep much. Follow her at seananmcguire.com, or on Twitter as @seananmcguire.

> "Ace, give me some of that Nitro-9 that you're not carrying. Quickly!"
>
> —The seventh Doctor to Ace, *Remembrance of the Daleks*

o. Sticks and Stones

This is an essay about companions of the Doctor and not my childhood, but I still want to open with an anecdote to illustrate why all types of companion are so important. Specifically:

When I was growing up, the true Golden Rule – before even "do unto others as you would have done unto you" and "do not feed bugs to your sister" – was "there is no excuse for hitting or kicking, ever, no matter what somebody may have done to you first." I knew this was untrue even before I started kindergarten, but just try telling that to the adults who controlled the universe. Violence Was Bad. No matter the situation, no matter the justification, Violence Was Bad, and girls who were violent, for any reason, were doing something wrong. Being a child who was perhaps overly fixated on being Good, I embraced the idea that if I hit anyone, ever, for any reason, I would be eternally cast down into the ranks of the Bad Children, and my life thus far would have been for naught.

Ever tried not to punch someone while being pinned down on a creek bed and having your face shoved into the muddy, crawfish-infested water? Because I assure you, if they gave medals for misguided childhood determination, I would have won one. *On the spot.* And then my savior arrived.

Leela of the Sevateem.

Introduced in *The Face of Evil*, Leela was a throwback, a primitive warrior from a devolved society. She was never seen without her trusty knife, she preferred to wear form-fitting leather "cavegirl" outfits, as she found them easy to move and hunt in, and she would cut you. Insult Leela or endanger her Doctor, and you could expect to be on the receiving end of a rather pointed smackdown. Leela traveled with the Doctor. The Doctor was essentially the definition of a force for good in the universe. Ergo, if Leela traveled with the Doctor, Leela was good. If Leela was good, then that meant it was occasionally okay to be a little bit violent, when the situation called for it.

1. Kiss With a Fist

While every *Doctor Who* fan probably has their own "one true companion," the greatest strength of the people who have traveled with the Doctor is their diversity. We have had ladies and we have had punks; we have had scientists and we have had flight attendants. There is, has been, or will be someone in the TARDIS for every one of us, although certain personality traits appear more often than others, either because they possess wide audience appeal or because they make for interesting stories.

Enter violence and the companion.

The Doctor has had multiple companions who were capable of aggression when it was called for, from Jamie McCrimmon – a Scottish piper from the eighteenth century – to Brigadier Lethbridge-Stewart who, you know, helped found UNIT. So there's that. But there have only been three companions whose personalities were really based around their quick tempers and willingness to solve problems with immediate and if necessary, extreme, levels of force. These are Leela of the Sevateem (fourth Doctor), Ace (seventh Doctor) and Amelia Pond (eleventh Doctor).

For purposes of this discussion, we are defining "violence" as a physical response to threat, not necessarily intended to be deadly, but definitely as a first reaction, rather than a well-considered choice. This is why River Song, who carries a firearm and is scary enough to intimidate a Dalek into begging for mercy, has been omitted: she never does anything without thinking about it first. If River pulls a gun on you, you had best make your peace with the god or gods of your choice. If Ace blows up your car, well... it's probably Thursday. This is also why Captain Jack Harkness, a former Time Agent, has been left out of the greater discussion. Jack and River are arguably the most militant of the Doctor's companions, and are among the most likely to consider violence as an option. This does not make them inherently violent. For Jack and River, violence is a tool. For Leela, Ace and Amy, violence is immediate and often unthinking.

Sara Kingdom, often regarded as the most aggressive of the first Doctor's companions, has also been omitted from this discussion. She was a trained security officer, and like Jack and River, her use of violence was always well considered and supported by her training. We're looking at visceral reactions in this essay, although there is plenty of ground to be plumbed by comparing innate violence with learned violence.

It is also important to note that, as I discovered in childhood, violence is not inherently bad. Leela moves to protect the things she loves and to protect herself. She does not react with deadly force unless the situation demands it – and sometimes, unfortunately, the situation does demand it. Ace is often belligerent and willing to present herself as more dangerous than she is, but this is largely for show, and is not matched by the sort of aggression that would take her out of the good column (and probably out of the TARDIS, as the Doctor has little patience for that sort of thing). Finally, there is Amy, whose tendency to slap people for small offenses is potentially the most problematic of our three, but who has never been seen to react dramatically out of proportion to what is happening around her.

There is an entire discussion to be had around whether violence is ever acceptable, and whether my starting premise of "some violence is healthy and not inherently wrong" is in fact correct. That being said, we have to start somewhere. So...

1. We have defined violence in this case as "a rapid and visceral response."

2. We are operating from the position that sometimes violence is a healthy and human reaction, and can even be positive if channeled correctly, rather than used as a justification for bad behavior.

Now that we're all on the same page, let's begin.

2. Bunny Fur Barbarians

Leela of the Sevateem first appeared on screen in 1977, and was intended to serve as the Doctor's Eliza Doolittle, a woman that he could civilize and mold in his own more respectable image. It is debatable whether he ever succeeded, as Leela had little interest in being turned into "a civilized woman." She was much happier being herself, even if maintaining that sense of self wasn't always easy as travel and experience broadened her horizons. By the end of her tenure in the TARDIS, Leela had mellowed without losing her dangerous edge, and was well suited to her new life on Gallifrey. Her time with the Doctor taught her a great many things. It never taught her to put down her knife, and that's a good thing. Leela's sense of self was in many ways tied to her upbringing, and her upbringing made her a warrior and a fierce protector. No one was going to hurt the people she cared about on her watch. Given the fourth Doctor's propensity for wandering wide-eyed and grinning into danger, this may be the only reason we took so long to get to number five.

Possibly apocryphal accounts state that Tom Baker originally disliked the character of Leela, finding her too violent for the show. This may actually have informed her performances: there's a fire to Leela that speaks of true actress investment, something that is easily explained by pointing out a personal stake in immediate acceptance. This is pure conjecture, however; it may just be that Louise Jameson was a fabulous actress (something I have no trouble believing).

From the beginning, Leela was quick to anger and to action, fierce in her defense of her territory, and fearless in the face of danger. These traits would not lessen during her tenure on the show, and even into the present day, Leela remains one of the most active and dangerous of the Doctor's companions. Not too bad for a primitive girl from the Sevateem.

Leela was in some ways a stereotypical example of the "cavegirl" cliché: Stone Age weapons, innocently sexy fashions, inexplicably good dentistry, and an endless supply of questions about the world around her. But she was also smart, and strong, and while her impulsiveness got both her and the Doctor into trouble, her curiosity was just as likely to save them as it was to put them in danger. By allowing her to leave the TARDIS essentially "untamed," the show made some very deep, if potentially accidental, statements about remaining true to your origins while also striving to become more than what you were when your journey began.

3. The Tea is Getting Cold

Of the three companions we are considering today, Ace is the only one not to receive an official, canonical send-off. She was the final television companion of the seventh Doctor (Sylvester McCoy), and the last shot of the original televised run of *Doctor Who* has her walking off into the sunset as the Doctor tells her about all the amazing adventures they still have ahead of them. I consider it one of the great tragedies of the cancellation (or hiatus, or whatever you want to call it) that we didn't get to see Ace's story completed.

If Leela was a primal character, whose violent reactions and reflexes were justified by her coming from a "less civilized" world, then Ace was a modern character, a confused and conflicted teen who was working her way through her problems in the best way she knew. It is perhaps unfortunate that the best way she knew involved blowing things up on a regular basis – when not beating the crap out of them with a baseball bat – but then again, maybe not. Ace was processing a lot of anger. Ace had good reasons to be angry. And Ace had access to a lot of explosives. So that worked out.

It is interesting to note that Ace, due to her arsenal of unstable explosives (the most famous of which, Nitro-9, I spent much of high school trying to recreate in the chemistry lab), was potentially the most dangerous of the Doctor's companions. River or Captain Jack could shoot you. Ace could blow up the whole building, with you inside it. She had the most capacity for wide-scale destruction, and yet channeled this potential largely in positive ways. Sure, she blew up a few quarries, but for the most part, she kept her explosives under wraps until the Doctor told her that she was clear to make the difficulties of the day go "boom."

Out of all of the Doctor's companions, Ace was the one I most identified with, and the one that I still do. She came from a troubled home situation; she was too smart in some ways for the school system, and too dumb in others; she was looking for a way to fit into the world. She latched onto the Doctor as a mentor and as something of a father figure, a replacement for all the adults who hadn't been there earlier in her life. It is thus interesting that even when his approval clearly mattered more to her than anything else in the universe, she insisted on remaining herself. She didn't stop carrying dangerous explosives just because the Doctor told her to; she didn't start second-guessing before picking up the baseball bat. Ace settles into the shape of her own skin. She does not redefine it for the sake of someone else.

Ace's violence is both distanced compared to Leela's or Amy's – she uses explosives preferentially, rather than a knife or her own fists – and as time goes on, more concentrated. She knows that her actions have the potential to kill, and so focuses them tightly on clearly defined enemies. It is no coincidence that of the potential futures suggested for Ace, one has her entering the Academy of Gallifrey (and presumably becoming a Time Lady, through some unknown mechanism), while another has her becoming Time's Vigilante, a law enforcement figure whose job is similar to the Doctor's, if on a smaller scale. She was in many ways shaped and defined by her tenure with the Doctor, and a final fate which placed her eternally within the ranks of the Time Lords would not have been out of line with her character. (While biologically human, both River Song and the eventual fate of Leela have shown that Gallifreyan genetics are flexible things. A little time in the company of Rassilon would have cleared that whole "born on Earth" problem right up. But I digress.)

Ace's last appearance in *Survival* (1989) very clearly illustrated the difference between her normal brand of "civilized" violence, which did a lot of property damage but didn't necessarily result in any injuries, and uncivilized violence, which runs and hunts and kills with little concern for the consequences. In the end, Ace was able to reject a lack of civilization, returning to her usual self, but did not reject that core components of that self: she would continue to fight for, and continue to protect, the things that she held dear.

Not a bad overall journey for a storm-swept girl from Perivale.

4. The Girl Who Waited

At last, we come to Amelia "Amy" Pond, who is, as I mentioned before, potentially the most problematic example of violent impulses in the Doctor's companions. In her very first appearance (*The Eleventh Hour*, 2010), she knocks out the eleventh Doctor and handcuffs him to a radiator. This was a perhaps understandable reaction, given that he'd just appeared inside her house without an invitation, but this sort of casual "hit first, ask questions later" approach would continue throughout her tenure.

I adore Amy as a character and as a companion, but I cannot deny the fact that her temper is a problematic, if realistic, character trait. Had the "slap your partner whenever things become stressful" tendencies been given to her fiancé and eventual husband, Rory, I doubt that he would have made it out of development and onto the show, much less out of Leadworth and onto the TARDIS. Because there is a certain amount of "violence is funny when it's female on male" double standard in our media, Amy was allowed to appear as Amy.

In many ways, despite the problematic aspects of Amy's character which I have pointed out above, this was a good thing. Amy is not presented as perfect, but she is presented as essentially good. She is surrounded by people who love her for who she is and for what she represents to them. Saying "we love her even though she is not some paragon of feminine ideals" is actually a wonderful thing. Would it have been nice to see Amy's temper more seriously addressed on the show, rather than written off as "oh, that's Amy" or the even more straightforward and dismissive "Scottish"? Yes. Absolutely. But she was granted a level of physicality that is normally reserved for male characters in media, and while the ways in which she used it were not always without their questionable aspects, she was never asked to change herself to be more like some female ideal.

Amy's violent impulses are more like Leela's than Ace's in many ways: they are primal and unthinking, and they put her very close to the action. There is no desire to remove herself from the conflict, not for Amy; she's going to be right up there on the front lines, forcing her way into whatever space she feels she can fit. Her actions are often driven by anger, but they are also based in a strong urge to protect. When she slaps the Doctor or Rory, it is usually because they have frightened her, or endangered themselves, and she is trying to remind them that these behaviors are not acceptable. (Again, slapping your friends because they scared you is maybe not such a good idea. At the same time, it is a very human impulse, and one that many people have acted on at least once in their lives.)

Like Leela before her, Amy was able to move through her entire character arc within the confines of the show, growing from an impulsive, emotionally damaged young woman to a more centered adult who had found passions both inside and outside her home. She found love; she had a child. She made her own choices, and she stood by them, even when they were not the choices that other people – even the Doctor – would have made for her.

In the end, while Amy's form of violence is not without its issues, it is a true and clear demonstration of who she is: fierce, protective and unafraid to confront the things that scare her. These are all valuable qualities, even if I maybe wish that Amy would spend a little less time slapping people.

5. Boom Boom Pow

Every companion of the Doctor has had their moments of heroism, and yes, their moments of violence: it's a part of the experience of travel. You cannot be put into constant danger and not eventually raise a hand to protect yourself and the people you are traveling with. But Leela, Ace and Amy represent the truest form of violence, the id that acts without hesitation or consideration for the consequences that might follow. They are a triptych, and they are unique. It is a statement on *Doctor Who* as a whole that it has given us three such women with so much in common, and so much that each of them holds absolute and without overlap.

I have loved all three of them, and I love them still, for the lessons they have taught me and the lessons they have yet to teach. Like sometimes, even if hitting should be the last resort, you can go ahead and push the bigger kids who are trying to drown you. It's okay.

The Doctor said so.

Companion Piece

Scheherazade and Galahad in an Exciting Adventure with the Daleks

Mags L. Halliday has been writing about, or for, *Doctor Who* since the late-80s. Her work includes a BBC novel, *History 101*, and various *Short Trips* along with work for the Bernice Summerfield, Faction Paradox and Iris Wildthyme ranges. Her more recent fiction includes a Sherlock Holmes story set on the Necropolis Railway. She gets strange looks when reading research books in a pizza place near the British Museum.

In 1981, I carefully loaded some black and white film into my dad's camera and pointed it at the television. I took a roll of shots as the first episode of *Doctor Who* was broadcast again for the first time in 18 years. From the prints I got back, only one was clear: I got an enlargement and kept it above my desk. For years afterwards, I saw Barbara Wright and Ian Chesterton's confused wonder at the inside the TARDIS every day. Over 50 years since they started the adventure in time and space, they've retained an iconic status for many fans and creators.

I'm going to look at Barbara and Ian not only as televisual companions to the Doctor, but as icons within the wider worlds of *Doctor Who*. Who were they, why were they key to the success of the series, and why do we still keep returning to them over 50 years after Ian was the first person to say "but it was just a police box"?

Barbara and Ian are the first companions to join the Doctor when he is traveling. The implication, from *An Unearthly Child* (1963) to *The Name of the Doctor* (2013), is that the Doctor and Susan left Gallifrey together. So Barbara and Ian serve a dual purpose in the first season of *Doctor Who*. They are the audience viewpoint: the regular, everyday people who feel the alien sand beneath their feet, and watch strange birds wheel in other skies. And they are also the agents of change: by bursting into the TARDIS, they disrupt the Doctor and Susan's world, causing the Doctor to run once more. And he's still running all this time later.

Barbara and Ian may seem unlikely viewpoint figures now, as they are impossible to replicate. They are contemporary, as most companions are, yet they are products of a time now as alien as Aridius. Although their ages are never specified, they are old enough to have grown up during World War II.

Ian is the right age to have seen National Service, 18 months of military conscription for all young men between 17 and 21 years old. He could easily have seen active service in the Korean War or the Suez crisis. The next contemporary male companion, Ben, is not a conscript, but a peacetime voluntary recruit to the Navy.[1]

It is simply impossible to have a contemporary male companion with Ian's mix of life experience. He's from a generation that saw the arrival of the National Health Service, the end of rationing, the death of a king. Ian is a male companion from before the dominance of youth culture and there is a sense, with Ian, that he is a grown-up.

Barbara, too, is hard to imagine as a twenty-first century woman. We have career women like Martha, and teachers like Clara, but they're not portrayed as grown-ups in the way that Barbara is. You can't imagine Clara sternly telling a younger girl to get over it, as Barbara does to Vicki after killing her "pet" in *The Rescue*. Like Ian, Barbara would have been raised in the kind of post-war austerity that would make twenty-first century people blanche.

One of my favorite character notes, though, is not her sternness but that she is making Vicki a dress in *The Chase*. It looks like such a strange thing to do now, in the world of infinite TARDIS wardrobes and "disposable" sweatshop T-shirts, but there she is, trying to cut a pattern on the TARDIS floor. That, more than the (obviously awesome) bouffant hair and sensible ballet pump shoes, marks Barbara out as different from every companion since.

Dig back, though, and both Barbara and Ian are designed to appeal to the audience in very precise ways. Barbara was to be "a handsome well-dressed heroine, aged about 30" to appeal to the older women and Ian was "the handsome young man hero" to appeal to older children. By which the program makers mean anyone over 15.

There were several drafts of their characters. Lola McGovern was to be "timid, but capable of sudden rabbit courage" who tended to get in danger, and Cliff was to be "a gorgeous dish" who can even be "brainy, in a diffident sort of way." Verity Lambert, and the rest of the nascent

---

1 In fact, except for Jamie, all the male companions after Ian and until Adric, are in some form of active – but peacetime – military service.

production team, sensibly toughened Barbara up and gave Ian rather more smarts. Combined, they became the heart and soul of the first TARDIS crew, and did their most important narrative function: they sold us the very idea of the show.

It is Barbara and Ian's acceptance of the TARDIS that enables us, as viewers, to accept it. The first 14 minutes of *Doctor Who* is a mystery story shot in a realist style. Who is this strange girl they teach, with her ideas about decimal currency in the UK and boredom with litmus paper? Barbara and Ian decide to investigate, in a gloomy fog, and find an even stranger, aggressive, old man. So far, the world of the show is our world. Everyone knew a kid who didn't quite fit at school, everyone has let their imagination run away with them, everyone has met a grumpy old man.

But when Barbara and Ian burst their way into the box that hums, they fall into an alien world. Todorov's theory of the fantastic posits the moment where the protagonist has to decide if what they are seeing is real (and the laws of the universe are different to what was previously believed) or an illusion. By having two audience viewpoints, *An Unearthly Child* manages to get both. Barbara believes the laws of the universe have changed first, whilst Ian continues to deny it.

> **The Doctor:** You still think it's all an illusion?
> **Ian:** I know that free movement in time and space is a scientific dream I don't expect to find solved in a junkyard.

When Ian finally believes, when he feels the alien sand beneath his feet, we too believe, and buy into the illusion that this is real within what has, until then, been a realist world. We accept free movement in time and space can be found in a junkyard because two very ordinary people have accepted it.

There's a second function they serve: over the course of the first year of the show, Barbara and Ian change the Doctor from the violent, selfish old man willing to brain someone with a rock, to someone capable of jokes, empathy and compassion. Yes, he lectures Barbara on her desire to save the Aztecs, but he also understands her sense of futility when she fails.

Barbara challenges the Doctor in a way that Susan would never dare to, and without the scoffing Ian employs. She cares, and argues from a position that – whilst maybe uncomfortably colonial now – wants everyone to live the best lives possible. You can easily imagine her sat in a Soho jazz club in the early 60s, vehemently arguing with someone over the rights of others.

What is curious about Barbara and Ian, aside from their sheer determination to go adventuring in time and space in cardigans, is their adultness. The characters were created in a period when teenagers were still something slightly bemusing, and by your mid/late 20s, you were fully grown-up. In *An Unearthly Child*, Ian is shown as being the embarrassing teacher who knows about pop music even though he is in his late 20s.[2] Even by 1965, this attitude – that there is a clear line between child and adult – is changing: in *The Chase*, both Barbara and Ian have heard of, and like, The Beatles.

Not only are Barbara and Ian coded as adults, but both Susan and Vicki are coded as children. When Barbara kills Sandy, her response is that of an adult telling a child to behave, rather than as an older person comforting a younger one. Their roles as teachers give them an authority that only a few companions have had since. This may be one reason why the character who is the first to encounter an utterly alien Dalek is Barbara. If she as an adult, an authority figure, finds these so frightening that she breaks her composure, then they really must be terrifying.

Before the BBC started their slow video release schedule in the mid-80s, the only way to experience old stories was through the novelizations. British Satellite Broadcast's Galaxy channel briefly ran old *Doctor Who* episodes in 1990, but had an audience in the thousands, needed a satellite dish and didn't repeat much of the black and white stuff anyway. The only mass market means of exploring Hartnell stories was to read the novelizations.

And of all the novelizations, the 1964 *Doctor Who in an Exciting Adventure with the Daleks* by David Whitaker was the first. Whitaker writes not merely an exciting but a *romantic* adventure. Any reader familiar with pulp romance will recognize the plot line in which the hero fails to recognize that the heroine has romantic feelings for him until the last page.

The romantic subtext of the original television version is made text by Whitaker's novelization. And that feeds back into the show. Whitaker's novelization – the first chance for anyone to re-experience a televised *Doctor Who* story – is published on November 12, 1964. *The Romans* goes into recording on November 18, 1964. And suddenly Barbara and Ian are acting like a couple, giddy like teenagers as they

---

2 Tom Lehrer's quip about "pop music and other children's ditties" in 1959 springs to mind.

lounge around a sunny villa. It's key to note the script doesn't indicate any change in the relationship – only the way it is played is different.

The next Whitaker novelization takes the romantic theme yet further. 1965's *The Crusaders* is supposedly set during a time of courtly chivalrous romance (although any historian would point out the fallacy of that). Ian becomes Sir Galahad to Barbara's Scheherazade. Not only does the novelization go further in suggesting the potential fate of Barbara – complete with illustration of her about to be whipped – but it adds a scene where the romance narrative crashes into the adventure story.

As a young teenage girl – equally fascinated by *Doctor Who*, *Jackie*[3] and boys – I found myself reading the novelizations seeking illicit romances. It was the 1980s, and like many other nascent fans, I'd discovered simple textual analysis and sought to apply it just about everywhere. I'd read a new novelization on publication, because here was a "new" story. But then during half-term holidays, I'd read all the stories about a specific pairing of companions, reading (or perhaps creating) a romantic subplot. So I'd read all the Jo and Mike stories (a tragic tale of missed opportunities culminating in treachery and transcendental meditation). Or all the Sarah and Harry stories (poor, silly old-fashioned Harry falling for a modern woman). But there was one scene in *The Crusaders* that blew them all out of the water:

> Barbara looked across at Ian, stretched out a hand and held his. A dozen unsaid words hung between them in the understanding of that moment. Modern people though they were, they had stepped into a world of chivalry and barbarism and Ian had not failed her. She had needed him and he had come for her. She knew, whatever the age, whatever the place, whatever the circumstances, he would measure up to her every expectation.
>
> She leant across from her horse, put her arm around his neck and kissed him softly on the lips.

I reread the novelization, as part of researching Barbara and Ian, and I was still surprised now by how startling that passage feels. This was *Doctor Who*, not a Silhouette romance! Even today, *Doctor Who* is frequently coded as a male, asexual format. It's about adventures in time and space, not kissing. And some elements of fandom feel adding romance to the series since 2005 has weakened what *Doctor Who* "should" be. But there it is, in a page from 1965: Barbara kisses Ian.

---

3 A teen magazine with photo-romances and pin-ups.

And that word order matters. It is Barbara who initiates their intimacy and this is something that recurs in all the Missing Adventures and Past Doctor Adventures and the Whatever-we-call-them-now Adventures. Barbara kisses Ian. In *The Eleventh Tiger*, she initiates sex, and proposes they marry. In *The Time Travellers*, for all Ian's attempts to express what he feels, it is Barbara who initiates their kisses at the end.

This romantic agency matters. In a period where the Doctor can act like an old-fashioned patriarch and "hand over" Susan to her suitor, Whitaker chose to make Barbara the one with control over her love life. He could just have easily had Ian kiss Barbara. As a reader, as a fan, I was being told Barbara dictated the terms of their relationship. It's unsurprising that I began admiring her.

The three 1960s novelizations were republished by Target books in the 1970s, and were the main way of "seeing" Barbara and Ian. There was the 1965 Amicus *Dr Who and the Daleks* film as well, but you were reliant upon it being shown on terrestrial television, or a local cinema showing a battered print of it on a Saturday matinee.

In the 1970s, Target began churning out novelizations in mass-market paperback form. Their primary focus was on the "current" show. Between 1973 and 1980, the Hartnell period was only represented by five novelizations. There were the reprints of the 1960s novelizations, plus two other iconic stories (*The Dalek Invasion of Earth* and *The Tenth Planet*).

By 1980, the publishers realized that their books sold not only to millions of children but also to collectors. Fandom had arrived, and we changed the business model. Collectors didn't pick a book because the cover had that monster from last month on it: we bought everything. Target realized there was a market not only for contemporaneous stories, but for the back catalogue of untouched 1960s stories. Between 1980 and 1990, all 22 remaining Hartnell stories were novelized.

In 1982, I stood in a bookshop beneath Birmingham New Street station staring at the motherload of Targets. I had a copy of every novelization stocked in my home city's W H Smith & Son, and I'd borrowed every hardback from the local library. But here were shelves of paperbacks! And a display with trilogy box sets. I couldn't decide what to spend my pocket money on. I picked up *An Unearthly Child* by Terrance Dicks.

There is a whole generation of fans who grew up experiencing earlier *Doctor Who* purely in this novelization form. When you talk to the people who wrote for fanzines and *Doctor Who* between 1989 and now, most of us learnt our *Who* lore from Whitaker, Dicks and Malcolm Hulke. These were the only way to revisit the stories, in the pre-video days, so how they decided to portray the characters and stories is how we perceived them to be. Whitaker, by making Barbara and Ian's romance an explicit part of the ongoing story, created a key theme that was continued into the 1980s novelizations.

Rereading that 1980s tranche recently, I was struck by how often the trope of unresolved sexual tension is used in some way. Sometimes, it's minor things such as Barbara and Ian hugging "for at least ten seconds" in Terrance Dicks' *The Dalek Invasion of Earth* and John Peel's *The Chase*. In Donald Cotton's *The Romans*, it is Ian's constant worry the headmaster will think they have eloped. My favorite, however, is Ian Marter's version of *The Reign of Terror*, which reads more like a Georgette Heyer[4] historical romance than a *Doctor Who* story. The physical similarity between Ian and Léon Colbert is drawn out, so that Barbara's attraction to Léon is clearly a sublimated attraction to Ian. And the book includes moments like:

> Léon looked at her and for a moment she thought he was about to seize her and kiss her passionately. But the moment passed.
> ...
> Colbert paused in the doorway. Again he seemed to be on the brink of rushing across to embrace her like a young blood out of an adventure story.

With these as our source material, it cannot be surprising that fanzines and then the official original novels produced by the pre-video generation of fans unfailingly treat Barbara and Ian as a couple. We'd been conditioned to perceive them as grown-ups with a secret – or not so secret – passion.

The first original novel to suggest that Barbara and Ian married once they returned to Earth is, in fact, *Timewyrm: Revelation* by Paul Cornell. That novel contains mention of Johnny Chess, a pop star whose real name is John Chesterton. In 80s fanzines, Cornell, Keith Topping and others had created a narrative in which Barbara and Ian marry, have a son (John), survive Barbara's cancer treatment and lead a happy life together.

4 Heyer pretty much created the historical romance genre, writing 32 novels set in the Georgian period between 1926 and 1972.

This fan narrative is brought into the original novels in the 1990s, in stories such as *The Face of the Enemy* and *Byzantium!*. Even the novels that don't stick to this narrative still buy in to the idea of Barbara and Ian as a couple.

A classic fanfiction plot – used for all kinds of stories from plot-what-plot fluff to high-flown romance – is that two characters with unresolved sexual tension are obliged to pretend to be a couple. It could be Mulder and Scully on a case on honeymoon cruiseship, or Bodie and Doyle doing a whole other kind of cruising in 1970s Manchester. Whatever the nominal reason, the aim of the plot device is that the two characters are brought into a situation where what they are pretending to be outside is how they secretly feel inside. Any physical contact is fraught with unacknowledged emotion and maybe, just maybe, they'll realize they are in love 4EVA.

There are no television stories, futuristic or historical, where Barbara and Ian pretend to be a married couple. You could argue they are acting as a couple in the final episode of *The Reign of Terror*, when they pretend to be running a pub in order to spy on Napoleon, but it is a fleeting pretence. In *The Aztecs*, Ian is a chosen warrior to Barbara's god. In *Marco Polo*, they never define themselves as anything other than traveling companions. In *The Romans*, they are friends. In *The Crusades*, Ian refers to Barbara as "a lady" when "my wife" may have made more sense to King Richard.

Open a historical original novel, and they'll be pretending to be married within two pages. In *The Witch Hunters*, the Doctor is horrified to find them sharing a room as Goodman and Goodwife Chesterton, until Ian says he sleeps on the floor. In *The Plotters*, they pretend to be married when they are in a pub. They spend the rest of the novel separated, but attempting to find their "spouse." Gareth Roberts takes a leaf from Ian Marter's style of writing when he reunites them:

> Ian crashed into Barbara's arms. She looked into his wounded brown eyes and felt like crying, 'Ian, Ian,' she sobbed. She pressed her head against his sturdy masculine shoulder and pummelled his upper back with her fist. The relief she felt was intoxicating.

Given the rest of *The Plotters* is a farcical Shakespearean romp, with gunpowder, I suspect Roberts was sending up the by-then established Barbara/Ian romantic trope.

In *The Eleventh Tiger*, set after *The Romans* and *The Web Planet*,

Barbara and Ian are not pretending to be married. There is no sub-textual coded romance. Instead, a lot of the text itself rests on the presumption by the audience that they are a couple. The idea has become so firmly established that the plot depends on it.

As readers, we are led to believe Major Chesterton is Ian, and that the photo he carries of a dark-haired woman is Barbara. Ian himself starts to believe it, and cannot comprehend what would have separated him from her. Barbara is distraught when Ian is beaten unconscious, and decides she needs to make things more explicit between them.

> He realized what was going to happen, just a heartbeat before Barbara kissed him.
> 'What are you doing?'
> 'Seizing the day.'
> 'I thought we'd seized this day before.'
> Eighteen hundred years before, he added mentally.
> 'But I didn't say I love you. And I do.' So saying, she kissed him again.

Later in *The Eleventh Tiger*, Barbara proposes, paving the way for their appearance as the Chestertons in *The Face of the Enemy*. On the 1999 VHS release of *The Crusade*, William Russell narrates links, to camera, in character as Ian Chesterton. Ian frequently starts to say "my wife," only to catch himself and switch to "Barbara."

The Rocket Men, a 2011 Big Finish audio by John Dorney, is pretty much a character piece devoted solely to the relationship between Barbara and Ian. Narrated by Ian, it opens with him asking, "When do you know [that you love someone]?" and episode one's cliffhanger is that he would rather face an uncertain fate than live without her.

Every medium treats their romance and their future together as a given. Even the *Doctor Who Magazine* comics, in 2013, feature Barbara and Ian's 1965 wedding complete with the eleventh Doctor as best man.

In 2010, the romantic narrative quietly slipped back into the television version again: Sarah Jane mentions various former companions in *Death of the Doctor*, including "the Chestertons."[5] The barriers between the TV series and its merchandise, sometimes policed by fans, are porous both ways. And they always have been, since Whitaker first wrote his Exciting Adventure.

---

5 In *The Day of the Doctor*, only Ian's name appears on the Coal Hill School sign. I like to think that's just because Barbara prefers to spend her retirement well away from the place.

Those key elements Whitaker set out in *The Daleks* and *The Crusaders* are retained, in all the different versions. Barbara always initiates a change in their relationship, whether it's a kiss, sex or marriage. She rarely gives in, attempting to dig her way out of a prison cell or convincing the Doctor the TARDIS is trying to communicate with them.

Barbara didn't become an icon for me just great because of her bouffant and cardigans, or her steely attitude, but for her self-possession. Ian, for all the many great qualities he had (and has), is in her shadow. He's the warrior to her goddess, the comedian to her campaigner, the knight to her storyteller.

Whilst writing this essay, I've consciously used "Barbara and Ian" rather than "Ian and Barbara." My fan conditioning twitches because it feels like saying "McCartney and Lennon" instead of "Lennon and McCartney." But there really is no reason for Ian to come before Barbara in the fan litany of companions. In fact, over 50 years ago, Barbara was the first one to step into the TARDIS.

Companion Piece

Steven Taylor, Space Adventurer!

L. M. Myles is the co-editor of Hugo-nominated anthology *Chicks Unravel Time*. She's the Scottish one on the Hugo-nominated *Doctor Who* fancast *Verity!* and she's written *Doctor Who* in both prose and on audio for Big Finish. She can be found procrastinating on Twitter as @lmmyles.

I'm not saying that Steven Taylor is *Doctor Who*'s Flash Gordon, but he's surely the closest thing the Whoniverse has got. Steven's a space pilot from the far future whose heroism is rooted in his fundamental decency. If something's not right, he'll step into the limelight, and he'd like to talk things out, but if that doesn't work, he's a dab hand with a blaster or a right hook. He's a character who seems to have stepped off the set of his own show (I like to call it *Steven Taylor, Space Adventurer!*) and into *Doctor Who*.

The departure of Barbara and Ian means a shake-up in the TARDIS team's family dynamics. Gone are the surrogate parents to orphaned Vicki, and the enigmatic Doctor no longer potters around in the background. The Doctor's ready to step in the limelight, now unequivocally the lead, and the dashing, cardigan-wearing Ian Chesterton is replaced by the dashing, stripy sweater-wearing Steven Taylor.

Unlike Ian, Vicki doesn't see Steven as any sort of authority figure. If he's lucky, she'll treat him as an older brother who'd be much better off if only he'd listen to her. The friendship that develops between them sets the pattern for Steven's tenure in the TARDIS. He travels with no less than four women, representing a broad range of character types. Each relates to Steven in a different way, showing off how, even in its earliest days, *Doctor Who* excelled at creating interesting female characters and character dynamics.

Pandas in Distress

Steven is thrown at us in the final act of *The Chase*. From the start, he's a winning combo of energy and charisma, delighted to meet the Doctor and friends. His enthusiasm might be a little overwhelming, but it's understandable since he's been locked up on his own for two years with only the robotic Mechanoids for company.

32

Ian and Steven don't immediately take to one another: there's a macho standoff as the dishevelled prisoner and cardigan-wearing science teacher size each other up. Tension is quickly diffused, however, when Steven introduces them all to his best friend: HiFi, a stuffed panda.

Steven may have spent two years growing his impressive beard and chatting to his panda whilst failing to find a way out of his cell, but the TARDIS crew are nothing if not overqualified at escaping. It's just ten minutes before Team TARDIS have their latest plan, and it's a doozy: they're going to rappel down to freedom via fifteen hundred feet of cable. What could possibly go wrong?

As it turns out, very little. Our heroes make their dramatic escape just as the Daleks and Mechanoids engage in an impressively well-directed battle scene, carelessly burning the whole city down around them. Alas, one of our noble heroes fails to descend: poor HiFi is left all alone in the cell. Steven, heroic fellow that he is, decides that he can't leave his buddy behind and dives back into the burning city to save the little guy. Has telly ever seen such loyalty towards a stuffed panda before, or since?

Meanwhile, the TARDIS crew have escaped, and assumed that Steven has died, but they're not too cut up about it. Don't be too hard on them: they only knew him for the better part of 15 minutes and besides, it's time for an emotional farewell as Barbara and Ian depart for good.

The Doctor and Vicki are left on their own, but not for long. They underestimated the intrepid Steven and his panda-saving abilities. While they've been mucking around with a Dalek time machine, Steven's snuck into the TARDIS and made himself, and HiFi, at home.

Steven Taylor vs. Time Travel

In some other universe, there's a charming sixties telly series called *Vicki and Steven: Space-Time Investigators*. It's about two intrepid humans from the future who travel through time and space, investigating stuff.

That's what I like to assume, anyway, based on Vicki and Steven's delightful relationship in *The Time Meddler*. Neither spends much time with the Doctor, who's entirely off-screen for episode two, and we're left to enjoy Steven being thrown in at the deep end of time and space adventures with Vicki as his reluctant guide and partner.

Steven, being young and manly, naturally assumes that when it comes to adventuring, he knows best. He also assumes that he's going to be in charge. *The Time Meddler* spends a great deal of time gleefully demolishing these assumptions.

Vicki's happy to share her knowledge of the TARDIS with Steven; what it means and what it does and where it goes. Steven doesn't believe a word of it. Vicki laughs as he tries to get the answers he wants from the Doctor, anticipating with delight the moment when he's going to be forced to admit that she and the Doctor have been telling him the truth all along.

The conflict set up between Vicki and Steven in these scenes characterizes their whole relationship. While affection and friendship grow between the pair, they never cease to argue. Steven may be older, but Vicki has the greater experience. She values caution and trusts the Doctor implicitly; Steven isn't entirely sure the old man can always take care of himself, and is quite keen on immediate and direct action to sort a situation out.

He does, however, take the time to dress for the occasion, and both Steven and Vicki enter eleventh-century England in sensible cloaks. Sensible, however, isn't the word Vicki would choose for Steven's solution when the pair of them get lost in a forest. The seasoned time and space adventurer is all for hiding; the guy who risked his life for a stuffed panda thinks the best plan is to accost a passing Saxon and demand to know where they are. It's enough to make Vicki lose her temper, sounding genuinely angry as she suggests he should actually listen to her, before she metaphorically hits her head against the nearest medieval tree when Steven engages in some mild fisticuffs with the first native he spots.

It doesn't work. The Saxon's no use at all, and Vicki and Steven spend a restful night on the cold, hard floor of the forest. Still, at least they have their excellent cloaks to keep them warm.

In the morning, Vicki discovers one of Steven's better qualities as he manfully wanders the forest picking fruit before he surprises her with the exciting breakfast choices of blackberries or... and here Steven pauses most dramatically... blackberries! Barbara never appreciated Vicki's daft jokes, but Steven's sense of humor seems to plumb the same depths of sophistication as Vicki's.

There's more bonding between the travelers when they're caught by the Saxons. Neither is impressed at their situation, and they have a right go at their captors, demanding to be released. Their indignation and anger is sufficient to not only secure their release, but to get them provisions. Vicki, clearly knowing that a bit of gratitude and some manners wouldn't go amiss at this point, glares at Steven until he gives their former captors a decent thank you, before adding her own, rather more heartfelt, one.

Together they engage in some medieval investigating to find the Doctor, questioning monks and sneaking into monasteries with abandon.

"Follow me!" they both declare confidently, and then head off in opposite directions. It's Vicki who wins this battle, with Steven trailing in her wake.

Their keen wandering-around skills yield further fruit when they discover the Monk's TARDIS, his prizes from other times, and his step-by-step plan for defeating the Norman invasion, complete with tick boxes. When the Doctor sabotages the Monk's TARDIS, he gives Steven another reminder of his place on the ship. The Doctor wants Vicki out of the Monk's console room while he does his work, and she goes without complaint. Steven, being the heroic young male that he is, assumes he can stay and assist in the dangerous manly work. The Doctor dismisses him with a heavy frown. "He's the crew," Vicki tells him, "we're just the passengers."

While Steven may have learned a few things on his first TARDIS outing, Vicki's an old hand at time travel and her experience shines through. The closing scene of *The Time Meddler* takes a few moments to emphasize the bond between the Doctor and Vicki, and their shared experiences: satisfied that all is now well in medieval England, Vicki chimes in with the Doctor's final words, her tone indicating it's an old lesson, well learnt. All's well, and "and history will be allowed to take its natural course," they say together.

Galaxy 4 opens with a charming domestic scene: Steven is sitting in the console room while Vicki is giving him a haircut. Lest we be fooled into thinking this is anything like the time Barbara rearranged Ian's hair in a scene laced with sexual tension, Vicki snaps at Steven to stop being a nuisance when he moves, and speaks of her efforts as if she's just participated in a casual beheading: "I've finished chopping this fellow," she says when she realizes they might have landed somewhere interesting, "can we go out and see?" Steven is suitably grateful for her efforts, assessing his stylish new do as "a bit amateurish."

Despite the mutual snark, and Vicki's greater experience, there are moments when we're reminded she's the younger of the pair. She names the charming, rotund robots that they meet the rather whimsical "Chumblies." They're "sweet little thing[s]" according to Vicki, but they're enough to put Steven off swimming on the rather creepy, silent world they've landed on.

It's the other way round when the team encounter the alien Drahvin. Vicki is initially suspicious, while Steven is more trusting. An ungenerous interpretation would be that the Drahvin are beautiful women and this has swayed Steven somewhat, but this is only his second time and space adventure; perhaps better to be kind and assume that he just hasn't had the time to develop the same sharp instincts as Vicki when it comes to discerning the motives of alien strangers.

Plotwise, it's interesting to note that both Vicki and Steven are held hostage by the Drahvin at different times. In fact, they deliberately swap round, sharing the role of the companion in distress equally. They also both attack the Drahvin in separate attempts to get a weapon, but where Steven fails, Vicki succeeds. Further competence is displayed when Vicki explains how she brilliantly outwitted one of the Chumblies: "I noticed, observed, collated, concluded, and then I threw the rock."

Galaxy 4 also gives Vicki a chance to show off her more diplomatic side as she forges an understanding with the Rill, an alien she initially screamed at, and saves them from the Doctor's cunning plan to sabotage their air supply. In contrast, when the next story – *The Myth Makers* – opens, the Doctor forbids Steven from going outside because he believes the natives won't be able to deal with his sarcastic mood.

Vicki, I'm sure, would gloat, except for the fact that she's not getting outside either; she's got a sore ankle.

Ironically, when they do finally get their chance to influence the Trojan War, it's Steven who ends up with a nasty injury, and Vicki who finds sarcasm is her go-to coping strategy when she's captured by the Trojans. King Priam, trying to assuage her fears, tells her, "You shall die when I say so and not a moment before." "That's very comforting," Vicki replies, her deadpan lack of sincerity flying clean over the Trojans' heads.

With Vicki captured by the Trojans, Steven puts on his heroic face and comes up with a plan to rescue her. It goes swimmingly, right up until the moment Priam has both of them thrown in prison. It's their last chance for a good bicker and they make the most of it. Vicki blames Steven for making everything worse just when she'd got Priam on her side, she criticizes his rescue plan, and employs a healthy dose of her well-practiced sarcasm after reminding him that she can, in fact, take care of herself. The best the poor fellow can muster in response is that if she's so great, surely she'll figure a way out of their prison cell.

In their final scene, we see how far their friendship has truly come. Thanks to the Doctor's inadvertent help, Vicki gets out of the cell, and she's the one who rescues Steven. He responds to her heroics by mocking Troilus's affection for her: "[He'll] be jealous if he knows you're with me." Instead of her usual snappy retort, Vicki expresses her hurt, and reveals her feelings for Troilus. Steven immediately apologizes for poking fun, because theirs is a friendship of snarky banter, but beneath that, they care very much for each other, and for their last moment together, they're both willing to admit it.

Steven Taylor Saves the Universe
(with a little help from his friends)

The TARDIS departs Troy losing one traveler only to gain another: Katarina, a Trojan handmaiden. Katarina enters the TARDIS believing it's a vessel to take her to the afterlife. She's dead, the people around her – Steven and Space Security agent Bret Vyon – are dead too, but she accepts this state of affairs serenely, without fear. She believes the Doctor is a god, and the TARDIS a temple, and that they are journeying to the Place of Perfection, the afterlife. She stays aboard the TARDIS for only the briefest of time, a breath of restful air between the irrepressible Vicki and ruthless Sara Kingdom.

It was Katarina who saved Steven during the sack of Troy and got him back to the TARDIS, badly injured but alive. They spend most of their time together with Steven semi-conscious and mumbling incoherently, while Katarina does her best to nurse him. It's an impressive bit of compassion, considering she believes they're both already dead.

Katarina's treated kindly by both Steven and the Doctor, but it's less a relationship of equals, and more like she's a rather odd pet. Steven's protective enough when Bret Vyon has a go at her, but when he says "she doesn't really understand," his tone suggests that he doesn't expect her to ever grasp what sort of story she's really in.

Katarina's a bit of a curiosity in that she's the only companion whose religious views we know in any detail. The closest we've come since is probably Rita, as she practically auditions for the role of companion in *The God Complex*. In a show where religion is often overthrown by science, it's interesting to see a character whose greatest strength is her religious beliefs. They're what allow her to accept and deal with the fantastic strangeness she's surrounded by with calm and grace.

How much Katarina understands of what's going on is never made clear. Even when she hits the button that opens the airlock, killing herself and the hijacker threatening her life, we don't know if she knew what she was doing, or if she was just panicking. It's an ambiguity that makes her death all the more poignant. The Doctor is obviously charmed by her, and she naively believes she'll always be safe with him. Her sudden death is met by a shocked silence from Steven and the Doctor, followed by the briefest of memorials: "I shall always remember her," the Doctor says, "as one of the children of the gods."

The innocent trusting priestess of the past could not be a more startling contrast to the TARDIS's next occupant: Sara Kingdom, a Space Security agent from the forty-first century.

The coy avoidance of mentioning Kingdom's gender before she appears on screen would be irritating in the twenty-first century, but, in 1965, it's a neat subversion of audience expectations. Kingdom's in command, we're told. Kingdom's hard and ruthless. Kingdom's here! Tell Kingdom to come in, then! Then Kingdom does, and Kingdom is a woman. And she's exactly what we've been told. Her character may develop through the story but, satisfyingly, it never softens.

Things between Steven and Sara don't get off to a great start when she kills Bret Vyon, who's become a bit of a pseudocompanion for the past couple of episodes, and then tries to kill Steven and the Doctor. He thinks she's a cold-blooded killer; she thinks he's a traitor who's destroying Earth's galactic peace efforts. It's not the best first impression on either side. She's no fool, though, and her composure breaks for a moment when she realizes that Steven is telling the truth, and she's killed Bret, her own brother, for nothing.

In contrast to Vicki and Katarina, Sara's colder and more logical, with a wealth of life experience. She's cool and competent under fire from Daleks, while Steven gets a smidgen excitable, and she's just as calm when faced with the prospect of an undead mummy attack in an Egyptian tomb. She's a practical person, getting on with the some TARDIS repairs while the Doctor and Steven have wandered off and into trouble. She's comfortable using a bit of physical force, opting to escape Earth's police with a neatly placed elbow, making her escape a quick affair, if not precisely in keeping with the Doctor's "let's try talking first" policy. Steven fights alongside her, but while he's no slouch in the fisticuffs department, Sara has the superior combat skills. Captured in an Egyptian tomb, they escape their bonds and, outnumbered, fight their captors, with Sara taking on two, while Steven struggles with just the one. And even that one is finished off only when Sara delivers a knockout punch. Marvelously, Steven isn't threatened by being outclassed, rather he admires her abilities.

Like Steven, she's from our future and she can handle space travel with aplomb. But she's from much farther into the future than Steven, far enough for her to mock Steven's technological knowledge when the team are trying to make a fake copy of the Daleks' Ultimate Weapon glow like the real thing. Steven's arrogant enough to ignore her comments and go with his plan anyway. It works, but he gets himself electrocuted and could have easily died. Worst of all, he earns a scolding from the Doctor, reminding him not to be so stupid again and that it's the Doctor who's in charge, so he can do as he's told or get out.

Perhaps it's a small balm to his pride when he later gets to say to Sara the very Doctor-ish line, "I'll explain later."

Steven's become quite a bit more relaxed when it comes to the Doctor. Sara's infuriated at the Doctor for not knowing what to do, then taking credit when sheer luck helps them out. Steven is sympathetic, but takes the Doctor's behavior in his stride, telling Sara that she's getting to know him quite well now, as Steven already does.

His experiences traveling in the TARDIS have affected him in other ways too. When the pair arrive in the Dalek city, Sara is eager to get on with things, just charge in (not entirely unlike a slightly younger Steven might have), while Steven counsels caution. They discover the city deserted, and Steven is suspicious as to why, but Sara dismisses the mystery. And though she's the one that suggests it may be some sort of trick, Steven has a healthy sense of their importance and points out that if the Daleks have caught the Doctor, they wouldn't be worrying about capturing the two of them.

In the final minutes of *The Daleks' Master Plan*, Sara, compelled by her sense of duty, stays behind to help the Doctor while Steven does as the Doctor says, and leaves him to go back to the TARDIS. Sara argues that they should stay because the stakes are too high for mistakes, while Steven has learned to trust the Doctor implicitly. His trust saves his life, but leaves him waiting helplessly for Sara and the Doctor to return to the TARDIS, unable to do anything except thump the console in frustration.

Sara escapes the Dalek city with the Doctor, but not quickly enough to escape the effects of the Time Destructor. She begins to age to death, but even as she's dying she yells at the Doctor to keep going. When he points out the obvious, she snaps out a sarcastic reply. In her last moments, impossibly frail, she still struggles to help the Doctor to his feet, before collapsing. It's a horrific, terrifying death that she faces with the same bravery, cool-headedness and practicality she's shown throughout her short time aboard the TARDIS.

And so *The Daleks' Master Plan* comes to end, and though Steven's helped save the universe, he's lost three friends across the adventure, and cannot take any joy in the victory.

Steven Taylor Rules the World

In *The Massacre*, Steven practically gets a solo outing. For four episodes, *Doctor Who* has taken a break, and it's *The Steven Taylor Adventures*, with our hero facing the nefarious forces of sixteenth-century France, and trying to get out alive. It's a maze of politics, religious discontent and reluctant swordplay, where Steven proves he has a terrible sense of direction as he wanders Paris determined to stop the assassination of a prominent Huguenot.

When the Doctor finally turns up again, he tells Anne Chaplet, Steven's pseudo-companion, to stay indoors and sends her away. Steven and the Doctor hurry to get back to the TARDIS and escape just as the eponymous massacre breaks out.

It's another harrowing adventure for Steven, and it takes a heavy emotional toll on him. The Doctor insists there's nothing he could have done to prevent the massacre, but Steven is furious they left Anne behind to die. He's disgusted by what he sees as the Doctor's callous disregard for life and he says goodbye before he storms off the TARDIS, furious. Is this the final end of Steven Taylor?

Thankfully, no. He's back five minutes later, compelled by loyalty to warn the Doctor about a couple of policemen coming towards the police box. They take off, with Dodo Chaplet on board. She dashed inside looking for a phone. It's another kidnapping, but unlike Barbara and Ian, Dodo doesn't care about getting home. Her parents are gone and she lives with a great-aunt who doesn't care much for her. And she's completely nonplussed by the extraordinary events taking place around her. Steven's much more concerned about her predicament than she is, possibly inclined to overlook how annoying he finds her after she introduces herself, and he's hopeful that she could be a descendent of his friend Anne.

As soon as the TARDIS lands, Dodo's out the door, much to Steven's irritation. He's learned to be cautious about new places, and check the scanner first, much to the Doctor's approval (Vicki would be proud too). He warns Dodo there might be "low gravity, poison atmosphere, all sorts of things," and she wanders off, ignoring him. She doesn't believe they've left Earth, though a clearly exasperated Steven tries to explain what's happened to her (Vicki would be greatly amused). Unfortunately, it's not all that convincing since there are plenty of Earth animals where they land, ones which Steven doesn't recognize but Dodo easily names.

Within 15 minutes of landing in *The Ark*, Dodo's decided that she's "beginning to enjoy this space travel or whatever it is." The fact that she's been effectively kidnapped by a strange man and is stuck wandering through time and space on random adventures? Such trivialities matter not to Dodo; she's more concerned about not being sent back home.

Her main contribution to her first adventure is to almost wipe out what remains of the human race with her cold. She does manage to find her way round the TARDIS and get the Doctor's list of supplies, and she copes with admirable good grace when the Doctor objects to her accent and use of the word "okay." One can only imagine his horror at a future where he'll be exclaiming "correctamundo" and "allons-y" with abandon.

Dodo's not terribly diplomatic, and she likes to poke things. Luckily, Steven's picked up a few diplomatic skills during his tenure and is there to stop her curiosity from crushing her beneath statues. But spaceships, aliens, revolutions? She takes it all in her stride. She also has a splendid line in hats. Her charming outfit, hat included, is one of the few redeeming features of *The Celestial Toymaker*.

In contrast to Vicki – very much the Doctor's partner-in-crime – Dodo is treated with kid gloves, while the Doctor's confidant aboard the TARDIS is now Steven. Where once he was prevented from leaving the TARDIS for being too sarcastic, in *The Ark*, Steven's trusted to give evidence in a trial where he must convince the locals that the Doctor should be allowed to try and find a cure for the infection ravaging the ship.

He's come a long way since the Doctor mocked him about believing Viking armor was "a space helmet for a cow." And he reaches a new height in his own heroism when he volunteers to make the final move in the Doctor's game with the Toymaker, offering to sacrifice himself to save Dodo and the Doctor.

Steven's not all heroic sweetness and light now, however. While Dodo copes admirably with the Toymaker's games, finding them amusing and being polite to the toys despite their homicidal tendencies, Steven's temper is quickly riled by the nonsense the pair are put through (he even tries to take a swing at the Toymaker).

He cheers up in *The Gunfighters*, however, and Dodo and Steven are united in glee as they discover they're in the Wild West and they can't wait to indulge in a spot of cowboy dress-up. Dodo even grabs a Stetson for the Doctor to wear, which he keeps for the whole story, almost 50 years before he declared that Stetsons are cool. Steven puts on an American accent and starts waving around a gun and calling himself "Dead-Eye Steve." Dodo joins in with a "darn tootin'!" in her own version of an American accent. She also plays a jaunty tune on the piano while Steven sings to a saloon of trigger-happy patrons. The story gives Dodo a chance to develop a friendship of sorts, when she spends some time with the charmingly blunt, unflappable Kate, aka Big Nose Kate, Doc Holliday's common law wife.

All companions deserve a few moments of awesome, and *The Gunfighters* is Dodo's time to shine, as she displays both humor and a steely determination in the face of legendary gunslinger Doc Holliday. To get him to return her to Tombstone, Dodo grabs Holliday's gun and turns it on him. Charmingly, she says, she'll "try not to kill [him], [she'll] aim for [his] arm," all matter-of-fact, only showing how fearful she is after Holliday promises that he'll have her back in Tombstone by nightfall.

In *The Savages*, the TARDIS team visit a fabulous advanced city where Dodo engages in the time-honoured companion pastime of "wandering off." Thanks to Dodo's exploring, the Doctor's able to piece together the ugly truth about the glittering civilization they've discovered: they extract the life energy from those outside the city to enhance the lives of those within it.

There's a lovely spot of foolhardy heroics for Steven in his final story. Cornered and defenseless, facing an armed guard, Steven taunts the man, basically yelling at him to come and get them, if he's not afraid. *After* attracting the guard's attention, he finds out from an ally how the strange light gun works, then improvises a plan nicked from Perseus and reflects the light from the gun back at the guard.

As soon as they take out another guard, Dodo grabs a gun for herself, and the pair head into the city. They're off to rescue the Doctor, and, at last, Steven is unambiguously the senior member of the companion team. Alas, he forgets the caution he's learned, and doesn't listen to Dodo's worry about how it's been rather too easy to break in. The pair are captured. But when there's an opportunity to escape, he puts the safety of Dodo and the Doctor first, risking himself to protect them.

At the end of the day, Team TARDIS have overthrown the parasitic society, and it'd normally be handshakes and cheery farewells all round before the Doctor and company leave, hoping there's someone left alive who knows how to rebuild civilization. These are the early days of *Who*, however, and the Doctor's still fairly new to empire toppling. When the inhabitants say they need a new leader for their united future, someone trustworthy, with a conscience, like Steven (they subtly hint), the Doctor's all for it.

His faith in Steven's ability to guide a new society is a testament to the value of his experiences in the TARDIS. Steven doesn't want to abandon the Doctor and Dodo (how will they survive without him?), but he agrees to stay. The man who spent two years trapped by Mechanoids and almost died rescuing his stuffed panda has been asked to lead a world, to work towards freedom and fairness for all its people.

And so, after tearful farewells, Steven walks away from the TARDIS for the last time. Somewhere out there in the multiverse, perhaps, someone saw enough potential in his character to give him a lovely spin-off. Something of a cross between *The West Wing* and *Yes, Minister*, but with more rocket ships and alien invasions. I like to think they'd call it *Steven Taylor: Space President*. Who wouldn't want to watch that show?

Companion Piece

Scintillating, Fascinating, Irritating

Liz Barr lives in Melbourne, Australia, where she writes, edits, blogs, volunteers for the local SF convention, drinks too much coffee, watches too much television, and occasionally acts as a chew toy for a cat with an anxiety disorder. She blogs with Stephanie Lai at no-award.net.

They say you never forget your first Doctor, and it's true, but I've never forgotten my first companion.

While my first Doctor was a small, sinister man, an otherworldly goblin whose clowning couldn't quite conceal his immense and terrible powers, his companion was a girl just like me – or, at least, like the grown-up I wanted to become. She was brave, facing the monsters even as she screamed in terror. She was clever and funny. And she seemed utterly unafraid of the Doctor.

If the Doctor was here to protect us from the monsters, his companion would protect us from the Doctor.

It was 1988. I was six years old, watching *Doctor Who* with my dad for the very first time. The story was *Paradise Towers*. The Doctor was Sylvester McCoy. And his companion, my Amazonian protectress, was Melanie Bush.

You can stop laughing now.

#

Mel was never a popular companion. The announcement of Bonnie Langford's casting triggered tabloid headlines and outraged letters to *Doctor Who Magazine*. Into the 1990s, when my sole knowledge of *Doctor Who* came from a couple of early Tom Baker stories on VHS and British magazines like *Starburst* and *SFX*, one thing I knew for certain was that Melanie Bush was the worst companion the show ever had. In 2007, the *Guardian* described her as "a screeching annoyance[6]" and gave

---

6   www.guardian.co.uk/culture/tvandradioblog/2007/mar/28/doctorwhothe-fivebestandw (2007) Accessed 19/06/2013

her partial credit for the series' ultimate cancellation.

The curious thing about Mel is that even though the revival of *Doctor Who* has brought a flood of new fans, ideas and perspectives into the fandom, Mel remains deeply unpopular. All companions have some value, the argument goes; all companions are appealing in some way.

Except Mel, of course. She was rubbish.

(Peri also gets a hard time from otherwise forgiving fans, and certain monochrome companions are sometimes forgotten altogether, but it's never hard to find a diehard Peri fan. And, frankly, it's easier to find someone willing to defend Adric, if only out of a vague sense of nostalgia, than someone who loves Mel.)

# # #

Mel was doomed from the outset. The first companion introduced since *Doctor Who*'s cancellation and revival had a lot riding on her shoulders: she needed to be bright and appealing; charismatic enough to take the place of the popular Peri; modern but unthreatening. Oh, and she had to be pretty. Something for the dads, right?

And they went and cast a former child star. A musical theater performer. A light entertainer.

From the very first announcement of Langford's casting, the tabloids and fandom were united in their accusations of stunt casting. *Doctor Who* was already on shaky ground, and now there was a shrill ginger in the TARDIS. And unlike Catherine Tate, whose casting 20 years later received similar reactions, she would not go on to become one of the series' most popular companions.

It didn't help that, within a short time of the announcement of Langford's casting, script editor Eric Saward quit the series and gave an interview to *Starburst* magazine that was mostly dedicated to criticizing executive producer John Nathan-Turner. ("I think he's a very paranoid individual. He probably feels that I've been slagging him off all over the place since I left," Saward mused, before going back to slagging him off.) Bonnie Langford became collateral damage:

Well, what did you think of the choice of Bonny Langford?[7]
Well my first question was like everyone else's – "can she act?"
And my first impression is that she will not be very good... I said
[to Nathan-Turner] "I don't think she can act, let alone bring
anything to the show."

Even in the days before *Doctor Who* had its own army of publicists
and media liaisons, not to mention the confidentiality clauses, this was
shockingly unprofessional.

Yet, when Saward goes on to say that, "given the fact we are in 1986,
the number of dozy female companions we've had doesn't actually
reflect modern womanhood very accurately[8]," he has a point, even if
one wonders why he didn't bother doing anything about the problem
when he was effectively second in command on the series. The Nathan-
Turner years were not exactly a great time for female characters – Nyssa
and Tegan, though full of potential and charm, were frequently sidelined, even as they were put into increasingly skimpy costumes, while
the production team evidently cared so little about Peri, they didn't
bother finding an actress who could do a credible American accent.[9]

In 1986, Random House published a guide to the companions of
Doctor Who[10] written by John Nathan-Turner. He previews the upcoming Mel: "Melanie is one of those annoying young ladies who is a feminist at all times, except at moments of great stress, when she relies heavily on playing the hard-done-by, downtrodden, crocodile-teared female."

The preview also includes some details about Melanie's past, and her
first encounter with the Doctor (helping him save the world when the
Master attempts to take over international banking systems). This is all
contradicted in Mel's very first episode, and on screen we never do find
out how she came to meet the Doctor and travel with him. Nor are the
timey-wimey shenanigans of *The Trial of a Time Lord* ever resolved.
(She's his companion! Then she's gone home! Then she's plucked from
her home and called as a witness, and then she's the companion again!
Then she leaves forever with Glitz – but when did they meet and when
and why did she first decide to leave the Doctor? Thankfully, Mel is

---

7 As if to reinforce the disdain for Langford, her name is misspelled throughout the
interview.
8 It probably wasn't okay in 1966 or 1976 either.
9 That Peri succeeds at all as a companion – and I'd argue that she does, especially
in her later seasons, when she got to be fully dressed – is mostly down to Nicola
Bryant's charisma and her chemistry with Colin Baker.
10 It's a great book. Really. JN-T's summation of Jo Grant, one of the most iconic and
popular companions of all time: "Katy now lives in Australia."

never actually portrayed as the part-time feminist/ manipulator Nathan-Turner promised.)

All these things considered, Mel's first appearance, in *Terror of the Vervoids*, is actually... pretty good.

It doesn't start off well. The Doctor, on trial for his lives, is still reeling from Peri's apparent death. Yet he, and we, are plunged into a new adventure with a completely unfamiliar companion bossing the Doctor about as if she has been around forever. Even the Valeyard remarks on the incongruence.

As if to make her first impression even more off-putting, Mel is introduced pressuring the Doctor to lose weight. Fat-shaming the hero, to apply a contemporary term to an age-old concept, is certainly a brave way to present the new companion; karmic payback, maybe, for the Doctor's treatment of Peri in *Revelation of the Daleks*[11], but not remotely as endearing as the writers seem to believe. Later in the story, she slaps the Doctor's hand when he reaches for a biscuit, as if he's not a grown Time Lord who can manage his own dietary choices.

To add insult to injury, after forcing the Doctor to swallow a glass of carrot juice, she starts jumping rope. In kitten heels. (One begins to wonder if it's *just* carrot juice she's been drinking.)

Luckily for the audience's patience, the plot finally moves into action, and here Mel's better qualities become apparent. She's eager for adventure – more eager, indeed, than the Doctor, who tells her, "Let's exercise the grey cells for once, shall we? Rather than the muscles?"

It's not that Mel isn't clever – the phrase "bright as a button" comes to mind – but she's also curious and unafraid of the unknown, and very much given to rushing headlong into danger. It is she who pushes the Doctor into participating in events and though she screams, loudly and enthusiastically, in the face of violent death, she's angry and outspoken when accused of complicity. She flirts her way into the hydroponics center, uses charm and persistence to make people open up to her, and it's her quick thinking that enables the stewardess Janet and the scientist Roland to escape the hijackers at the climax of the story. Six, the most verbose of all Doctors, even lets her speak for him.

And that's just her first story.

Response was mixed. In *Doctor Who Magazine* #122, Richard Marson was "positive, with reservations," highlighting Mel's first scene in the TARDIS as a low point, but noting, "She is refreshing in many other

---

11 The sixth Doctor era provides a whole essay's worth of bodyshaming and fatphobia, from the dialogue to the tabloids' treatment of Colin Baker. Luckily, this isn't it.

ways, most of all in the energy with which [Langford] imbues the part."
On the other hand, the official BBC website, effectively offering an official perspective, quotes Lance Parkin:

> Bonnie Langford is terrible... Can anyone find a scene or a single line in which she is anything other than awful?

Unfortunately, like most companions, Mel suffers from uneven writing. Some writers, such as Pip and Jane Baker, seem to enjoy giving her material. Others, starting with Eric Saward, find her irritating and write her as such. *The Ultimate Foe*, with its cavalcade of writers, demonstrates both attitudes. The first draft of the first episode was written by Robert Holmes and rewritten by Saward following Holmes' death. The second part was thrown together at the last minute by Pip and Jane Baker after Saward quit and refused to let the BBC use the script he had already prepared.

In Holmes and Saward's first part, the companion role is temporarily passed to the roguish Sabalom Glitz, introduced in *The Mysterious Planet* as a charming and ambiguous criminal type – a sort of proto-Jack Harkness, but with a much worse haircut. Mel is left behind in the courtroom, pleading mercy for the Doctor and feeding straight lines to the Master:

> **Mel:** How utterly evil!
> **The Master:** Thank you.

Then the Bakers take over and suddenly Mel has much more to do. Initially, it appears that she has risked her life and the wrath of the Time Lords to venture into the Matrix and rescue the Doctor. This turns out to be one of the Valeyard's deceptions. In reality, she stops to give the Time Lords a good telling off, *then* goes to rescue the Doctor. (He doesn't need rescuing by the time she arrives, but it's still impressive.)

The Ultimate Foe isn't one of *Doctor Who*'s greatest stories, but it comes to life when the Doctor and Mel are together. They have a sparky repartee that occasionally borders on the flirtatious and Mel seems to delight in the Doctor's theatrics even as she pointedly rolls her eyes. There's none of the bullying that marked the sixth Doctor's early time with Peri; for all the Doctor's condescension, he and Mel feel oddly like equals.

Sadly, it wasn't to last. Colin Baker was fired, and although John

Nathan-Turner promised there were no plans to replace Mel or Bonnie[12], she would only have a short time with Sylvester McCoy.

Season Twenty-Four opened with *Time and the Rani*, a story remembered largely for featuring Sylvester McCoy in a wig for the regeneration scene and the Rani fooling the amnesiac Doctor by posing as Mel.[13] These are generally not considered good memories, and *Time and the Rani* is not as strong as some of Pip and Jane Baker's earlier work. But it has some wonderful moments for Mel as she showcases classic companion behavior: demonstrating compassion for a man who has just tried to take her prisoner; wearing white trousers in a quarry; having an implicit, out-of-the-blue romance with a male guest star.

She's also the first companion who, on meeting a newly regenerated Doctor, throws him over her shoulder and gets him in an arm-lock. Watching Langford and McCoy demonstrate their stage fighting skills has all the hi-octane, adrenaline-pumping energy of watching kittens wrestle, but it's oddly charming.

Langford's performance is much more restrained, more naturally girlish, which makes Kate O'Mara's work as the Rani-as-Mel even more hilarious. The Rani's imitation is terribly perky and earnest, and she plainly hates every minute of it. Mel isn't particularly enchanted by the Rani either. She might be terrified of Tetraps, but she's awfully keen to give the Rani a taste of her own medicine.

On the downside, the legendary inconsistency of companion writing comes to the fore: this time, Mel is keen to hightail it away from danger. Her disregard for the Rani's victims contradicts even her future actions in the story, let alone past adventures.

That inconsistency recurs in *Paradise Towers*, where Mel is more reactive than usual, and spends a lot of time being passive and fearful, needing Pex to save her from the various dangers of the decaying Towers.

True, she does sensible things like making plans with the Doctor for if (when) they're separated, and finding a map instead of wandering around aimlessly. But then, in a building she knows is full of deadly threats, she goes swimming.[14] This is possibly the silliest decision she has made and that includes every single outfit she has ever chosen.[15] Mel

---

12 *Doctor Who Magazine* #124. Never, ever trust a showrunner.

13 Also a giant brain, and the Doctor playing the spoons on the Rani's chest.

14 On the other hand, you could argue that getting her hair wet is a very brave choice.

15 To this Australian viewer, the whole premise of the story – that you can have every beach in all of time and space to choose from, but what you *really* want is an indoor swimming pool – is a bit silly.

does rescue herself from the monster in the swimming pool, but it feels like too little, too late. It's true that no mere human companion could possibly be as proactive as the seventh Doctor when it comes to pursuing adventure, but Mel is much diminished from her earlier appearances.

She has a slightly more active role to play in *Delta and the Bannermen*, a cheery story about rock 'n' roll and genocide, in which Mel finds herself in a setting even she has trouble enjoying: a holiday camp in 1950s Wales. It's not exactly the trip to Disneyland she was promised, but a busload full of hyperactive alien tourists is well within her comfort range. It is she who recognizes that Delta, alien queen and genocide survivor, needs a friendly ear, even if she goes from promising that "Discretion's my middle name" to telling the Doctor everything.

She does get captured and used as bait, but she also helps evacuate and then defend the holiday camp. This marks the second story where Mel gets to wield an alien weapon, and for a computer programmer, she's remarkably proficient with guns. (Bonnie Langford: secret action heroine.) But the Doctor's involvement in events is set in motion when Mel gets the reserved Delta to open up to her.

This is a skill she demonstrates again in *Dragonfire*, her last story. Most of Mel's scenes are with Ace, almost as if she's mentoring her replacement, except that Ace seems to be doing all the teaching. They bond over a love of anarchy, Ace instructs Mel in the use of deodorant-based explosives, and both women share a mutual and vocal hatred of being arrested.

Ace, for her part, seems to regard Mel as somewhere between an apprentice and a pet. She addresses Mel as "Doughnut," gives her a look of disbelief when Mel screams at the first appearance of the "dragon," and helps her release her inner pyromaniac. Ace also looks after her when Mel trips and suffers a minor head injury while they're fleeing ice zombies. That's only fair: earlier, Mel had saved Ace from the (metaphorical) seduction of the criminal Kane.

And it is to Mel that Ace reveals something of her past, her sense of alienation growing up, her fear that there is nothing else for her but a life of inescapable drudgery, and her real name, Dorothy. (As promised, Mel doesn't laugh, but she does smile a little.)

In exchange, Mel gets to introduce Ace to the TARDIS and dimensional transcendentalism and ensures that the Doctor takes Ace with him when she leaves.

Because Mel is going. This is a terribly bittersweet scene, featuring

Bonnie Langford's best performance, but we never actually find out why she's leaving. Let alone why she's going with Glitz, who opened the story by selling his crew into slavery. (Apparently, we're still meant to find him charming. Mel pointedly sulks at him when she finds out, and the Doctor looks mildly disapproving, but everyone's on the best of terms again by the end of the first episode. Except for Ace, who regards him as beneath contempt, and why not?) Mel wants more adventure: "Who said anything about home? I've got much more crazy things to do yet." But why she can't stay with the Doctor is never explained. Maybe the lure of space piracy was stronger than the call of the TARDIS. All we know is that she's going, and as the Doctor rambles about time and missed encounters, it's clear he's going to miss her terribly.

# # #

Mel's scenes with Ace encapsulate a curious pattern that developed under Andrew Cartmel's script editing: Mel as a focal point for class consciousness and mild class conflict.

Cartmel entered the series as a new, young writer with an avowed left-wing agenda, and once he started commissioning scripts himself (*Time and the Rani* was leftover from the sixth Doctor's era), Mel was frequently displaced in favor of substitute companions from groups previously marginalized in *Doctor Who*: working class and Welsh women. This is admirable, but it had the side effect of minimalizing Mel's importance to the stories.

Take, for example, *Paradise Towers*, in which Mel's scenes do little to advance the major plot. The role of companion is filled by an entire gang of girls – the Red Kangs – but principally by their leader, Bin Liner.

Mel's reaction to the Kangs is particularly interesting. She's polite to them, but seems quite repelled by their appearance, their lack of manners, and even their names and manner of speaking. Suddenly, she has become a middle-class woman surrounded by working class urban youth, and she's completely out of her comfort zone.

It is Mel's very middle-classness that makes her so appealing and vulnerable to Tilda and Tabby, the cannibalistic Rezzies. They make much of her good manners and pleasant appearance; she in turn is only too glad to meet people who seem to be like her. The appearance, of course, is deceiving, and she eventually warms to the Kangs.

Perhaps that experience in Paradise Towers is what makes her so open to friendship with Ace. It is Mel who invites Ace to join their little group, and although she frequently seems shocked by Ace's behavior and attitudes, there's none of the defensive hostility she showed towards the Kangs.

Nevertheless, there is an element of class-based conflict between the two women. They are only a few years apart in age, but they couldn't be more different: polite, middle-class Mel and the hostile teen from Perivale. Mel initially tries to take an authoritarian, almost maternal role with Ace, inquiring about her school and home life and attempting to defend Glitz's sexism and general unpleasantness, but she seems enthralled when Ace pours milkshakes over dreadful rich women, and laughs when Ace admits to blowing up the school art room. By the end of the story, they feel like best friends. Had Mel stayed on longer, we might have gotten to see that friendship grow.

Mel appeared in only six stories and she never got the rich characterization that Ace and the companions of New *Who* would enjoy. But we know who she is. She's an exercise junkie. She waves at cows. She loves adventure. She screams when she sees a monster, but then she stops to get a good look at it.

She admires people who are constructive and positive. She hates liars and dishonesty. She considers herself "truthful, honest, and about as boring as they come," but she will lie to protect someone in need. Her uncomplicated candor was used against the Doctor by the Valeyard, but it also enables Mel to befriend troubled, lonely women like Delta and Ace. "I'd help anyone in trouble if I could," she tells Delta, and these aren't just empty words.

A character who is *nice* and *honest* and *uncomplicated* can be difficult to like, and even more difficult to write well. Big Finish has produced some marvelous audio dramas featuring Mel, but the one most commonly recommended is *He Jests at Scars*, in which Mel has become bitter and cynical after years of hunting the Valeyard. For an audience accustomed to the candy-colored nihilism of the sixth Doctor's era, Mel must have seemed deeply incongruous. In the twenty-first century, with the fashion for sociopaths and shades of grey, she seems odd, but also refreshing.

Mel marked the end of an era. No more would companions be automatically middle-class, uncomplicated, devoid of family connections. A new template was created with Ace, one that would eventually carry *Doctor Who* into the twenty-first century.

But Mel came from a long and respectable line of characters. There's a dash of Jo Grant in her determined positivity. There's an echo of Polly

Wright in her capacity for unrecognized competence. And her sheer determination to help people brings to mind the magnificent Sarah Jane Smith. Although she was a product of a difficult era and uneven writing, she doesn't deserve her reputation as the worst companion ever. She played her part, and played it well, and she must have gone on to be a really *nice* space pirate, making friends and reassuring little girls all over the universe that, however scary the monsters might be, she would always do her best to protect them.

Companion Piece

I Don't Want Her to Go

A lifelong lover of science fiction and fantasy, **Amy Gaertner** would like to be forgiven for discovering *Doctor Who* relatively late in life. She actually went to school with a girl called Amy Pond, and now kinda regrets not getting to know her better. In the present day, Amy works in a library and is pursuing her Master's degree in Library and Information Science. When not stapling things to bulletin boards or panicking over deadlines, she enjoys many more hobbies than could reasonably fit into her very limited spans of free time. Those hobbies include gardening, cooking, knitting, fooling around on Twitter, writing fiction in the genres of science fiction and queer romance, and many other highly unprofitable ventures. Some day, she will finish one of the many novels she's started and abandoned over the years. (Either that, or she will manufacture her own TARDIS from bits of old computers and empty yogurt tubs. At this stage, it would be difficult to tell which outcome is more likely.) If you should stumble across her on the Internet, do say "hello"; especially if you're not quite over your first companion, either.

Though I was there for the tenth Doctor's final goodbye, his era was never really mine to mourn. Amy Pond was the first companion who was *mine*.

The first episode I ever watched on its initial run was *The Next Doctor*. Looking back, the theme of loss was so completely apropos to my experience as a fan. By now, David Tennant had already announced that he would be leaving the show after one last year of specials. Donna was lost, her adventures with the Doctor erased from her memory forever; Rose was sealed off in another dimension with the Doctor's handy lookalike; Martha was off to continue saving the world with Mickey and Jack. The Doctor was looking for a sign that life would go on. What he finds is a man crippled by loss. Though the man calls himself the Doctor, his redemption does not belong to his namesake. When Jackson Lake regains his son and his identity, the Doctor loses hope of a life less lonely. His friends are gone. Everyone will always leave.

The rest of David's episodes are a countdown, slowly unraveling toward Ten's demise. His companions were the best of him and when they leave, he's left to battle his own demons. While he misses the beautiful people they were, I can't help but realize that while I grew to love them, they were already gone. Rose was always trapped in another dimension. Martha was always walking the earth. Donna was always a woman robbed of her memories.

Amy is my companion. The same way fans both old and young will point to an incarnation of the Doctor and boldly declare, *that one's mine*, I feel the same proprietary stab of jealousy about Amy Pond. We share a first name, a hair color and a somewhat temperamental disposition. We're both in love with Rory and the Doctor. Neither of us can resist a Keep Out sign. And, perhaps more than anything else, she was the first companion I ever fell in love with, and the first I ever had to say "goodbye" to.

I loved her from the start. Who can't love a girl who invites in the man who crashes his spaceship in her backyard for a midnight meal? Who, without hesitating, rushes off to pack a suitcase when offered a chance to see the stars? Who grabs a cricket bat and a kissogram costume when confronted with an intruder? Who would trade domestic bliss for adventure, so long as she could always keep tomorrow just an arm's length away?

All right, yeah, so there's plenty of people who can't. Some people like Earl Grey while others some prefer Darjeeling, and for many, Amy Pond just isn't their cup of tea. There are 50 years of characters to love and hate about this show, and it's the loving *and* the hating both that comprise the passion of the Whovians.

Defending Amy against her detractors was part of what made her my companion. Her short skirts, her job as a kissogram, her clumsy attempt to seduce the Doctor, her choice of boyfriend, her treatment of said boyfriend... I've defended it all. How could people say that Amy just isn't "vulnerable" enough when we see her heart broken twice in the first episode alone? How could they say that she doesn't love Rory when she's willing to fight (and die!) for him at every chance she gets? How could they argue that getting married was giving up her dreams when she celebrated her honeymoon on the TARDIS and her first anniversary in the deserts of Utah being chased by the Silence?

As I watched Amy's story unfold, I got to celebrate the triumphs of vindication when I watched her be just as awesome as I said she was all along. And I suffered the agony of disappointment when I watched her make choices that I really wish she hadn't. Knowing that a character can disappoint you, and standing by her anyway; watching that character redeem herself and be better than you could have ever dreamed (or written down in fanfic); surfing through the agonizing ups and downs of fan opinion and coming out the other side; all of that made her mine.

All good things must come to an end, and that's doubly true for television. Amy and Rory left the show in a spectacular, heart-rending finale that left me a sobbing puddle of feelings weeping into my keyboard. While the tenth Doctor's era was never mine to mourn, with Amy's departure I had to live the lesson that every Whovian must eventually learn: that actors come and go, but the show lives on. That when a beloved character's time is over, you have to ask yourself: is it the show itself or a particular face that you really fell in love with?

I didn't actually think that I had anything to worry about – after all, I'd loved our first glimpse of Oswin/Clara Oswald. I had been cautiously tweeting, pinning and reblogging pictures of Jenna Louise Coleman for months, in a show of good faith that I was *definitely* going to like her as the new companion, and I was *not* going to sulk my way through the new episodes and waste my breath whining all over the Internet about how much I miss Amy. It was so *annoying* when other fans did that: barge into the middle of a perfectly good discussion of a new episode to wistfully pine that *Rose would have never acted that way!* Or *Martha would have done it better!* Those characters were awesome, but their time was over; wasn't it best to move on? When it was my turn, I was *definitely* going to move on, no question about it. The new companion was going to be great and I was going to be just as excited about the show as I'd ever been.

I'd spent so much time convincing myself that I was going to like the new companion that it was a relief to *actually like her.* She was great! She was, first of all, adorable, and I loved her feisty personality. "Feisty" is one of those terms that tends to grate like nails down a chalkboard to a well-trained feminist ear, but as she flirted with Rory, made fun of the Doctor's chin, and bragged about her own intellectual prowess – all while the TARDIS gang is fighting for their lives against the Daleks – I found I didn't mind the trait at all; the ability to make fun in the face of danger is a telltale mark of a suitable companion. She was clever, she was funny and, in the end, she was very, very brave.

It was a weight off my mind, knowing that I *was* going to fall in love with the new companion. I could savor the last handful of episodes with my beloved Ponds safe in the knowledge that, after a suitable grieving period, I would seamlessly transition to a certified Clara/Oswin fangirl.

After all, didn't I love the flirty chemistry she had with Rory? Wasn't it fun how much Amy enjoyed Oswin teasing the Doctor? Wasn't it great that Oswin didn't hesitate to stand up to Amy's Scottish anger when she was turning into a Dalek? And... oh. Crap. Isn't it strange how much of what intrigues me about her character is based on her interactions with the Ponds?

Perhaps that was only a revelation fully realized after the fact, because I was still completely convinced that Clara was going to be My New Companion when *The Snowmen*, her first episode without the Ponds, aired at Christmas. It didn't bowl me over, but, then again, most of the Christmas specials don't. Her character was still fun and brave and clever and everything I had loved about her in *Asylum of the Daleks*. She was still going to be my new favorite companion. Any minute now.

Back to Series Seven proper, and the magic still wasn't there. The episodes were fun and full of lots of creepy/silly/madcap *Doctor Who*-style adventuring, and I enjoyed them. I know I've given up on a show when I start forgetting to watch it. I'm out when the show first airs and never quite find time to get to it on my DVR. I skim through friends' blogs and see their reaction posts and analyses and think, "Oh, I'll have to come back and read this once I've seen the episode," but the essays and gifsets are soon forgotten. That didn't happen with *Doctor Who*; it hasn't happened! I still eagerly await new episodes and what the future will bring. But I am waiting for that same magic feeling I felt back when I seriously considered not attending my friend's actual wedding because she'd been foolish enough to schedule it on the same day as Amy and Rory's fictional nuptials. (I'm still jealous she shares their anniversary.)

It's not that Clara hasn't lived up to my expectations, and it's definitely not that I don't like her. In fact, I really love the dynamic she has with the Doctor! She looks up to him without being in awe. She challenges him without making herself an adversary. They are friends without any of the jealousy, insecurity and sexual tension that cropped up in so many of the relationships he had with his previous companions.

Clara was an excellent companion to help the Doctor get over Amy and Rory. The man is an ancient nine year-old, capable of childish wonder and bone-weary sadness, often in the same breath. He faces disappointment like a child, unbelieving and unaccepting, but with the memories of a man whose heart has been broken over and over again. The mystery of Clara – who she is, and why he's met her so many times – was just the thing to distract him from his loss. She is a puzzle he just has to solve and, in the meantime, she's a really great friend.

Clara's mystery doesn't last forever. All those little glimpses, all those hints that pointed to the Impossible Girl lead us to the Doctor's end. The Doctor knows the journey will lead them to his grave, but he does not know if it will necessarily lead to his demise. It is because of Clara that he survives. We knew that she was clever and we knew that she was brave, but in *The Name of the Doctor*, we discover that she is selfless: willing to sacrifice her life for that of the Doctor. She enters his time stream, traveling back through all his lives to save him from the Great Intelligence, not stopping to wonder how she'll make it back to her own life. She is not only the Impossible Girl, but the girl who has saved the savior of many galaxies. What greater proof could there be that she is a worthy companion?

I loved my first sight of her and I went on to love many other things about her; but I have never felt that she was mine the way Amy was. I haven't recaptured that same excitement.

It makes me wonder if I'm that second type of fan: the one that falls in love with a character, and not the show itself.

Perhaps the new Doctor will make the difference. Amy Pond doesn't belong to just me alone – I share her with the eleventh Doctor. Yes, the "eleventh Doctor" is not a separate character; he's the same brilliant alien Whovians have been following for 50 years. His face changes, but the man inside...

I know what I'm supposed to say here as a "proper Whovian." The face changes, but the Doctor stays the same. Only he doesn't really, does he? The friendships he makes, the lessons he learns: they never look the same through the lens of regenerated eyes. You can love more than one, you can even love them all, but when a fan says, "this is my Doctor," you know they have a point: each Doctor is special, each a signpost of his own era. The eleventh Doctor? As far as I'm concerned, he belongs to Amy Pond.

Maybe Clara will be a Twelve Girl. Maybe Twelve will be a Clara Guy. Perhaps they'll each come into their own together, building a new era of *Who*, and rewriting the rules we all got too comfortable with under Eleven's long and prosperous reign. I can picture the adventures now, and I'm excited.

I'm still ready to accept Clara as my new favorite companion: the best thing since bowties and bananas in daiquiris. The Impossible Girl, the Girl With Many Lives. I know I'm going to fall in love... any minute now.

In the meantime, though, I'm an Amy girl.

"What a Splendid-Looking Roman You Make!": The Male Companions, from Ian to Rory

Emma Nichols still thinks of herself as a *Doctor Who* newbie, even though it's approaching a decade since she reluctantly agreed to watch *Rose* and then spent the next year catching up on the show in its entirety (not to mention the books, the comics, the Big Finish audios...). When she was a little girl, she thought she'd like to be a scientist, so she became a scientist. She works in physics outreach at the University of Manchester, and one of the best parts of her job is when kids tell her that *Doctor Who* has made them want to be scientists when they grow up. While writing this piece, she tried multiple times to put together a list of her top ten companions, but was forced to give up when each attempt was completely different.

There's a paradox in my life as a *Doctor Who* fan: I've loved every companion who's ever set foot on the TARDIS, every last stupid one of them[16], but I'm always excited to see them go. The ever-changing cast is one of the few fundamentals of *Doctor Who* and all companions, no matter how much you love them, will one day ask to go home, accept a marriage proposal from someone they met that morning, or find themselves on a doomed freighter hurtling towards prehistoric Earth. Cheer up! The next one will be along in a minute, and they'll be brilliant.

The wait for a new companion is even better than the wait for a new Doctor, since instead of arguing over lists of actors and the canon minutiae proving why the latest one does/doesn't have to be a youngish white male, we get to speculate wildly about the new companion's background. I think we know, really, that it's going to be a woman from modern Earth; outside of a few specials and the four-year Leela-Romana(s)-Adric streak, there's been a contemporary human woman in the TARDIS since the show went into color. But when people have their hearts set on the new one being a Zarbi, or a plucky Bletchley Park

---

16 If your immediate reaction *wasn't* "She can't possibly mean Mel/Adric/Dodo," we should be friends.

Wren, or a clog-dancing lesbian ninja from the future[17], a little thing like 50 years of precedent can't stop the peevish disappointment when she's inevitably a twenty-first century London nanny instead.

In the midst of this, there are always people suggesting that, hey, why don't they do something radical this time? Why not make the companion... a *man*?

The obvious answer is "because if your cast consists of a male Doctor and one companion, making that companion a man means a show that's had a half-century of terrific female characters suddenly doesn't have any women in it, that's why." But why is that the model for companionhood, when it wasn't always that way?

A handy fact, should you ever find yourself in either a *Doctor Who* pub quiz or (just as likely) some sort of Celestial Toymaker scenario, with your life depending on your ability to answer trivia questions posed by aliens in dubious costumes:

How many *Doctor Who* episodes (counting the whole show so far, 1963 to 2013) feature a male companion?

A) None. There won't be a male companion until the Doctor's played by a woman. That's how it works.

B) Around ten percent. Rory died in most of them.

C) About half.

D) There's a huge range of possible answers depending on what you mean by "companion" and whether you're including robots with male voice actors, since if we're counting the men of UNIT and one-off characters like Craig and Wilf and Bret Vyon, then the number gets considerably higher, and if you bring in the books and the comics and the Big Finish audios, then [answer redacted because it could fill the rest of the book].

All right, in a strictly accurate sense it's D; it depends how you count. But taking a hard line on who is and isn't a companion – not including the Brigadier or anyone else who doesn't actually travel in the TARDIS, and leaving out K-9 and Kamelion – we're left with ten male companions. Ian, Steven, Ben, Jamie, Harry, Adric, Turlough, Mickey, Jack and Rory[18]. How many episodes between them?

It's actually C – a bit over half if you just look at classic *Who*, a bit

17 Martha's wonderful just as she is, but I still wish this had been true.
18 I may have been the one person who liked the ninth Doctor's other (not-really-a-) companion, but I was being ruthless in my judgments, so... I'm sorry, Adam Mitchell, from the far-flung future of 2012, but you didn't make the list.

under if you add in the new series, and if that seems higher than you might expect, it's largely down to the first seven years of the show. For the whole of the Hartnell and Troughton eras, more than 250 episodes (this was the good old days before this "six episodes a year is plenty" nonsense), the Doctor traveled with a mixed-sex entourage.

Ostensibly, the show started out this way because of William Hartnell's age. A younger male character had to be part of the cast, the story goes, so there was somebody to do the fight scenes and the action sequences; a dynamic, heroic type. I'd heard a lot about classic companions from various Whovian friends before I watched any of the pre-Eccleston Doctors, so I went in expecting the women to scream and fall down a lot, and the men to rescue them and hit things.

Both these things were untrue, as I realized when I saw Ace introduce a Dalek to a baseball bat, and Peri shout down the Master, and Barbara do almost everything she does. The female companions were brilliant. And so were the men... just not quite in the way I'd been led to expect.

Take Ian, since he has the distinction (with Barbara) of being the first companion. I'm not suggesting for a moment that Ian doesn't hold his own in the action department. You don't get knighted by Richard the Lionheart without some serious heroics. Ian leads the Thals to revolution and is the first character ever shot by a Dalek for his troubles (he gets better); he battles giant ants (twice); he gets challenged to a ritual fight to the death seemingly every other week, including one notable stint as a Roman gladiator. Famously, he stops the Doctor – the *Doctor* – from bashing in the skull of the injured man who's slowing down their escape attempt.

It all sounds like it fits in with my preconception of the male companions as dashing but humorless punching machines, but that image couldn't sustain itself for long against the reality of Ian Chesterton, mild-mannered mid-1960s science teacher. Ian, with his various cardigans. His dismay at losing his school tie to a puddle of alien acid. His frankly astonishing "dancing" to "Ticket to Ride." Obviously, I loved him from the very start.

Nothing will convince me that Barbara didn't love him too, but she has a point in *The Keys of Marinus* when she complains that he treats her and Susan "like Dresden china." It's a trait that carries over when she and Ian find their way home and future space pilot Steven joins the TARDIS. Steven is funnier and snarkier and more laid back than Ian – except when he runs back into a burning building to rescue his toy panda, but two years marooned on a deserted planet with only robots for company would do that to anyone – but he also has a habit of telling his female fellow travelers that "the Doctor would never forgive me if I let anything happen to you." It's a pity he doesn't get to hear the speech at the end of *The Massacre,* so he doesn't know how much his threat to leave saddens the Doctor. I tend to assume Vicki and Dodo spend a lot of their time quietly not letting anything happen to Steven, because they'd never hear the end of it.

The Massacre, incidentally, is one of only three Doctor Who stories with no female companions at all, at least until the last scene when Dodo makes her entrance, dragging her wandering accent across Wimbledon Common to startle Steven with her resemblance to a woman he's spent four episodes failing to save. It's also the first time we see the Doctor with just one companion. In a parallel universe where Steven was as iconic a companion as Sarah Jane would become, "Doctor plus one male companion" could have become the accepted standard, and this would have been a different book. As it is, we're back to teams of two or three right away, as Steven leaves to lead a warring group of aliens and the next story introduces his replacements, Polly and Ben.

By this point, enough companions have come and gone that certain patterns are starting to emerge. Ben is from contemporary Earth – London, in fact – and like Ian before him and Mickey and Rory after, he only meets the Doctor because of his relationship with a female companion. Aliens and men from other times might fall in with the Doctor on their own, but the modern man is either assigned to him by UNIT or brought along by a woman. Ben's a sailor, as Steven was a combat pilot. More cautious and more serious than Ian or Steven, unimpressed by the Doctor but drawn into his world anyway, smarter than people give him credit for and present for the very first regeneration, he reminds me quite a lot of Mickey Smith.

A third companion joins Ben and Polly not long after their own entrance and Dodo's abrupt exit. Picked up from Culloden, Jamie's the first companion from the past (if you don't count poor doomed Katarina) and his time as companion almost perfectly overlaps with Patrick Troughton's tenure as the Doctor, coming in on Troughton's second story, leaving on the regeneration. It's a completely new Doctor / companion relationship; oh, the first Doctor doted on the companions who reminded him of Susan, and "my dear"ed and "my boy"ed everyone else to within an inch of their lives, but with Jamie it veers away from the paternal and becomes a more or less perpetual state of sheer co-dependent cling. Their separation (from each other and Zoe) in *The War Games* is so crushing, it's been retconned into a whole other series of adventures we mostly didn't see, but it's a shake-up as major as the first regeneration. For the first time, the entire cast changed at once. When the show returned, everything was different.

In 1970, the third Doctor arrived in color, on film, and with a new Time-Lord-plus-one-modern-woman dynamic that was going to define the Doctor/companion relationship for most of the next 40 years – to the point that answer A in our quiz was a verbatim quote from a casual viewer friend of mine who assumed that there was only ever one companion at a time, Highlander-style. I can see where he got that from, even if he must have been channel-hopping when Mickey and Jack and Rory were on screen. Rose leaves before Martha arrives, and Donna only starts to travel with the Doctor after Martha's gone, and Donna never meets Amy, who never meets Clara. That starts here, with Liz and Jo and Sarah Jane.

If the male companion was only meant to act as an action stand-in, it's not surprising there are none in the Pertwee years. The third Doctor Venusian Aikido-s his way through his own fight scenes and never met a vehicle he couldn't involve in a high-speed chase. Still, with the TARDIS stuck on Earth, it's possible for the first time to have a regular supporting cast beyond the Doctor and the people traveling with him. The fine fighting men of UNIT are in all but about half a dozen of the Pertwee stories, but aside from a few short trips (which the Brigadier, in particular, doesn't seem to enjoy), they're strictly a ground crew. It's not until the third Doctor comes to a nasty end on Metebelis III that a UNIT man gets to join the TARDIS.

Harry Sullivan's more explicitly a comic relief character than anyone before him (the Doctor in *Revenge of the Cybermen*: "Harry Sullivan is an imbecile!"), but Ian Marter pulls it off with enough charm that it's not embarrassing or mean, as similar slapstick material later seems with Mickey. When Harry's had enough of the Doctor's lifestyle, he just decides he's off, and gets the train home. He has the lowest-drama entrance and exit ever, chumping amiably into the story and back out of it again without too much in between aside from his titanic battle with a giant clam. "Oh, Harry," Sarah Jane says years later, in a Russell T Davies-scripted episode of kiddie spinoff *The Sarah Jane Adventures*: "I loved Harry." So did I.

Sarah Jane leaves without meeting Leela, and Romana (both of her) replaces Leela without so much as an episode of overlap, and once the

Doctor stops dropping by UNIT HQ the recurring cast fades out. He also regenerates again. With the youngest actor yet playing the Doctor, there's no need for a male companion to sub in for the fighting bits. Well, not after his opening story, a significant chunk of which he spends incoherent or unconscious, but even then it's Tegan and Nyssa who do much of the heavy lifting while Adric gets captured by the villain. This is a bit of a problem of Adric's; when he's not being held prisoner by the bad guys, he's joining their side, usually as a misguided attempt at being a double agent (three times may not sound like much, but considering that he's only in 11 stories...).

Doctor Who fandom never agrees on anything, but it's a safe bet that Adric won't be topping any companion popularity contests any time soon. All companions are someone's least favorite, but there's a particular kind of sci-fi fan vitriol that's reserved for teenage boy geniuses. Even the sweet, eager-to-please teen prodigies – your Wesley Crusher types, say – inspire furious loathing, and Adric knows very well how clever he is, thank you very much. He's got the badge for mathematical excellence to prove it, after all.

I have a soft spot for Adric, who even at his worst – and despite his genius – seems a fairly typical awful teenager who simply never has a chance to grow out of that awfulness. If he has a match among the companions who went before him, it's not Ian or Jamie, but Vicki, Dodo or (perhaps especially) Susan. Adric's relationship with the Doctor is far more fractious than the girls', though, and his exit doesn't even have the bittersweet hope of Susan, who is abandoned on an alien planet but left with the man she loves. He dies, accidentally wiping out the dinosaurs in the process, with silent credits rolling over a shot of the same shiny maths star broken on the floor – the first companion death since 1965, and (arguably[19]) the only long-term companion death at all.

Turlough is harder to compare to anyone else, because it's the first time a companion starts off working against the Doctor. Even Ian and Barbara got over their distrust of him within a couple of stories, and that was after he'd kidnapped them. Turlough, meanwhile, blags his way onto the TARDIS on the say-so of a duck-hatted alien being who wants him to murder the Doctor. It's my single favorite companion history, even before you get into the part where he's secretly an alien political prisoner forced into an exile that, for some reason, involves him attending an English boarding school ("the worst place in the universe," he

---

19 Wikipedia has a list of companions who we assume to have died after they left the TARDIS – though taking the long view, that would include everyone except Jack.

says, never deigning to elaborate on why he continues to wear the uniform long after escaping on the TARDIS). It's as if the writers knew he was going to be the last male companion of classic *Who* and decided to throw every backstory they'd ever wanted to use at him.

Even after choosing the Doctor over the Black Guardian, Turlough doesn't fit the faithful sidekick role quite as well as companions past. He's more of a pragmatist, giving the Doctor up for dead within 20 seconds of his apparent drowning in *Warriors of the Deep*, and in *Frontios* he gloomily agrees with the assurance that nobody expects him to save the day: "Of course they don't. I'm Turlough." He's selling himself short, considering that in the same story he discovers a hat stand can easily be mistaken for a deadly weapon, but it's still some way from Ian and Steven's weekly companion heroics. I can't imagine him telling Nyssa or Tegan "the Doctor would never forgive me if I let anything happen to you" with a straight face, or that they'd believe him if he did, but he's sincere in his final scene, as he tells Peri, "Look after him, won't you? He gets into terrible trouble."

We've shifted from multiple companions taking care of each other to a single companion taking care of the Doctor: after Peri, Mel, then Ace, without so much as a robot dog for a supporting cast. That Doctor-plus-one model was to continue into the series' 2005 revival under Russell T Davies, and it's nicely appropriate that the 1996 TV movie, coming as it does just about halfway between the end of the original run and the ninth Doctor's debut, has a foot in both camps. Grace's emotional arc and her romance with the Doctor make her a prototype for the Roses and Marthas and Amys of New *Who* and Chang Lee brings the first racial diversity to the companion line-up, but he's also solidly in the tradition of Turlough and Adric, pulling double companion duty by spending half the story working with the Master.

He does make a promising early bid for companionhood by sticking with the mortally wounded seventh Doctor – which doesn't sound like much until you consider that the gang who shot him were aiming for Chang Lee, and that at least one of his friends was killed in the same firefight – but it all goes a bit wrong when the Master hunts him down. With a combination of mind control and a flimsy sob story about the Doctor being the real bodysnatching villain, Chang Lee switches sides. Luckily for him, a tendency to be duped by the villain is where the similarity to Adric ends; he does die, killed by the Master, but the temporal grace reset button means it isn't permanent. He's back on team Doctor by the end, but all this duplicity is probably why it's Grace who gets the big, fireworks-backed kiss and the invitation to travel in the TARDIS, while he's sent on his way with a bag of gold and a cryptic warning about the future. What might have been a pity for those of us who enjoy companions with ambiguous loyalties turned out to be a moot point – the TV Movie didn't lead to any more screen outings for the eighth Doctor, and *Doctor Who* was gone again for nine years.

The show came back in 2005 with a new companion and first episode both called *Rose* – although Rose Tyler, like Grace, declines the chance to travel in the TARDIS, at first. "Someone's got to look after this stupid lump." The lump in question is her boyfriend, Mickey, who's understandably not at his best, having spent the day being kidnapped by Autons and eaten by a bin. The Doctor returns to repeat his invitation, pointing out that his spaceship is also a time machine. Rose kisses Mickey goodbye and runs, beaming, into the TARDIS.

In the old series, we would never have seen Mickey again. Barring some plot contrivance, it wouldn't even have been possible for the first nine seasons of the show, when the Doctor had no control over where he headed next. If you got caught up in one of the Doctor's adventures and didn't leave with him at the end of it, that was your lot. In some ways, Jack is the most traditional of the new series companions: he has a major role in his first story, but it's not *about* him. We don't see his home or his family, and he integrates into the TARDIS family between stories. He's even fairly Steven-ish, both of them being snarky space-adventurers from the future; I'm not sure Steven did quite so much flirting, but he *was* very pleased to find himself on a planet of beautiful ladies in *Galaxy 4*, and with so many of his episodes missing, who knows?

Mickey, and later Rory, have quite a different character arc. New series Doctors can more or less steer the TARDIS – the "less" becomes apparent when Rose goes home after what should be a few days and finds she's been missing for a year, with poor, luckless Mickey suspected of her murder – and that lets us have characters who don't start off as companions but grow into the role. Mickey starts off dismissed as "Mickey the idiot," explicitly "not invited" to come with the Doctor. A year and a regeneration later, he invites *himself* along, with no less a TARDIS veteran than Sarah Jane Smith backing him up, and the Doctor agrees. There's only so many times somebody can save the world before you have to admit your first impression might have been a bit hasty.

Rory seems at first to be in the same vein as Mickey; the companion's boyfriend back home, an obstacle to any potential romance with the

Doctor, the occasional comic relief. Since they're not part of the Doctor's world by their own choice, they get to point out the downsides of the way he lives and his effect on the people he meets. They even both get replaced by Nestene duplicates.

The major divergence in their arcs comes when the eleventh Doctor, alarmed by Amy getting amorous, abducts Rory from his stag party and takes him on a would-be romantic jaunt to vampire-infested Venice. From that point until both Amy and Rory leave the series – and setting aside the times when Rory's busy being dead – the Doctor has two companions. Jack and Mickey only joined the TARDIS for a few episodes each; Rory has a longer tenure that either Martha or Donna. It's the first extended period with a TARDIS team since the days of Tegan and Turlough, but in Amy and Rory's later episodes – once they're not only slightly older, and a married couple, but the Doctor's in-laws – it's more reminiscent of Ian and Barbara.

It does seem fitting that if Jack is Steven, and Mickey is Ben, then Rory's our parallel to Ian. They both give me the impression of fundamental human decency wrapped in a comfy cardigan. Ian could certainly have locked Hitler in a cupboard, and I'd fancy Rory's chances against a giant ant any day. And they do both end up as Romans, though Ian for a matter of weeks instead of two thousand years (wouldn't he have done it, though, for Barbara?).

As I write this, in the fiftieth anniversary year, Peter Capaldi has been announced as the twelfth Doctor. At 55, he's quite a bit older than the last few Doctors; older than any of them, in fact, except William Hartnell himself. For all I know, someone at the BBC is at this very moment insisting that a young male companion needs to be brought on board to handle the action scenes. While I don't think that's necessary – Clara has protected every single Doctor across his entire lifetime, she can cope – if some young stud does turn up, I'm sure I'll love him just as much as the rest. In fact, I'd like to suggest harkening back to the show's earliest days and returning to the earliest almost-companion of all. The very first scene of *An Unearthly Child*, Foreman's junkyard, the policeman peering through the London fog; he was so close to greatness, whoever he was, if he'd only paid more attention to that mysterious police box.

Companion Piece

A Different Way of Living

Julia duMais is from Washington, D.C. In her free time, she enjoys swimming, video games, embroidery,and informing her cats of their cuteness. She also enjoys sharing her many feelings on pop culture, which she typically does on the Bossy Britches podcast and on Twitter (@juleshastweets). She is a web developer by day, and by night she's asleep.

In 2005, I was barely 20, working a retail job that made me unhappy, and just coming off my annual *Peter Pan* reread, itching for Adventure with a capital A, with all the 20-year-old (okay, teenaged) exuberance and naïveté that embarrasses me now in my ancient, wizened late twenties. I was longing for more stories of girls who ran off on wild adventures, and then came back and grew up, changed but not unrecognizable. Then my friends started buzzing about this *Doctor Who* thing. I never stood a chance. I, not to put too fine a point on it, couldn't have projected onto Rose Tyler more if my name was IMAX.

I gulped down the Eccleston episodes and was left longing for more. And then I got it, at Christmas, and more a few months later, and... it seemed like something had changed. I couldn't put my finger on what, exactly, but something was very different, and not just the Doctor's face. Something was different about Rose, too, and the change wasn't for the better. I ultimately stopped watching altogether for awhile, not finishing the series until years later.

I couldn't say, on finally finishing the series, that I was sorry I'd waited. Suddenly Rose – Rose, who had saved the world and the Doctor; Rose, who scrawled across history a message to herself not to let the Doctor write her future – was weeping on a beach, lamenting that her life, that *she*, was nothing without him. I could handwave that moment, sure – I'd gone through rough breakups. A few weeks of crying, a steady stream of chocolate, she'd be fine. But I shouldn't have to tell myself that – the Doctor was supposed to make people's lives *better*. Following the retcon of Sarah Jane Smith's departure early on in Series Two, it wasn't a surprise, but it was still a disappointment.

And all throughout Series Two, Rose seems to become less substantial, less necessary. In *The Idiot's Lantern*, she is literally rendered just a body – she's baggage, with no face and an impractical costume; more disturbing still, it's her investigating, asking the right questions, that gets her there. The entire series, for me, is similarly uncomfortable to watch, sometimes even upsetting or disturbing (*Love and Monsters*, looking in your direction, though at least that has some wonderful moments of Jackie Tyler). But there's more to it, I realized, when I finally did watch the whole thing, especially in combination with Series Four.

Together, they drag each other in circles. It's only when the Doctor and Rose separate that they can start growing again. She illustrates the paradox of the companions: the Doctor is the title character, the constant, but *they* are the ones whose lives change the most – it's just that the very nature of his relationship with them means that we don't see it. He changes their lives, but they're the ones who go out and live, while he keeps on going in circles.

The Doctor-Peter Pan comparison is so on the nose as to be a cliche; on the other hand, it's a cliche because it's so on the nose. Peter, who can't grow up, is "the tragic boy"; his entry into someone's life is a "tragedy." Wendy is the hero, the one who grows up, and it's the companions who go on and have lives. "Everything has its time, and everything ends," the Doctor says – everything but him. Rose's story illustrates this brilliantly, but, in keeping with the paradoxical nature of the issue, the weakest parts of her story do so at least as much as the strongest.

The End

"Oh no, he isn't grown up," Wendy assured her confidently, "and he is just my size." She meant that he was her size in both mind and body; she didn't know how she knew, she just knew it.

—J.M. Barrie, *Peter and Wendy*

In Series One, Rose and the Doctor complement, even parallel one another. Russell T Davies says that in giving Rose a family, a life on Earth, and "a sad story" in her father's death, he was setting her up with "her own mythology, to match the Doctor."[20]

The idea seems laughable at first – a boyfriend, a mother and a father who died when she was a child make her a match for the Doctor, who's lost his family, his entire people? But, what's a companion if not a version of the Doctor who doesn't get to do it all over and over? What's a companion if not the Doctor on a slightly different scale?

---

20 "Time Trouble." *Doctor Who Confidential*. Series One, episode eight.

"I did it again," he berates himself, and her, in *Father's Day*, "I picked another stupid ape." Making it all about himself, about his own choices, acting as though, as Rose says at the very beginning of their time together, the entire Earth revolves around him.

She *used* him, he rages, she planned this all along. She initially declined to travel with the Doctor in space, only agreeing when he said "time machine." The Doctor's implication here, the question even he never dares ask out loud, is that he was only ever a means of saving her father. But he was there, both times she witnessed her father's death, and he *took* her there to see it in the first place. He knew that there could be no satisfactory outcome or even a good choice – even if there was a *right* one – and she had to choose anyway.

Sound familiar?

"I couldn't save your planet, I couldn't save any of them," the Doctor tells the Nestene Consciousness in *Rose*.[21] We know early on that the Doctor blames himself; that it was his actions that ended the war and killed his own people becomes terribly clear as the episodes unspool. There was no good choice in the Time War, but there may have been a right one. And there is the choice he made. We don't know until years later, in *The Day of the Doctor*, whether they are the same – and perhaps more importantly, neither does he.

Rose and the Doctor learn together that some things can't be changed, only, maybe, made a little less awful. Her father dies, but not alone, and Rose learns to think of the story as something a little less terrible, in which she isn't helpless.

# # #

The first time Rose meets the Doctor, he blows up her workplace. The second time, her mother is already talking about how she needs to find the right *kind* of job – one that will keep her from being a burden, but won't encourage her to get above herself, to put on "airs and graces." And here comes someone strange and clever and funny and part of a much, much bigger world than Rose ever imagined existed. He wants her with him, he *needs* her with him... and he asks her to come with him. Every step of the way, he asks.

Until, suddenly, he doesn't.

In *The Parting of the Ways*, he sends her away. He tricks her into the

---

21 Not to be confused with one of the big questions fanfic writers deal with, of what exactly the Doctor says to Rose at the end of *Doomsday*.

TARDIS, locks it and sends her back to her own world, tells her to let it – and him – die, and to forget that he ever existed. He asked her to see a new world, showed it to her – and then took it away, without asking her what she thought of the whole matter.

"Is it always this dangerous?" she asked, when he first invited her. "Yeah," he said, and she *chose* to go with him anyway. He took her to see her planet burn, and asked her, again, if she still wanted to stay. In *Father's Day*, she saw the terrible consequences that result from doing the right thing, and he let her make those terrible choices anyway. And now – hardly the first time she's been in danger with him, not even the first time she's seen the Earth destroyed, or its destruction threatened – *now* he decides for her?

"The Doctor showed me a better life," she says, trying to explain to Jackie and Mickey, in what comes out as a criticism of their lives. Combined with other comments she makes, in Series Two in particular, it's hard not to resent what she says here. Whose fault is it that her life isn't more exciting, more interesting? Do you think you're entitled to adventure? You've got to go out and make it interesting for yourself.

Which, of course, she did. She said yes when the Doctor *asked* if she wanted to go away with him, and when he brought her back and they saved the world from the Slitheen, she packed a bag and went with him again.

It's telling that it's not a better life the Doctor shows her, it's "a better way of living":

> "I don't mean all the traveling and seeing aliens and spaceships and things. That don't matter. The Doctor showed me a better way of living your life. You know he showed you too – that you don't just give up. You don't just let things happen. You make a stand. You say no. You have the guts to do what's right when everyone else just runs away."

In *The Parting of the Ways*, Rose does what no human is meant to do, what no human *can* do and survive: she gazes into the heart of the TARDIS, takes the time vortex into herself. And the ninth Doctor, who saved the universe by killing billions, a man whose own later incarnation describes him as "too dangerous to be left on his own, full of blood and anger," gets to destroy himself, and save the woman who saved Earth (by killing millions, Daleks though they were) in doing so. Someone else – someone intimately connected to him, but *not* him – has done the ugly part, and now, finally, he gets to *fix* something.

"You need a Doctor," he says to Rose before he kisses her. There's a lot of light, and even more when she wakes up – and at the end of all this cosmic violence, there's a new Doctor. The series ends.

The Middle
Then Peter knelt beside her and found his button. You remember she had put it on a chain that she wore round her neck.

"See," he said, "the arrow struck against this. It is the kiss I gave her. It has saved her life."

—J.M. Barrie, *Peter and Wendy*

The first series of New *Who* looks different from the rest. There's a hazy, dreamy glow about everything, and the colors are brighter, more saturated. Conversely, Rose and the Doctor look entirely ordinary, even Spartan: in *Dalek*, she spends most of her time running around in jeans and a white tank top, rocking the John McClane look. The Doctor, too, wears jeans, a shirt and a leather jacket; a minimal, practical outfit. Their clothes are for running in. And they wear bold, dark colors; Rose wears almost no non-denim blue the entire season.[22] She's in blacks and reds and bright fuschia pinks.

With the tenth Doctor, things are different. The colors are less vibrant – *Tooth and Claw*, in particular, is all blues and grays, so that it almost looks black-and-white at some points. The Doctor's Converse shoes, made for running, are impossibly, impractically clean, and the rest of his outfit – a tailored suit and glasses – is downright professorial, or at least professional. Rose is, usually, still in jeans and T-shirts, but the two of them are no longer color-coordinated. She still wears pink, sometimes, but it's hidden under jackets or sweatshirts, and it's a softer, paler pink – the bubblegum of her fluffy, shiny dress in *The Idiot's Lantern*. Her hair is shorter, and it's more carefully styled – for that matter, so is his, gelled into spikes or moussed neatly. And she wears blue – blue jackets, blue sweaters, etc.

In *The Christmas Invasion*, immediately following the Doctor's regeneration, both Harriet Jones and Rose Tyler deal with the same question: what does one do without him? Jones deploys a super-weapon to protect Earth – and the Doctor punishes her for it, destroying her career.

Rose decides that she'll be the Doctor herself, facing down the Sycorax and boldly trying to bluff. She fails. The Sycorax laugh at her,

---

22 And really, denim is basically a neutral anyway, so that hardly counts.

her "stolen words." They're ready to kill her for her audacity, for daring to think she can be the hero here. If it wasn't for the Doctor,[23] she'd have died there, punished for doing exactly what he taught her to do.

"When I'm stuck at home, I'm useless," she says, while the Doctor is unconscious. Hardly – it's Rose who notices that something is off about the alien pilotfish. She gets her mother, Mickey, and the Doctor to the safest place: the TARDIS. She faces the Sycorax herself. But that, right there, is the problem: her actual *home* isn't safe. She faces the Sycorax because "someone's got to be the Doctor."

"You need a Doctor," he said to her. She's forgotten a lot of what happened at the end of the fight – but it's hard not to think that this, at least, she's retained, even taken too much to heart.[24]

Watching Series Two, it seems that the biggest lesson Rose has taken is that she *does* need the Doctor.

# # #

While he's unconscious in *The Christmas Invasion*, she comments that she forgets that the Doctor isn't human. This becomes a recurring theme: Rose trying to mash the two parts of her life together, refusing to accept that they won't stick.

The gap between her life on Earth and her life with the Doctor always existed, but in Series Two, it widens to a chasm. The difference is glaring because Rose herself is so torn: she has trouble accepting that the ordinary human life she expects with the Doctor can never actually happen, that he can't grow old alongside her, that he really, truly isn't human – but she no longer fits into life on modern-day Earth, either.

The two of them are unbearable in *Tooth and Claw*, acting "like smug idiots" in the words of Graeme Burk and Robert Smith?.[25] There's a straight line between their obnoxious behavior here and their violent separation in *Doomsday*, one that's explicitly made in the text, when their behavior results in Her Majesty telling them precisely how dangerous they are:

---

23 The Doctor, it's worth noting, is revived by Jackie's tea – the very domesticity he so openly loathes, from the one person (except perhaps Mickey) he's mocked most since meeting Rose.

24 When we see her again, it's because she's working to save the world – by bringing together everyone who's ever traveled with the Doctor, in the hopes of contacting him. She sacrifices her life in the attempt, and is allowed to go out a hero, having apparently learned that worldsaving is best left to the Doctor.

25 Burk, Graeme; Smith?, Robert. *Who is the Doctor*, ECW Press, Ontario, 2012.

"You consort with stars and magic and think it fun. But your world is steeped in terror and blasphemy and death, and I will not allow it. You will leave these shores and you will reflect, I hope, on how you came to stray so far from all that is good, and how much longer you will survive this terrible life."

The Queen creates the Torchwood Institute, the organization through which the Earth is very nearly destroyed at the end of Series Two, specifically to protect her people from creatures like the Doctor. It's through Torchwood that Rose and the Doctor are ultimately separated, universes apart.

Which makes it so interesting that it's in a parallel world's Torchwood that Rose finds herself a career, a life, a way of saving the world herself... and the Doctor again.

The Beginning

That was the last time the girl Wendy ever saw him. For a little longer she tried for his sake not to have growing pains; and she felt she was untrue to him when she got a prize for general knowledge. But the years came and went without bringing the careless boy; and when they met again Wendy was a married woman, and Peter was no more to her than a little dust in the box in which she had kept her toys. Wendy was grown up. You need not be sorry for her. She was one of the kind that likes to grow up. In the end she grew up of her own free will a day quicker than other girls.

—J.M. Barrie, *Peter and Wendy*

Suddenly, she's back.

Well, no, it's not really sudden at all. Rose is gone, but she's still a *presence* in Series Three, which does the show, and the Doctor, no favors – Martha Jones deserved far better than she endured from the Doctor, a fact which even Rose seems to wake to, come the Series Four finale. "Oh, she's *good*," she says of Martha to the Doctor, before she and Martha wrap each other up in a joyful hug.

Indeed, Rose seems to get on well with all of the Doctor's assembled companions, however rocky her relations with them might start: she's initially put off because Martha seems to have taken her place on Harriet Jones' emergency network, not to mention the embarrassing catfight-style tension between her and Sarah Jane Smith in *School Reunion*. But the two of them end up close, laughing at the Doctor and understanding one another as few other people in the universe can do.

The companion Rose interacts most with, though, is Donna. They have some obvious parallels: women working jobs they feel disconnected from, with strong-willed mothers offering no end of advice. It's Donna that Rose finds in *Partners in Crime*, Donna who is tasked with warning the Doctor when Rose can't make him hear it for himself.

Somewhere along the line, it seems, Rose has remembered the meaning of "Bad Wolf": she's not powerless in the face of the Doctor's choices for her, she can come back and help him. But it's through Donna that she passes the message first, and it's later in *Turn Left* that we really get a sense of who Rose is becoming.

"I've been pulled across from a different universe because every single universe is in danger," Rose says. The passive voice is interesting: Rose has on the same outfit in all her Series Four appearances, suggesting that each time she's "pulled" across from her own universe, it's the same day. But she knows the details of what's happening as she spends more time with Donna – she works for Torchwood now, so she's got the resources to research it (not to mention the giant gun she brings with her in *The Stolen Earth*). She talks tech at lightning speed to Torchwood officials, not just reciting information that Torchwood has given her – she's confident, practiced.

The *Turn Left* version of Donna is confused, even frightened, by Rose, who takes the reaction in stride. "You'll come with me," she says, "when you want to." And, indeed, just as someone else kept popping up in her life, so Rose keeps popping up in Donna's. "You're the most important person in all of creation," she tells Donna, before, with incredible sadness, sending her to a point where she must sacrifice her own life.

Rose is, in short, sounding an awful lot like the Doctor.

But she's come into her own; without a Doctor whose shadow she can retreat into when she fails at imitating him, she's become a version of him without losing herself. The Doctor recognizes this, sending his part-human double with her to the parallel universe where she now lives.

"He destroyed the Daleks," the Doctor says of his counterpart. "He committed genocide." So did Rose, though, when she saved Earth in *The Parting of the Ways*. If that's what makes the other Doctor "too dangerous to be left on his own," then presumably it applies to *her* as well. The other Doctor is "full of blood and anger and revenge," and "our" Doctor entrusts Rose with the job of helping him, again, learn to live in the world after the war is over.

This new Doctor isn't the only one who's different, after all: so is Rose. She still has her family, but it's a *larger* family, one where she's got a new sibling to think about. She still has a job, but it appears to be a proper career, one where she takes what the Doctor showed her and saves the world – in short, she has a life. And his double ("me when we first met," the Doctor says) will eventually have a death. They can, once again, complement each other – but on *her* terms, this time, complete with the domesticity he's always rejected about her life on Earth.

It always seems like a cop-out to try and explain Rose's more frustrating moments with "well, she's very young." But I think it's worth looking at Rose as someone who's trying her best to grow up – and it's a messy, scary process, that. Sometimes, there are a few steps backward for every step forward, and sometimes you need to get away from the people you most want to be so you can figure out how to be yourself.

We, Robots

Erika Ensign is technical producer and co-host of the *Doctor Who* podcast *Verity!*, co-host of *The Audio Guide to Babylon 5*, co-producer of *Uncanny Magazine Podcast*, and a frequent panelist on *The Incomparable*. She tweets about all kinds of things as @HollyGoDarkly and blogs about *Doctor Who*, knitting and other random geeky (and non-geeky) pursuits at fan girlknitsscarf.wordpress.com. She started watching *Doctor Who* in 1983 at the age of five because she has the coolest mom in the world. She met her now-husband Steven online through his *Doctor Who* podcast (*Radio Free Skaro*), and they got married at the *Gallifrey One Doctor Who* convention. Her fancy university degree in communications, which concentrated on editing and production, is finally serving her in the real world (at least, she tells herself podcasts are part of the real world). In addition to *Doctor Who* and oodles of other SF and fantasy, she likes spreadsheets, Canadians, the Oxford comma and pop punk music. Not necessarily in that order.

I'll admit it straightaway: I was a kid when K-9 first graced my screen. I was at that perfect age, when my eyes got big as saucers and my grin nearly popped off my face at seeing a metal doggie – who talked! And wagged his tail! And did Important Things within the context of the show! (Heck, even when he wasn't *doing* things, he was often important – if not for the memorable waggling of K-9's tail, the Doctor and Romana might still be stuck in that pesky chronic hysteresis.) So my views on K-9 are a bit clouded by the rosy view of a six-year-old. I own this. I feel no shame. I apologize for nothing.

That's not to say I'm completely blinded to the troubles inherent in adding a mechanical companion to a low-budget BBC program in the 70s. Old Hollywood wisdom holds that you should never work with children or animals. I suspect the BBC production team in charge of *Doctor Who* at the time might want to add robots to that list. The mechanical characters certainly had a troubled behind-the-scenes history. They often had to be written out or written around because of their real-world failings. (Of course, the same could be said for the live actors. How many times in the first and second Doctor eras was one of the leads imprisoned for an episode or knocked unconscious, simply because the actor needed a vacation or contracted chicken pox?) But I don't think it's fair to hold these not-in-the-*Doctor Who*-universe issues against the characters themselves. When I look at K-9, I don't see him as a metal prop trundling along halting and awkwardly; I see an adorable, lovable, incredibly smart, occasionally smug robot dog.

The on-set troubles K-9 caused were nothing next to those caused by the show's other mechanical companion, Kamelion. No one even knew how to operate him (due to the untimely death of one of his designers), so he had an introductory story, a farewell story and pretty much disappeared entirely for the five stories in between. Even so, when I look at Kamelion I see a noble, self-sacrificing soul whose entire story is tragic, touching and beautiful. I realize I'm probably in the minority here. That's alright. I've made myself a nice little fort in *Doctor Who* fan minorityland. Feel free to come visit. I'll bake cookies.

Kamelion's tenure on the show may have been brief, but I think he was a wonderful idea, poorly realized. A robot that can make himself look like anything or anyone? Yes, please! My imagination is running away with me just thinking about it! Sadly, we got next to no payoff for that inspired idea. Damn real world. Why must you hinder my *Doctor Who*? I wondered why they didn't just cast random actors to "be" Kamelion in some of the stories for which he resided on the TARDIS, until I realized actors cost money. And I suppose if the nifty idea can't be realized fully, it was easier for an overworked crew to forget about the poor robot. His disappearance does make for an amusing game though. While watching *The Five Doctors* through *Resurrection of the Daleks*, it's fun to play Spot Kamelion, and try to guess what random object in the TARDIS is actually the robot in disguise.

Game or no game, I like Kamelion. He had a kind soul (or whatever the robot equivalent of a soul is) and simply wanted to help. It wasn't his fault that he was weaker than the Master, a freaking *Time Lord* who has a long history of messing with the Doctor's friends. Poor Kamelion was just another in a long line. In the end though, he's able to throw off that control long enough to save his human comrades. He then requests that the Doctor destroy him so it can't happen again. Just thinking about that has me misting up a bit. (It also has me a bit cross with the Doctor for not seeming sorrier about doing it.)

So yes, I've officially outed myself as a lover of the mechanical companions, the "mechompanions," if you will. You won't? Okay. Fine then. Whatever you want to call them, I think they're aces. Over the years, *Doctor Who* did (and still does) a great job of including a variety of different types of characters as companions. Yes, it skews heavily in favor of cute young girls, but to the show's credit, it's broken out of that mold several times – nearly always to great effect (as far as I'm concerned anyway). The decision to attempt companions that are not only non-human, but non-living, was a leap further and one that I think works.

It's an even bigger leap when you consider the Doctor's attitude toward mechanicals. He has a storied and inconsistent history with machines and computers. The first Doctor seems to be interested in and fascinated by them. In *The War Machines*, he's genuinely impressed by WOTAN, but treats it and its creations a bit like wayward children. The second Doctor is vocally opposed to computers in *The Invasion*, as is the third (BOSS in *The Green Death*). By the time the fourth Doctor rolls around, he seems to have a more genial and trusting relationship with mechanicals (despite the fact that he occasionally has to destroy the bad eggs and tells Romana not to trust "gimmicky gadgets"). I suppose it makes sense that this Doctor is the one to adopt the first mechanical companion.

Personifying inanimate objects is something children do all the time. It's also something people with a nerd-brain (like mine) seem to do very well. I'm not sure if it should be surprising or not that it's something the Doctor excels at too. K-9 and Kamelion aren't properly inanimate, but they're certainly not living breathing human beings (despite Kamelion's ability to look that way occasionally). What they do have, like the human companions, is personality.

The show does a great job of displaying these personalities. K-9 is a rascally little scamp. He loves his master and mistresses (at least insofar as he's programmed to do so), and he defends them unquestioningly. While there's an emphasis on the fact that he's a mechanical creature, it's played out by way of his logical brain and his inability to understand colloquial turns of phrase. While a show like *Star Trek: The Next Generation* often focuses on Data's inability to feel emotions, *Doctor Who* neatly sidesteps nearly all discussion of that aspect of its mechanical characters. K-9 is treated, in great part, like the dog he's built to resemble. Kamelion, being humanoid, offers more opportunity for such existential examination, but the show almost seems to take it as read that he does have some sort of emotional response to stimuli – even if that response is simply to be sorry and frustrated at being possessed and used by a more powerful entity. Kamelion *asks* to be destroyed in the end. Maybe that could be chalked up to purely rational and altruistic decision-making, but (certainly as a child) I read it as the noble self-sacrifice of a soul in torment. Parse it as you will, Kamelion's stories themselves didn't focus on his differences from humanity. Some folks might think that the show missed a trick there, but I appreciate that these mechanical pals are simply characters. I found it easier to love them because less time was spent on highlighting how "other" they are.

Of course, the Doctor's sentimentality extends beyond objects shaped to mimic people and dogs. His love for the TARDIS (even before she got all humanified in *The Doctor's Wife*) is obvious... perhaps not at the very beginning, but it did become a theme. He talks to her constantly, fiddles with her unceasingly, and it's clear that however much he loves his companions, he cares about the TARDIS just as much. And then there's his sonic screwdriver, which he mourned almost "like a friend" when a Terileptil blasted it in *The Visitation*. Perhaps it comes down to the fact that people, and Time Lords apparently, personify the "things" they love the most.

Now we know (through the magic of retconning) that the TARDIS really isn't a machine after all. Still, the TARDIS isn't a "person" except for a few brief hours. Machine or not, she's at least partially mechanical and not at all humanoid. When you think about it, the Doctor's number-one-most-favorite companion ever is his nearly constant companion, the TARDIS herself – and I don't assign the female gender just because of the body she happened to inhabit as Idris. The Doctor has referred to the TARDIS as female for centuries. Sarah Jane may have rankled at being called "old girl," but the TARDIS never did. (Or if she did, she expressed it more subtly – perhaps some of those mechanical failures and missed destinations were actually her version of grumbling.)

The Doctor treats K-9, the TARDIS, and his sonic screwdriver like they're beloved friends (okay, so he never really treats Kamelion that way), but the program itself certainly doesn't show the same affection. Living breathing companions occasionally got short shrift, but that was nothing compared to what the robots had to deal with. Kamelion's five-story disappearance seems somewhat understandable given the limitations of the robot itself, and occasionally K-9 isn't a viable companion. (K-9 in a swamp? No, of course not.) But there are plenty of times K-9 could have been helpful, and just chases a ball into the water or has a Marshman bash his head off. And how many times does he spend most of a story dismantled in the TARDIS because he's undergoing repairs? Even when he's part of the story, he's attacked by Wolfweeds or damaged by time winds. Or nearly destroyed by an Ogri or melted down. Or left stranded in a boat, plaintively calling for his master. Poor little K-9.

And then we have the unfortunate and battered TARDIS. She's

kicked around even from the first season of the show: she's damaged in *Marco Polo* so much that she can no longer produce power, water or light. She's covered in fungus and webs, dragged across planets, knocked off cliffs and all that happens before she takes the worst beatings – during the John Nathan-Turner/Christopher Bidmead era. She's used as a battering ram, shrunk, has part of her jettisoned (twice!), and is eventually blown up and scattered underground! The Doctor is appropriately concerned by these occurrences, but I almost picture the production team sniggering just off camera. Silly, I know, but boy do they lay it on thick. The Doctor wants to protect his mechanical companions from the world in the show. I want to protect them from the production team!

Don't even get me started on the destruction of the fifth Doctor's sonic screwdriver. The Doctor was disheartened. I was *shocked* and *appalled*. I didn't quite cry, but little Erika felt like she'd lost a friend too. That, as much as anything else, speaks to the show's ability to convince the audience that these "things" are worth caring about.

Despite their real-world limitations, these mechanical companions managed to capture the hearts, minds and imaginations of audiences all over the globe. The TARDIS is one of the most iconic symbols in television history. Sonic screwdrivers are currently selling like hotcakes in stores all over the world. And I wasn't alone in my longing for a plush K-9 to hug (something I still wish for at times). I just may even have a K-9 poster hanging proudly in my living room. (I totally do.) K-9 finally left the show in 1981, but he was such a memorable character he kept coming back. He had a cameo in *The Five Doctors* and even scored the title role in the spin-off *K-9 and Company*. It may not have gone beyond the pilot episode, but the catchy theme song will live on forever.

Yes, I'm leaving poor Kamelion out of this bit. He has been largely forgotten, and much as that pains me, I accept it. I'll keep his memory alive in my heart, since no one else particularly seems to want to.

Even decades later, K-9 wasn't to be forgotten. He appeared in *School Reunion* in 2006 – twice, technically, as K-9 Mark III sacrifices himself, and the Doctor gifts Sarah Jane with K-9 Mark IV. (I shan't get into the ins and outs of the various iterations of K-9. There are plenty of resources better suited to that kind of detailed info-dumping.) He goes on to be an occasional star of *The Sarah Jane Adventures*, and he even gets his own show again in Australia, *K-9* (which may or may not be in the canonical *Doctor Who* universe, depending how you look at it). This good dog simply cannot be put down any more than the TARDIS. And I wouldn't have it any other way.

Companion Piece

The Damned Don't Cry: Adric as Outsider

Sarah Groenewegen was born in Sydney, Australia, but now lives in London, UK. She's a writer who has had features and reviews published in various periodicals like the *Sydney Star Observer, Lesbians on the Loose* and *SFX Magazine*. She has had essays published in anthologies including the *Time Unincorporated* series and *Queers Dig Time Lords*. Her short fiction has won awards (Scarlet Stiletto, 2002) and been published in Big Finish's *Doctor Who* line, including the award-winning *Short Trips: Zodiac*. She writes a blog at nyssa1968.blogspot.co.uk. She is currently working on a science fiction novel trilogy when she's not out walking in the British countryside and sampling the fine ales of that land.

I am going to assume that if you are reading this, then you are a *Doctor Who* fan and you are reasonably well-versed with the concept of time travel. Excellent. Now, take my hand and I'll take you back to a specific time and place so you can understand what I'm going to share with you. A little secret that will help you form your own opinions, and not worry quite so much about what the fan elders think.

Yes, even about Adric.

I'm going to take you back to early 1982.

Hold on, hold on, you're thinking. *Adric became a companion in 1980. Full Circle first aired in the UK on October 25th, 1980. Earthshock episode four first aired in the UK on March 16th, 1982. Oh, okay, that is what you're on about.*

Well, partially. You see in 1982 I was a kid growing up in Sydney, Australia, and where I was Adric first turned up on our telly screens on March 22nd, 1982. In these twenty-first century days, when a new *Doctor Who* story is watched globally almost instantly, it's difficult to think of a time when international phone calls were prohibitively expensive. You needed to be incredibly rich to afford to listen to an episode down the phone lines; even a long call with friends or relatives telling you the story cost a lot. Video recorders existed, but were far from everyday household items. Besides, the fastest way to send a video recording – or even an audio on cassette tape – from the UK to Australia was by airmail, and that was expensive, too. Being a fan back then, and in Australia, was a very different experience to what it is now.

So, here's my hand. Take it and we'll head back to the time when aerobics – thanks to Jane Fonda – were about to be the next best thing, along with both fluorescent lycra and leg-warmers; when women and men wore their hair big and their make-up bright. A time when the genderqueer New Romantic bands ruled the pop charts.

# # #

I'm a kid again. Thirteen and a half years old. I am interested in politics and global affairs, and science fiction, but my high school doesn't encourage such interests. It's a state school, all girls, and it rather fancies itself a snooty private school. Us girls are meant to be preparing ourselves for finding a nice fella to marry and raise a family.

My parents have ruled that I can only watch television in the late afternoon after I've finished my homework. I tend to watch before our dinner. My favorite shows include *Doctor Who*. In fact, it's a bit of an obsession.

The Australian Broadcasting Corporation (ABC) had shown *Doctor Who* from 1966. I grew up watching *Doctor Who* and I love it. I know I must have seen Patrick Troughton stories, but I've gotten used to watching various Jon Pertwee and Tom Baker stories on an endless repeat cycle. "My" companions are Jo Grant and Sarah Jane Smith, joined later by Leela, K-9 and the two Romanas.

Then, disaster – the ABC decided to stop buying and showing *Doctor Who*.

I discovered *Doctor Who* fandom in 1979. The timing was dreadful. When *Doctor Who Monthly* turns up at local newsagents, I'm one of the loyal purchasers. Unfortunately, it doesn't turn up regularly, and I don't have the money for a subscription, and because it arrives by boat, it is always several months out of date. That and the Target novelizations are what tide me over in that television drought. It is through *Doctor Who Monthly* that I find out about John Nathan Turner taking over as producer, and of the changes he brought. I read about Romana and K-9 leaving, and about the three new companions joining by the end of Season Eighteen. One of them an Australian! One of them a boy. The first male companion in, oh, ages.

At 13 going on 14, I am at that awful and confusing age when boys and girls are supposed to be discovering each other. My classmates are obsessively into Duran Duran. I am in Year Nine (also known as Third Grade or Third Form), and I'm desperately thinking of an actor or pop star I can paste all over my school books. A constant war in my head is the need to conform to the social norms set by my peer group and establish my individuality. I feel different than everyone else, like I don't belong, and these are feelings I don't like very much. I'm not brave enough to stand out, but stand out I do. Sigh. Being a teenager is such a bundle of intense contradictions.

The publicity pictures of Matthew Waterhouse in *Doctor Who Monthly* look sweet. He has a nice smile. Bonus, he's in my favorite television show ever. Yeah, he'll do. In February 1982, the *Doctor Who* drought is at last ended. Two years after Britain saw the new title sequence and heard the new version of the theme music, I am eagerly watching Tom Baker's last series. Not that I want to see him gone, mind.

Doctor Who back in its cherished spot, Monday to Thursday. But, new episodes. Glorious.

# # #

Full Circle debuted in Australia at 6:30pm on Monday, March 22nd, 1982. It introduces Matthew Waterhouse as Adric in a story written by the young Scot, Andrew Smith. The story has some great scares (the spiders hatching from the marsh fruit, the marsh men emerging from the misty swamp) and introduces some concepts new to me (political oligarchies). I like the idea of the Outlers actually being brought back in when the society starts to collapse in on itself. They're adorably rubbish teenaged rebels. I'm not the only one in my group of fannish friends to identify with them. Bonus, they aren't all boys.

But, really, I am watching the story avidly for Adric. Just who is this new companion? What's he like? In *Full Circle*, he's a kid who doesn't belong in the rarefied atmosphere of the academically gifted, nor does he belong in the Outler gang with his brother, Varsh. Adric is arrogant, but it's that awkward young teen arrogance of trying to prove himself when still trying to work out who he is. It's not really surprising that he stows away in the TARDIS when he's given the chance. I love his debut story and I love the complexities in his character. Initial thoughts are that there's a story to be told here. I want to get to know him more. I start to think of some fan fiction ideas to explore his background and relationships with his brother and the other Alzarians.

I also think he is cute, especially with his little worried frown.

Happily, I cut out and stick pictures of Adric on my schoolbooks.

State of Decay is a stonkingly good vampire tale, let down by some of the special effects. Most of them are evocative and imaginative; it's the space ship-as-giant-vampire-stake at the end that's the problem. It's weird how we as fans obsess about the one that doesn't quite work. There are some lovely scenes with Adric and the Three Who Rule that echo his relationship with the Doctor, Romana and K-9. He quickly convinces Aukon that he really does want to become a vampire – and perhaps he is tempted by the promise of power and eternal life, but that doesn't mean he's turning his back on his friends, and he does try to help Romana escape. I like Adric wearing the villager's outfit more than the pyjama-like Alzarian gear, and sadly have never found a publicity shot of him wearing it.

The next story, *Warriors' Gate*, says farewell to Romana and K-9. I love the Tharils and the special effects. Unfortunately, there's not much more to learn about Adric in this story, but I forgive it because I'm fascinated by how Romana gets to escape the wrath of the Time Lords.

The Keeper of Traken has Adric as the Doctor's sole companion. It's a set-up I'm familiar with (the Doctor and Jo, then Sarah Jane, and then Leela until K-9 comes along), but it's interesting that now it's a wise old man and a young lad who is also a genius rather than a wise old man and young but adult women whose knowledge of everything is considerably less than the Doctor's. Adric is brilliant at times, but can still be endearingly left behind by the Doctor's intellect and experience. *Keeper* is one of my favorite stories in part because of this subtle character stuff.

Keeper also introduces Nyssa, whom I already know – thanks to *Doctor Who Monthly* – will become a companion in the next story, *Logopolis*. When Adric and Nyssa work together, they have a meeting of minds and become instant best friends forever.

I have eagerly anticipated *Logopolis* for a long time, but with trepidation. Tom Baker's long reign is ending, but with promise of a regeneration far more interesting than the one at the end of *Planet of the Spiders*. Also, the Australian companion was being introduced. I am a bit confused by my schoolmates starting to tune into *Doctor Who*, not because of Adric, but because of the promise of Tristan from *All Creatures Great and Small* (Peter Davison's signature role prior to this) turning up as the Doctor.

Adric's mathematical genius has a chance to shine in both *Logopolis* and *Castrovalva*, which we in Australia are seeing back-to-back. I love all the science Christopher H. Bidmead has brought to the show. He wrote both tales and also did script editing duty. The opening scenes of the Doctor and Adric in England are lovely continuations of their relationship in *Keeper*. The forbidding sense of doom permeates it all along with the mournfully tolling cloister bell.

Adric is central to the story in *Castrovalva*. Without him, the Master's plans wouldn't amount to much at all. It's a cracking tale and I like the new TARDIS team. Tegan and Nyssa become instant friends and they are concerned about Adric, who tries his best to thwart the Master's plans. Given how much of an outsider Adric was on his homeworld in his home universe, it makes me smile that he now has friends. A made family to comfort him after the horrors of what the Master has done to him. They bond because of the Master's evil.

Four to Doomsday is an odd little story. It has some great ideas in it, but the treatment of the Aboriginal Australians and Tegan's bizarre knowledge of a 35,000-year-old language throws me out of enjoying it. Worse, Adric turns out to be sexist and enthralled by the bad guys over his friends too easily. It jars.

Kinda, however, is the show back on form. I watch the first episode while recovering from an operation I had under full anesthetic. The dreamy, nightmarish quality of it all enhanced probably by my wooziness. Adric's petulant anti-childishness is an effective counterpoint to all the adult men (except the Doctor) being childish. This is another story in which Adric drives the story along, and in a sense is the Doctor's sole companion again while Nyssa is asleep and Tegan is caught in the Mara nightmare.

Adric spends most of *The Visitation* wandering about a little lost between the Doctor, being captured with Tegan, and helping Nyssa build an anti-android weapon in the TARDIS. He can fly the TARDIS, which is cool. It's a busy story and about a period of British history I know a little bit about. I do like the little joke at the end about the Great Fire of London. But I'm not sure about how we've now had three stories in a row where the family unit isn't behaving as it should, and it's Adric who's being sidelined. Is he destined to suffer a repeat of what happened to him on Alzarius?

Black Orchid brings back just how much Adric is an outsider. Tegan and Nyssa share a bedroom in the TARDIS and the Doctor, despite his friendly enthusiasm, is his usual solitary self. Adric is an awkward teenager, and painfully alien while at the party thrown by the Cranleighs after the cricket match. Tegan and Nyssa are at home at it, but Adric resorts to stuffing his face. A classic cry for help. We've been learning a bit about eating disorders in our personal development classes at school and I can spot the signs. But *Doctor Who* is *Doctor Who* and not *Grange Hill* or some other series that delves into the problems faced by people who do not fit in. Yet, that's what *Black Orchid* is all about when you look beyond the cocktails and cricket and dancing and lookey-likey hi-jinks. Once again, the main plot is echoed by what is happening with the TARDIS crew.

Earthshock. It's the end of May 1982 and – due to the vagaries of sea mail and our local newsagent – I hadn't seen *Doctor Who Monthly*'s take on the story, so I didn't have a clue. The Cybermen are cool, as is the flashback. Of all the clips, it's only the one from *Revenge of the Cybermen* that's familiar, so that frisson of seeing even just a tiny snippet of the show's past is amazing. This is *Doctor Who* as gritty sci-fi military (I am reading a lot of Heinlein and Asimov at the moment and I like that military stuff – only *Doctor Who* has women, too, with guns). I love all the attention Adric gets in a TARDIS that is too full. I feel sorry for him, wanting to go back home and yet again proving himself and making it up with the Doctor after their silly little spat. I had no idea...

At a bit before 7pm on Tuesday, June 1st, 1982, I sit watching the silent end credits as they roll over the shattered gold badge with my mouth hanging open. And, yes, I have a few tears rolling down my cheeks.

They killed Adric. I don't know what to think. I can't quite trust the series any more. No one is safe.

# # #

Okay, let's return to the present.

Go to any fan forum, read a plethora of articles and reviews of these stories, listen to the commentaries and watch the documentaries, and you'll see the established wisdom that Adric was the worst companion ever. No one, it seems, but a very tiny number of fans liked him except to make fun of him. His over-eating. His stupidity and his awkwardness.

A big part of all this is tied up with a view of Matthew Waterhouse, his acting skills at the time and stories of his youthful arrogance. I've deliberately kept away from all that in this essay.

I'm more interested in the character of Adric and how he interacted with the other main characters in the TARDIS at a time of great change with the series as a whole. I truly did like Adric back when I was a kid, and much of what I've written here comes from my diaries at the time.

I wasn't the only one who liked him then, either. I had a few pen pals from around Australia who liked him as I did. Older fans didn't, though, and in the pages of all the fanzines started the jokes that still abound. I tried to defend him in letter columns, but got shouted down by the fan elders.

I re-watched all the Adric stories to prepare for writing this essay, and found it an interesting experience. I can still see what I liked at the time, and I can see the flaws my elders did back then. Waterhouse isn't the greatest of actors, but actually nor are terribly many of the others. At least, not in their roles in *Doctor Who*.

Looking back on those first stories with John Nathan Turner as producer, the incoherence of vision is astonishingly obvious. The documentaries talk a lot about how Nathan Turner wanted a team of companions, but he also wanted at least one strong guest star per story. I was struck by how just about every story had another character in the companion role – especially in the early Davison stories: Bigon in *Four to Doomsday*, Todd in *Kinda* and Richard Mace in *The Visitation*.

I think that inherent contradiction affected the character development for all of the companions. Adric lurched from clever, to naïve, to a sexist beast, to best friends with both Tegan and Nyssa, to a glutton. While Tegan was always a "mouth on legs," her character also shifts from incredibly brave one second to a gibbering wreck the next – and not for coherent reasons. Startlingly, Nyssa is a violence-loving and gun-toting rebel in the two stories written by her creator, Johnny Byrne, but a gifted and peace-loving scientist in most of the other stories. When she's not asleep, that is.

When I was an older fan, I raved about how Ace has a storyarc that was important for the whole series. Actually, so does Adric (if you take *Four to Doomsday* out of the mix). And it's a tragic story.

Adric was an outsider twice over on his homeworld. He wasn't really included when Romana and K-9 still inhabited the TARDIS, in part because he had stowed away and in part because he had difficulty in working out who he should take as a mentor. Unsurprisingly given his upbringing where, despite his recognized genius, he was slipping between the social cracks. Aukon may have tempted him, but was ultimately unconvincing (Adric was more inclined to join Monarch, later, which makes me think *Four to Doomsday* makes more sense as a Season Eighteen story in the context of Adric's arc), and while the audience is meant to think his choice of the Doctor as mentor is the right one, I question whether that's really the case. After all, the Doctor is incredibly chaotic, and despite all the standing up for the oppressed, he can be morally suspect.

Adric shines when he's with Nyssa, but it's never a romantic thing. At first, he is embraced by the new Doctor, Nyssa and Tegan as a direct result of what the Master has done to all of them, but then slowly that relationship starts to disintegrate as the girls bond (despite Tegan always wanting to leave) and the Doctor becomes a bit of a recluse.

It culminates in Adric wanting to go home, too. An impossibility, except he proves it isn't, and then he sacrifices himself for a human race that hasn't really been the friendliest to him.

And it's all that which makes Adric one of the best companions ever.

Companion Piece

Stories and Fairytales: Feminism, Agency and Narrative Control with the Pond Family Women

A recovering ex-pat, unrepentant fangirl and absent-minded academic, **Karen K. Burrows** writes about popular culture for fun and profit (mostly fun). Her interest in *Doctor Who* started with Sarah Jane Smith: that early exposure to the awesomeness of the companions has colored her experience of the program ever since. Previous publications have focused on queer identity in *Battlestar Galactica* (2003) as well as American identity pre- and post-9/11 in *La Femme Nikita* and *Alias*. She recently completed her doctoral thesis on the representation of the female spy on television, so if she told you where she works now, she'd have to kill you. Karen tweets about pop culture, feminisms and whatever else catches her fancy at @karenkathryne. She likes to drink tea, read books and go places.

> "Well, you'll remember me a little. I'll be a story in your head."

> —The Doctor, *The Big Bang*

Throughout his tenure as showrunner of *Doctor Who* and *Sherlock*, Steven Moffat has received significant criticism for his representation of female characters. Fans and critics alike have variously branded his creations insipid, heteronormative, without agency and plain offensive. I don't disagree with some of the charges, but I believe *Doctor Who* presents a more complex position, and I want to offer a different, reparative reading of two of Moffat's most polarizing female characters on *Doctor Who*: Amy Pond and River Song.

The parallels in Amy's and River's story lines are even more apparent when their relationship as mother and daughter is taken into account – but let's set that aside for a moment. Critics of the characters and their storyarcs have complained that they are defined entirely by their relationship with the Doctor and their marriages (a double blow to River's character). To an extent, this is true: the Doctor reshapes Amy's entire life and history in *The Big Bang*, while River is trained from birth to kill the Doctor and subsequently organizes her life and academic career around him. Without the Doctor, neither woman would be the same.

Yet the reverse is also true: without Amy and River, the Doctor as we know him would not exist. He is Amy and River's creation just as much as they are his.

# # #

"I hate good wizards in fairytales. They always turn out to be him."

—River, *The Pandorica Opens*

When I say "creation," I mean that quite literally.

The Moffat eleventh-Doctor seasons have been concerned with what being the Doctor *means* and how that meaning is formed. In *Asylum of the Daleks*, the Doctor is information: deleting it changes what he means to the Daleks. *The Name of the Doctor* and *The Day of the Doctor* ask how the Doctor's actions affect his self-definition. We've seen duplicate and alternate Doctors in *Amy's Choice*, *The Rebel Flesh/ The Almost People* and *The Wedding of River Song*. River makes the theme explicit in *A Good Man Goes to War*: "Doctor. The word for healer and wise man throughout the universe. We get that word from you, you know. But if you carry on the way you are, what might that word come to mean? To the people of the Gamma Forests, the word Doctor means mighty warrior."

The Doctor is a story, the meaning of which is determined by how it is told – and Amy Pond overwhelmingly shapes that story.

Amy's first imaginary friend is the Doctor; he's a story she clings to despite "twelve years and four psychiatrists." Her imagination is strong enough to transcend even the space-time continuum: in *The Wedding of River Song*, the drawings and models of the TARDIS in her alternate-universe office are the same as those in her bedroom in Leadworth. The Doctor suggests in *The Big Bang* that the crack in Amy's wall somehow expanded her mental capacities; regardless of the reason, Amy's powers of imagination and her ability to create from those imaginings are impressive. We first see the true strength of her mind in *The Pandorica Opens*.

To create a trap for the Doctor, a temporary alliance of all the Doctor's foes pulls information from a psychic imprint left in Amy's house. On the strength of her memory alone, they construct not only the Pandorica itself, but an entire Roman legion with a Rory-reincarnation so realistic, her memory of him allows him to override his programming as a Nestene duplicate. The combined strength of Amy's memories, her imagination, and her emotions is enough to transcend advanced alien technology.

Emotion is key to Amy's feats of creativity: she is not detached from, but rather passionately engaged with, the creative act. This emotional component is evident in her most audacious creation: summoning the Doctor back into existence in *The Big Bang.*

Amy's ability to remember the Doctor and to reintegrate him into the universe such that everyone else subsequently regains their own memories is grounded not in unformed imaginative play, but in language: "Raggedy Man, I remember you... I found you in words, like you knew I would." The Doctor sets a trigger and River toggles it, but it is Amy's reinterpretation of the "something old, something new, something borrowed, and something blue" wedding proverb that allows her to access the quasi-incantation she uses to bring the Doctor back into reality. She literally re-calls her Raggedy Man to life at her wedding reception.

The timing here is key: while retaining her own identity (after all, Rory becomes "the new Mr. Pond," rather than vice versa), Amy's first act of creation after her marriage is not one of reproduction. Rather than a biological occurrence, it is a feat of mental skill.

Amy faces significant criticism from viewers for her body and appearance, with her jobs as kiss-o-gram and model derided as sexist. But Amy's methods of earning a living are not only the choices of an independent young woman, they are also constantly driven by her creativity. A kiss-o-gram plays a role akin to that of an actress: Amy must create and embody a character other than herself. The characters' stereotypical nature doesn't reduce the effort Amy must put in to perform them. She also shows improvisational skills in her performance, first of a police officer and then of Amy-not-Amelia, during her first meeting with the Doctor as an adult.

Her subsequent role as a model includes similar requirements of performance. More interesting, however, are the suggestions that Amy's role as model extends further than merely being the voice of the products. In *Closing Time*, she is billed as "the girl who's tired of waiting"; the scent she advertises is named "Petrichor." These are references to her travels with the Doctor; as we learn later that Rory is not involved with her modeling career, she is the only person who could have contributed them to the campaign. Amy is important to the advertising, yes, but she is clearly firmly in control of her own professional narrative as well.

Amy's creative abilities are, interestingly, perhaps more apparent after she has herself left the story. In *The Angels Take Manhattan*, when Amy and Rory are sent permanently and irretrievably into the past, she manages to communicate with the Doctor one final time through an afterword in River's novel. Her written words draw the Doctor out of his grief in a way even River's presence cannot. Just as she brought him back into being with her words in *The Big Bang*, she draws him back to himself with them in *The Angels Take Manhattan*.

More, Amy again literalizes her control over her own story. Though she asks the Doctor to once more return to little Amelia Pond, waiting in her garden, the story she asks him to tell is *her* story: she lives it, and she gifts it to the Doctor to teach her younger self how to grow up. She is the heroine of her own story, quite literally. We learn in *The Bells of Saint John* that – as Amelia Williams – Amy later became a novelist, suggesting that her creative abilities allowed her and Rory further financial security. That she passed this creativity on to her daughter should not be a surprise.

# # #

"The Pandorica? Ha! That's a fairytale."
"Oh, Doctor – aren't we all?"

—The Doctor and River, *Flesh and Stone*

It's no accident that we first meet Professor River Song in a library. River is constantly associated with knowledge – specifically, knowledge beyond that held by the Doctor. We as the audience are used to being in a position where the Doctor holds all the cards and reveals them as necessary to his schemes (and the plot). River reverses this position: her knowledge is literalized in the form of the diary, to which she has access and the Doctor does not. River and the diary are largely conflated; in *The Name of the Doctor*, she makes the comparison explicit, describing herself as "left… like a book on a shelf." Although by the end of *Forest of the Dead*, we (seem to) know the end of River's story, its contents remain mysterious to us and to the Doctor.

River retains control over her own narrative during our and the Doctor's non-chronological encounters with her. She insists in *Flesh and Stone* that her story "can't be told, it has to be lived." Though she asserts that everyone has a story or a fairy tale of her own, River is in fact more story-like than most. She is constantly associated with and defined by writing. Even the revelation of her identity in *A Good Man Goes to War* is dependent not on her own confession, but on an act of translation – of being read – by the Doctor (who reads the Gallifreyan lettering on the cradle) and Amy and Rory (who read the writing on the prayer-leaf). River's very self is mediated by the act of understanding text.

In *A Good Man Goes to War*, River can also be found hidden in proverbs ("the only water in the forest is the river") and nursery rhymes (the Demon's Run chant includes the lines "the battle's won, but the child is lost"). Lest she be seen as without agency in her own story, however, I remind you that while she may be part of a fairy tale, she is equally adept at manipulating words to her own advantage. The Doctor hints at the power River can summon in *The Time of Angels*, when he describes the writing on the homebox he and Amy encounter in the museum: "Old High Gallifreyan. The lost language of the Time Lords. There were days, there were many days, these words could burn stars and raise up empires, and topple gods." Its power is in fact still evident, as the message – "Hello, sweetie" – effectively compels the Doctor to rescue River. Not bad for two words – but after all, as we learn in *The Pandorica Opens*, they are the very first words in recorded history: on Planet One, the oldest planet in the universe, River has burned them into a diamond cliff face in an untranslatable language. Though the Doctor accuses River of having "graffitied" the cliff, her summons (which is, again, effective) represents the first successful instance of written communication. It's a pretty good trick for an archaeologist.

Though the Doctor initially mocks River's career, she proves its worth in *The Time of Angels* and *Flesh and Stone*. Yet in *Let's Kill Hitler*, questions of agency surrounding both her motivation for her career and her defining attribute, her diary, come to light. The Doctor gifts her the diary, anticipating her writing, and instructs her in its use in the DVD extra *First Night*. Additionally, she claims to be interested in archaeology as a "search for a good man," ie, the Doctor. These two elements had previously placed her on even footing with the Doctor; to have them both effectively dictated by him seems to devalue her own abilities and decisions. Yet by giving River the diary, the Doctor communicates the importance of her knowledge. It could be dangerous; it must be kept from him. His is an act of trust as well as submission: he subjugates himself to the knowledge that River will hold in her future.

River's research on the Doctor similarly ensures that her knowledge is neither limited nor controlled by anyone, not even the Doctor. Her research is an act of defiance against the brainwashing of the Silence; she is determined to develop her own conclusions about what kind of man the Doctor is. Her knowledge eclipses that of the Doctor himself in *A Good Man Goes to War*, when she is able to understand the impact of his mythological status as a warrior as well as a healer. When the Doctor's existence is erased from the universe's records, she retains her own memories, making her *the* expert on the subject. Even when she is merely a book on the Library's shelves, an echo of her former self, she retains control. The Doctor does not "read" her in *The Name of the Doctor*; she chooses to speak his name and open his tomb on Trenzalore. Just as her false grave is the entry to the TARDIS-tomb, so too is she the key to the Doctor's life.

River does not guard her knowledge jealously; rather, she makes it available when it can be of use. Like Amy, River becomes a novelist. Her book *The Angel's Kiss*, published under the suitably noir pseudonym "Melody Malone," becomes a blueprint by which she, Amy, and the Doctor are able to rescue Rory. Again, the power of story – of words – is literalized through the impossibility of escaping its effects: neither River nor the Doctor can avoid breaking River's wrist once that point in the text has been reached. Flesh and bone are no match for the narrative.

The Angel's Kiss is a collaboration between Amy and River: River writes the story and Amy the afterword, while Amy is able to decipher the clues River leaves in the table of contents and River understands the impact Amy's words will have on the Doctor. The Doctor himself is not easily able to translate the words into meaning. Though he arguably impels both Amy and River into their acts of creation – Amy by subliminally implanting a suggestion, River by giving her the diary – by the time of *The Angels Take Manhattan*, the pupils have decidedly surpassed the teacher.

# # #

"Time can be re-written."
"Not once you've read it. Once you know what's coming, it's written in stone."

—Amy and the Doctor, *The Angels Take Manhattan*

The focus on the powers of female creativity is itself an impressive message within the show. The Doctor provides a positive message of male non-aggression, while Amy and River emphasize the importance and breadth of female resourcefulness. Both Amy and River challenge the stereotypes of feminine passivity and of the "helpless" companion; they are not only active but more action-heroic than the Doctor himself, as well as more likely to make morally ambiguous decisions.

Yet in the context of the show, it is their creative aspects I find most fascinating and, in fact, most transgressive. In the midst of two and a half series apparently celebrating the importance of the heterosexual wedding, *Doctor Who* explicitly divorces a woman's worth from her ability to bear children and ties it to the strength of her mind.

The emphasis on heterosexuality seems particularly evident throughout Amy's tenure as companion. Both Series Five and Series Six literally end with a wedding saving the world: Amy and Rory's wedding allows the Doctor to re-enter their universe in the former, and the Doctor and River's wedding re-aligns the deteriorating time streams in the latter. The grand arcs of all three series can be seen as making it possible for those marriages to occur. For much of those two and a half series, there were two married couples in the TARDIS. Even Amy and Rory's final episode is explicitly concerned with the importance of their marriage to their survival. Both they and the Doctor and River refer to marriage as a way of "changing the future," which can be read as reference to procreation.

On the surface, this narrative is explicitly heteronormative, establishing the heterosexual married couple as both the norm and as something to strive for, and, indeed, as the backbone of even a culture as advanced as that of the Time Lords. Yet today's society often suggests, erroneously and reductively, that the importance of the heterosexual marriage lies only in its impetus to the future: its reproductive potential. It is this emphasis on childbearing that *Doctor Who* deliberately refuses. In doing so, it presents a much more realistic and inclusive picture of relationships as they exist in reality.

This may seem an odd claim for me to make, given that the first half of Series Six is devoted to the mystery of Amy's pregnancy and that her child turns out to be River. And yes, concern over "the child" – the concrete child that is Amy's stolen baby, the unknown child of the astronaut suit, Melody Pond who inhabits them both – certainly drives the characters at various points in the show. But the child is never actually saved; the child becomes a threat; the child as child never exists within the narrative. More, there is never a future to be concerned about. The Doctor points out to Amy and Rory in *Let's Kill Hitler* that while he can search as much as he wants to for baby Melody, they already know the outcome because they have already had several adventures with adult Melody-as-River. What he forgets, though, or deliberately chooses not to mention, is that we know that Melody's story leads to River, but we also know how River's story ends: with her death in the Library.

If the importance of heterosexual marriage lies in its ability to produce children, the Doctor's relationship with River actively opposes this narrative. It embraces the death drive: it has, as Lee Edelman would put it, no future. River dies before her relationship with the Doctor begins: there is no literal, procreative future for it, and there can therefore be no hidden reason for it save that it brings pleasure to its participants. As Edelman's work shows, the child is an image that defines the "hope for the future" rhetoric that characterizes cultural identification with the ideal of working for a better world. Rather than adopting the perpetual deferment of that "better" state to benefit a theoretical future child, Edelman claims that embracing the queer idea of taking pleasure in the now, for oneself, is a radical act. Although the Doctor and River's marriage is heterosexual (at least until we get the Helen Mirren regeneration we've all been waiting for), it is in Edelman's sense a queer one: with its ending already known, it circumvents the reproductive futurity that defines society's views on the institution of heterosexual marriage. Its non-chronological progression marks it as out of step with society's norms. By revealing it as a relationship unconcerned with reinforcing reproductive tropes, the show manages to avoid uncritically supporting the reproductive imperative.

Though River's identity as queer, non-reproductive child is a subtle commentary on societal norms, the show also grapples more directly with the idea that marriage is inherently tied to childbearing. In *Asylum of the Daleks*, Amy and Rory's marriage is ending: they are separated and in the process of divorcing. Rory assumes that Amy has grown tired of him; her new, glamorous job as a model seems to bear this out. But when Rory confronts Amy directly, she corrects him:

> **Rory:** Amy, you kicked me out.
> **Amy:** You want kids. You have always wanted kids. Ever since you were a kid. And I can't have them... I didn't kick you out. I gave you up.

Amy has internalized the narrative that says a marriage can only be valid if it is capable of producing biological children. With River an unsuccessful – a queer – child, Amy has not yet fulfilled her reproductive destiny; she believes her inability to do so in the future invalidates her relationship. By divorcing Rory, she intends to allow him to find a "real" marriage – one that will produce heirs.

Rory's choice to privilege love over procreation challenges Amy's presumption and asserts her importance regardless of her infertility. Like the Doctor and River, Amy and Rory's relationship is not determined by its ability to contribute to the future through biological reproduction. Though they repair their marriage, it too is ultimately literally removed from the linear timeline in *The Angels Take Manhattan*. Their marriage and the connection that defines it makes it possible for them to survive, but it also draws them out of their timeline permanently when a Weeping Angel sends them back in time. Neither Amy's desperate jump with Rory off the Winter Quay roof nor River's attempt to hide her broken wrist from the Doctor are successful attempts at changing the future. Yet Amy's sacrifice to join Rory in the past and the Doctor's use of regeneration energy to heal River demonstrate that even when a marriage has no influence on the future, it remains valuable to its participants. And just like Amy's infertility didn't end her marriage, Amy and Rory's absence from their and the Doctor's timeline does not end their influence. Amy's writing outlives her: it affects not only the Doctor, but many others, as seen in *The Bells of Saint John*. Instead of being survived by a future generation of children, she provides a legacy in the form of her creative output.

# # #

"We're all stories in the end. Just make it a good one, eh? Because it was, you know. It was the best."

—The Doctor, *The Big Bang*

As a child, Amelia Pond sounded like a character in a fairytale. When she grew up, Amy Pond tried to deny fairytales existed; she created a no-nonsense persona and held on to her own conception of herself. Only as Amelia Williams did she become able to take control of those fairytales for herself: she recaptured her childlike sense of wonder and used it to create a career and an identity with which she was finally at peace.

River Song similarly emerged from a muddle of identities: Melody Williams (the schoolteacher – and she does become a professor), Melody Pond (the superhero – yes, she's that too), Mels (the delinquent – well, no one's going to argue with that either). The name by which she is most widely known is the result of an error in translation – the Gamma Forests "don't have a word for Pond, because the only water in the forest is the River." Yet the way her identity is most often defined is through records of her deeds. Both the Teselecta in *Let's Kill Hitler* and the Dalek in *The Big Bang* understand and explain River by reference to her historical presence. This narrative is one that River herself has already built through her actions. Like her mother, River ultimately chooses and defines her own identity for herself, rejecting any other attempts to guide her own story – even by the Doctor; in her first appearance as "herself," she rejects his narrative of heroic martyrdom and substitutes her own.

Though the narratives of Series Five through Seven appear in many ways to privilege the heterosexual marriage and reproductive futurism, the show in fact interrogates those assumptions both subtextually and explicitly. Within what appears to be a highly regressive framework, the characters and narratives of Amy and River are privileged above (or at least equal to) the Doctor's.

More, the female characters control their narratives conclusively and unapologetically. This narrative control is literalized in the show by giving both women creative control over the stories they tell. Their creative output defines both marriages, challenging patriarchal assumptions and societal norms by removing the reproductive drive from the story being told in *Doctor Who*.

Neither Amy's nor River's narratives are unproblematic, nor are they unchallengeable models of feminism. Yet both characters achieve a sense of agency that makes them impossible to write off. That this agency is couched in terms of words and imagination, and that it is a celebration of mental skill rather than physical characteristics serves – especially in the context of the marriage narrative that permeates the show – to draw these characters into a new position. It queers the traditional marriage by removing it from its insistence on reproduction, and it transfers control into Amy and River's hands. Amy brings the Doctor to life and River drives his adventuring: their creativity provides a future for the time traveler.

Companion Piece
The Shakespeare Race Code

Amanda-Rae Prescott is a journalist based in New York City. She is currently attending the Master of Science program at Columbia School of Journalism. She received her BA in Journalism and History from SUNY Purchase. She co-founded *TheDailyHeyNow.com* to combine her passion for pop culture as well as professional journalism. Her interest in Martha Jones began in 2007, when she watched *Doctor Who* for the first time. Her appreciation of Martha sparked an interest in cosplay. Since then, she has been active in *Doctor Who* cosplay discussion online and at local conventions.

Whenever I watch historical *Doctor Who* episodes, my thoughts always wander towards the realities of each place and time. The first time I watched *The Shakespeare Code*, I was intrigued by the interactions between Martha and the Londoners of 1599. As a multiracial woman, I expected a reaction closer to what she experienced in *Human Nature/ Family of Blood*, where Martha had to stand up for herself while living in a society intent on seeing her as inferior. In 1599, all Martha encountered was outdated racial remarks. Unfulfilled expectations and curiosity led me to research into the period to compare the fictional depiction to historical reality...

Shakespeare's England was in a state of transition. England and the other European powers were expanding their knowledge of the world beyond the Mediterranean. Explorers were busy mapping the "new worlds" of North and South America, sub-Saharan Africa and the Far East. Although interest in differences in religion, skin color, social structures and culture increased dramatically, few people were able to – or desired to – travel to distant lands to see these societies for themselves. As time progressed, the perceived differences between themselves and the expanding knowledge of the "other" widened. This was the time of the development of the concepts of race that would lead to colonization and chattel slavery in later centuries.

The Globe Theatre and other theaters in England were incredibly influential in forming public opinion. The Doctor and Martha are also in a position to influence the opinions of Londoners of 1599, but they use this ability carefully. Shakespeare's life and works are a fixed point in history, but they are meeting him in the earlier stages of his career. There are several points in the episode where they quote or refer to plays written after 1599, just as Martha introduces Shakespeare to concepts that evolved long after his death.

At first, Martha is excited about seeing what London is like in the past, but it fades quickly once she realizes she is now in a time where she is vulnerable:

> **Martha:** Oh, but hold on. Am I all right? I'm not gonna get carted off as a slave, am I?
> **The Doctor:** Why would they do that?
> **Martha:** Not exactly white, in case you haven't noticed.

This quote not only contrasts Martha's racial awareness and the Doctor's lack thereof, it also brings up the status of non-white people in Tudor England. Current research on this topic has yielded mixed results. Records from London and other areas indicate non-white infants and adults were baptized and the deceased were buried in parish graveyards Royal records indicate Elizabeth I and other members of the elite had servants of color. Robert Cecil, a member of the Privy Council, employed an African by the name of Fortunatus. Black people are present in numerous sixteenth-century European works of art and literature.

Some of Martha's fears are justified. Only a few years before the episode takes place, tradesmen staged riots protesting "strangers" and foreigners. Elizabeth I published an order calling for the deportation of blacks in 1599 and 1601. Experts believe this was unsuccessful, because non-English names continued to appear in later records. However, they are divided about Elizabeth I's intent. Some believe international politics motivated the orders, not personal prejudice. In the years after the Armada, England was seen as a place of asylum for those fleeing Spanish persecution of Muslims and Jews. Others believed fears about the assimilation of outsiders and racial blending motivated the proclamations. Some sources use the evidence of harassment and expulsions of "gypsies" to argue these edicts targeted the Romani and other migrants.

After walking around the vicinity of the Globe and watching *Love's Labour's Lost* without incident, the Doctor and Martha meet Shakespeare in a pub. The conversation that follows is a strange mixture of flirting and outdated racial and ethnic terminology:

> **Shakespeare:** Who are you exactly? More's the point, who is your delicious blackamoor lady?
> **Martha:** What did you say?
> **Shakespeare:** Oops. Isn't that a word we use nowadays? An Ethiop girl? A swarth? A Queen of Afric—
> **Martha:** I can't believe I'm hearing this.

Martha is shocked that he's insulting her with a smile. She expected unkind remarks and a lack of understanding, but it's all the more shocking because Shakespeare is so revered in our culture. Since the companion in *Doctor Who* often becomes the eyes of the audience in the plot, the viewer is also taken by surprise. These are terms usually only seen in history books or in older media. The Doctor, in reply, jokes about political correctness because he knows Martha is incredibly offended.

Shakespeare's words as well as attitudes are likely historically accurate. Beneath the stated romantic attraction lies confusion. He has never met anyone like Martha before. Even though there were characters of color in his works, he, too, knows about the world through the stories and views of others. Europeans were beginning to create maps of the world beyond, but many areas were still unknown. Much of the published material consisted on myth and accounts many times removed from their original source. There was even less agreement in the past compared to today on the correct terms of identification for other ethnic and racial groups. Many of the terms we would consider highly offensive were commonplace and acceptable; others did not exist.

Some terms were indicative of skin color, others were based on location and some referred to religious affiliation. Many terms combined one or more of these elements. The term "swarth" or "swarthy" was used to refer to people of color regardless of geographic location. Explorers of the so-called New World as well as Asia and the Pacific referred to native peoples as "swarths," as did works referring to residents of Africa. "Ethiop" was a short hand for Ethiopia as well as the area south of Egypt.

"Blackamoor," a term which also appeared in a few different forms, was the all-encompassing term for people of color at that time. Many records indicate "blackamoor" was used to refer to any person of African descent regardless of culture or location. In many instances, the "moor" in "blackamoor" usually referred to the descendants of the Berbers who brought Islamic culture and religion to the Iberian peninsula in the eighth century. The difference between Moors and Spaniards hinged on religion and culture; physically, their appearances were similar due to centuries of assimilation. In the Tudor Era, the Moors were a sizable minority who were seen as threats to the unified Catholic and white nation of Spain. Many works from this period also use the term "blackamoor" to indicate a person of North African background. At this point in time, Europeans called this region the Barbary States.

These definitions indicate people in 1599 had vastly different conceptions of race compared to the modern day. Even the word "race" was not used to refer to a group with common skin color and defining physical features. In Tudor England, the word "race" was used to indicate class distinctions, not physical traits. Each class was seen as a separate species of people, because status was seen as something passed on by birth, and couldn't be changed by improving one's situation.

Views on all of these cultures were based heavily on stereotype. People from North Africa, Ethiopia and Egypt were seen as powerful, wealthy and having ancient traditions. Sub-Saharans were seen as savage, depraved, lewd, hypersexual, ugly and unchanging. Despite the differences, all of these cultures were seen as inferior to European culture. English merchants and elites were, however, interested in expanding trade with the North African region at this time.

Religious ideas at this time played a major role in creating ideas about race; skin color was believed to reflect the inner personality and moral state. These ideas can be traced back to the Crusades. European Christians saw the Islamic Saracens as black physically and in personality. A popular Tudor era play had the Devil take the likeness of a black man. Some writers believed the black skinned could be washed white, while others believed the color of the souls of non-Europeans could not be changed. As colonization progressed, ideas of class were added to negative racial stereotypes.

Standing up to prejudice appears to be nothing new for Martha. She realizes that Shakespeare is not malicious in his intent, and chooses to educate him about the future. "Freedonia" becomes the code word for modern society. Despite the rule of Elizabeth I, Shakespeare still had trouble comprehending a place where women and people of color could pursue any career they wanted. At this point, many believed the royals were placed by divine intervention, which explained the queen's deviation from the norms of the time.

The last conversation between Martha and Shakespeare solves a well-known literary mystery, given that many have speculated about subjects of Shakespeare's sonnets:

Shakespeare: Martha, let me say goodbye to you in a new verse. A sonnet for my Dark Lady. Shall I compare thee to a summer's day? Thou art more lovely and more temperate...

Sonnets 127 through 152 are widely believed to be about loving a woman who has dark skin. Her beauty throughout these poems is praised as more pure than others, especially those who use makeup. Attempts by scholars to identify the Dark Lady as a woman who lived at the time have failed. Martha's appearance in 1599 is a Whovian solution to an historical mystery.

How likely was an interracial relationship in Tudor England? Traditionally, scholars have analyzed the plays produced in Tudor England to gauge the views on interracial relationships. Very few of these relationships ended well, because black men were believed to have an inferior state of mind. The black female body was seen as simultaneously repulsive and desirable. A European man could seek pleasure with a black woman, but any sort of serious relationship would be out of the question. There is, however, evidence of marriage between black Africans and white English people of the time: a report from 1578 says, "I myself have seene an Ethiopian as black as cole... taking a faire English woman as wife [they] begat a sonne in as respects as blacke as the father." Based on research into the sex trade in Tudor England, it is also entirely possible Shakespeare would have encountered someone with a similar appearance to Martha if he visited a brothel. Black women could have served as hostesses as well as valuable entertainers of the men who frequented such establishments. Earlier in *The Shakespeare Code*, Shakespeare alludes to Martha becoming his mistress while in town. Martha declines, because she knows that he's married. Although Shakespeare was portrayed in the episode as a man ahead of his time, the racial controversies found in his plays are not mentioned. In fairness, some of these were written after 1599; characters of color feature in *Othello*, *The Merchant of Venice*, *Antony and Cleopatra* and *Titus Andronicus*. Shakespeare never used race to refer to skin color, but used the other terms highlighted earlier. Shylock in *The Merchant of Venice* can never move beyond being a Jewish outsider. Christians described Jews as a race despite not having attachments to one geographical location. Cleopatra is seen as an exotic woman who emasculates Mark Antony and convinces him to abandon his people and his responsibility. Othello goes through the motions of assimilating into Venetian society, but his skin color prevents him from being truly accepted. *Titus Andronicus* features Rome in the last days of the empire battling German invaders as well as a black villain of unknown origin. All of these plays end in tragedy, demonstrating the impossibility of interracial relationships. Although many academics disagree on matters of interpretation, the collective whole highlights how Shakespeare is responsible for mirroring and perpetuating negative stereotypes.

Doctor Who is famous for using mysteries, disappearances or a lack of records as opportunities for historical stories. Counterfactual history, also called speculative history, is defined as the inquiry into the effects of an event unfolding in a different way compared to what is known fact. The entirety of *The Shakespeare Code* is based on counterfactual history. Historians believe *Love Labour's Won* was lost to the ages because no written copies survived. Staving off a Carrionite invasion meant the play needed to be erased from history so they would never threaten humans again. *The Shakespeare Code* depends on taking many liberties with history and literature, but one issue the episode leaves untouched is the state of racial relations at the time, leaving Martha to bring enlightenment to one of history's most famous figures.

Sources

Oxford Shakespeare Topics: Shakespeare, Race, and Colonization. Loomba, Ania. 2002, Oxford University Press New York

Shakespeare and Race. Eds Alexander, Catherine M.S. And Wells, Stanley. 2000, Cambridge University Press Cambridge UK

"What's in a Name." Oneyka. *History Today*: pgs 34-39: October 2012.

Blacks and other Minorities in Shakespeare's England. Harry Lee Faggett Prairie View Press 1971

"Black people in Tudor England." Sherwood, Marika *History Today*; Oct 2003; 53, 10; ProQuest Research Library pgs 40-42

Shakespeare Jungle Fever: National-Imperial Re-Visons of Race, Rape and Sacrifice. Arthur L Little Jr. Stanford University Press, Stanford CA 2000

Companion Piece

"I Can Do Your Part if You Can Do Mine": Romana II as the Girl Doctor

Gwynne Garfinkle lives in Los Angeles. Her fiction and poetry have appeared in numerous venues, including *Strange Horizons*, *Interfictions*, *Mythic Delirium*, *Goblin Fruit*, *Shimmer*, *The WisCon Chronicles*, *Clean Sheets*, *Big Bridge* and *Exquisite Corpse*. Her reviews and features on music and poetry have appeared in such publications as the *Los Angeles New Times*, *LA Weekly*, *BAM* and *News Clips and Ego Trips: The Best of Next... Magazine 1994-98*. She fell in love with *Doctor Who* when the new series began, then proceeded to devour classic *Who*. Her other TV obsessions include *Buffy the Vampire Slayer*, *Gilmore Girls*, *Dark Shadows*, *General Hospital* and other soap operas (both vintage and contemporary). For more about her work, visit her website: gwynnegarfinkle.com.

> **Romana:** I told you you'd got the time wrong, Doctor.
> **The Doctor:** Yes, but you're always saying that.
> **Romana:** You're always getting the time wrong.
>
> —*Shada*

I first encountered Romana II in *City of Death*, Douglas Adams' witty, joyous fourth Doctor story. Christopher Eccleston was my first Doctor, Rose my first companion – but I immediately liked Romana, with her nonchalant genius, gravity-defying straw hat, schoolgirl outfit and girlish looks that belied her Time Lord age. I loved the way the Doctor and Romana grinned at each other and ran through Paris holding hands in a manner not dissimilar to the ninth Doctor and Rose. Knowing about Tom Baker and Lalla Ward's brief marriage only added fuel to my enthusiasm – but I quickly discovered that the relationship between the Doctor and Romana, though delightful, was by no means the most interesting thing about her.

Prior to Romana II's introduction, Romana I (played with great flair by Mary Tamm) shared the TARDIS with the Doctor and K-9. At first Romana and the Doctor had an adversarial relationship, characterized by the clash between his age and experience and her relative youth and academic training. (When they first met, in *The Ribos Operation*, the Doctor told Romana to stay out of the way and even asked if she could make tea!) Soon enough, however, skepticism and distrust developed into mutual respect.

Icy (especially at first), brilliant and glamorous – and womanly as opposed to her girlish successor – Romana I nonetheless did not take on the role of the Doctor in the same way that Romana II does in *Destiny of the Daleks* when, apparently on a whim, she regenerates. She chooses the face and form of Princess Astra, the character Lalla Ward portrayed in the previous story, *The Armageddon Factor*. At first the Doctor thinks she *is* Astra, until Romana casually informs him she's regenerating. He's appalled that she should steal someone's appearance, whereupon she tries on a series of other identities, modeling them for the Doctor as though shopping for clothes.

The scene is played for laughs, but we can't discount the fact that Romana, unlike the Doctor, seems able to regenerate (and even to choose what she's going to look like) without breaking a sweat. More often than not, Romana II makes whatever she's doing – from fixing spaceships to facing down assorted evildoers – look effortless. Where the Doctor goes in for rhetorical flourishes, she is matter-of-fact. In *Nightmare of Eden*, the Doctor boasts, "I like doing the impossible." Romana replies, "If it's possible to get into the situation, theoretically it should be possible to get out of it." The Doctor, slightly crestfallen, says, "I preferred it when it seemed impossible."

Romana doesn't go in for Time Lord angst. When, in *City of Death*, the Doctor tells her, "You and I exist in a special relationship to time, you know – perpetual outsiders," Romana retorts, "Don't be so portentous." (I can only imagine how she'd react to the tenth Doctor's angsting over "the curse of the Time Lords" in *School Reunion*.) What's more, the Doctor's relationship with Romana is strikingly lacking in the inequality inherent in so many of his companions' stints on the TARDIS. Most of the Doctor's companions are human or humanoid, with much shorter life spans than that of a Time Lord. Most of the companions are brave and resourceful; some are quite brainy too (notably Zoe, Liz Shaw and Nyssa), but because they're not Time Lords, their power relationship with the Doctor remains unequal. The first Doctor does travel with Susan, but because she is his granddaughter, their power relationship is still skewed.[26] But Romana and the Doctor are equals. Perhaps she puts

---

26 It can be argued that Donna Noble, in her all-too-brief DoctorDonna period, is a

on his outfit – first his actual costume, then her own pink version – as an outward sign of their equality and even their interchangeability, a sign that Romana is trying on her own version of the Doctor role, with all the genius and moral authority that goes with it. Or perhaps she wears his outfit to let him know *she* knows they're equals.

I Wish I'd Thought of That

The equivalence between Romana and the Doctor is especially striking in *The Horns of Nimon* – which might as well be titled *The Two Doctors*. In this story, Romana and the Doctor trade off who gets to play the Doctor role at any given time; sometimes it's just one of them, sometimes both simultaneously. Romana strides through *Nimon* in her hunting outfit with bold red jacket like she's running the show – which, more often than not, she is. While the Doctor and Romana are trying to work out how to repair a foundering Skonnan spaceship, the Doctor learns that Romana has made her own sonic screwdriver! He looks it over (it's smaller and sleeker-looking than the Doctor's), calls it "a bit basic," and immediately tries to steal it.

It is Romana who figures out how to power the broken down spaceship. "Brilliant! I wish I'd thought of that," the Doctor says. With a sunny grin, Romana replies, "Oh, you *will*, Doctor. You will!" The Doctor laughs happily, though it could be construed as an insult (i.e., that she's quicker on the draw than he is). Neither of them seems to regard it as such – rather that if Romana hadn't been there, the Doctor would have figured it out soon enough. The Doctor and Romana's roles are at this point identical (though if we're being honest, Romana might be slightly more awesome).

When the Doctor returns to the TARDIS, Romana's Doctor-esque adventures really begin. She repairs the spaceship, gets to know Seth, Teka and the other young Anethans slated to be sacrificed to the Minotaur-like Nimon, tells off the co-pilot ("despicable worm!") when he flies off without the Doctor, tries unsuccessfully to get the Anethans to help her overpower the co-pilot, helps land the spacecraft, meets the histrionic Skonnan leader Soldeed, and faces danger in the labyrinth with the Anethans. Meanwhile, the Doctor is puttering around trying to repair the TARDIS – though he does get a bit of excitement when he's

female Doctor, but the fact that the Doctor wipes her memory (even if it's to save her life) shows how unequal they still are. River Song is an even more complicated case – she's not a Time Lord, but she can regenerate, and she knows the TARDIS like the back of her hand – but her lack of a moral compass might disqualify her for Doctorhood. Come to think of it, River might make a fantastic female Master.

almost smashed by an asteroid. When he does finally arrive on Skonnos, he reclaims the Doctor role, saving Romana and the Anethans from being attacked by the Nimon. Next, he and Romana work in concert to figure out the Nimons' plan of planetary conquest. They function as two Doctors at this point, practically finishing each other's sentences. Then the Doctor goofs and accidentally sends Romana to the Nimon-infested planet Crinoth (a very un-Doctor-ish move).

When she finds herself cornered by Nimons on Crinoth, Romana, usually so cool under fire, cries out and squeezes her eyes shut, cowering. This might seem an un-Doctor-like response, but while the fourth Doctor tends not to exhibit much fear in the face of danger, other Doctors do (notably the second Doctor – and, for that matter, the ninth Doctor when he first encounters the Dalek in the episode of the same name).[27] Romana II is smaller and slighter than the fourth Doctor, and she cuts a less imposing figure (and unfortunately doesn't seem to know martial arts like the third Doctor does). This, combined with her girlish appearance, sometimes causes her adversaries to make the mistake of underestimating her, but on a practical level, when she doesn't have a weapon in hand (or K-9 with his blaster at the ready), she's more physically vulnerable than the Doctor – which only underscores her bravery in constantly walking into dangerous situations.

Stranded on Crinoth, Romana is aided by Sezom, who was tricked by the Nimons into giving them access to his planet. Strikingly, when Romana finally makes it back to Skonnos, she is the one who utters the grand moral pronouncements that the Doctor ordinarily would. Soldeed calls her a "meddlesome hussy," and she lets him have it: "It's all over, Soldeed. You're finished." Armed with what she's just witnessed on Crinoth, she makes Soldeed face the truth – that there isn't just one Nimon in existence, as he'd been led to believe, but a whole army of them ready to invade Skonnos. "[The Nimon] told you what you wanted to hear, promised you what you wanted to have... They're parasitic nomads who've been feeding off your selfishness and gullibility!"

---

27 Other instances of Romana's overt fear include her freaked-out reaction to the Daleks who capture her in *Destiny of the Daleks* (though she soon recovers her composure and fakes her own death to escape them), her unnerved response to the sight of the drained bodies and the blood in the fuel tanks in *State of Decay*, and her blood-curdling scream when Lazlo the Tharil reaches for her when she's trapped in the navigator's chair in *Warriors' Gate*.

Ask It How To Handle a Woman

Throughout Romana II's time with the Doctor, his attitude toward the power balance between the two of them is mixed – sometimes he downplays it, sometimes draws attention to it. In *Nimon*, when Soldeed asks if he was the one who fixed his spaceship, the Doctor replies, "Yes... well, with a little help from my friend... nice girl," though it would be more accurate to say that Romana fixed the ship with a little help from the Doctor. But he then describes her as "blonde, about so big, always sticking her nose in things that don't concern her." This last bit describes the Doctor himself to a tee.

It is perhaps in *Shada* that the Doctor most explicitly acknowledges both Romana's brilliance and their interchangeable roles. *Shada* is the story in which Romana rides (in the TARDIS) to the Doctor's rescue when he's on the verge of being attacked by Skagra's mind-stealing sphere. The sphere does eventually manage to take a copy of the Doctor's mind – and the Doctor is at a loss as to how to defeat Skagra, until Romana reminds him that the Doctor's mind is in the "melting pot" along with all the other brilliant minds Skagra has stolen. At this, the Doctor pins a medal on her (in the script, the medal reads "I AM A GENIUS"[28]), kisses her on both cheeks, and they salute each other. Soon after, when Romana points out how slim the Doctor's chances are of surviving their attempt to defeat Skagra, he says, "Listen, I can do your part if you can do mine," and adds, "You're a hero, remember?"

Though, strictly speaking, it does not belong in *Doctor Who* canon, I can't resist mentioning one of the Tom Baker-Lalla Ward ads for Prime Computer – the one entitled "Dr. Who meets his match." Romana wears her pink version of the Doctor's outfit. The Doctor sits before a Prime computer, while Romana stands behind him, puts her arms around him and nuzzles his neck. The Doctor spiels on about the wonders of Prime. "Ask it how to handle a woman," Romana says. Her tone undercuts the sexist ad copy: it's a command. No sooner does the Doctor touch the keyboard than the words appear on the monitor: "MARRY THE GIRL DOCTOR" (with no comma). The Doctor can barely get a proposal out before Romana accepts.

Of course, in *Doctor Who* canon, the Doctor does not marry the Girl Doctor (which would have been quite a surprising turn of events in the world of classic *Who*). Instead, Romana II was written out of the show partway through Season Eighteen. An argument can be made that

---

28 According to Lee Horton's *Doctor Who* Scripts Project: http://homepages.bw. edu/~jcurtis/Scripts/Shada/shada6.html

Romana's Girl Doctor persona is the reason she was jettisoned in favor of new companions. *Doctor Who* may have been too much of a closed system for some viewers when the TARDIS crew consisted of the Doctor, Romana II and K-9. Perhaps having companions who kept asking the Doctor questions rather than providing him with answers gave young viewers more of a way into the show (though surely many young female viewers found the brilliant Romana someone to aspire to). Perhaps some members of the *Doctor Who* production team felt such a brainy crew made for too few obstacles to overcome – though all the adventures featuring the Doctor, Romana and K-9 are full of perils and problems. In "A New Beginning," a special feature included on *The Leisure Hive* DVD about the various , mostly terrible changes he made to the show in Season Eighteen (less humor! more science!), John Nathan-Turner sourly says he "didn't like the whole lineup. They [the Doctor, Romana and K-9] were all so bright. I didn't like it." Of course, Nathan-Turner brought on Adric and Nyssa, no slouches in the brains department, and it does seem a bit odd that he wanted more of an emphasis on science and, at the same time, a less intelligent TARDIS crew.

I've Got To Be My Own Romana

At the end of *Meglos*, the Time Lords summon Romana home. At the beginning of *Full Circle*, she is visibly agitated as she tells the Doctor, "I don't want to spend the rest of my life on Gallifrey – after all this." Romana clearly has the makings of a Time Lord renegade like the Doctor himself, and one would think he would empathize with Romana's position and come to her aid. Their similarity is once again emphasized by matching costumes, Romana wearing a dress the same burgundy color as the Doctor's new outfit. The Doctor's reaction is strangely casual. "You can't fight Time Lords," he says, not looking at her. "You did, once," she points out, but he replies: "And lost." She is clearly disappointed at his reaction. The scene feels like a realistic disagreement between a couple – underscored by the fact that the scene takes place in Romana's room, with her moping on the bed when the Doctor enters. It's unclear whether the Doctor is unwilling to help Romana fight her summons solely because he fears what the Time Lords may do to her, or whether there are more complex reasons. Perhaps on some level, he (like John Nathan-Turner) is beginning to feel that there is one Time Lord too many in the TARDIS.

Fortunately for Romana, she and the Doctor are stranded in E-Space before they can reach Gallifrey. They have one last love-fest in *State of*

Decay (in which the Doctor tells her, "You *are* wonderful"). But by the beginning of *Warriors' Gate*, they're bickering over the TARDIS controls and how to get out of E-Space, and it does feel like the TARDIS, bigger on the inside though it may be, isn't big enough for the both of them. Unbelievably, the Doctor asks her, "Don't you want to get back to Gallifrey?" "You *know* I don't want to get back to Gallifrey!", Romana cries, seeming at her wits' end. Soon after, when the Doctor leaves the TARDIS, Romana asks Adric, "What if the Doctor and I went different ways?"

Throughout *Warriors' Gate*, we see Romana chafing under the "assistant" role she's long outgrown. When the slave-trading Rorvik and his crew arrive outside the TARDIS, Adric sees their guns and says he wishes the Doctor were there. Romana replies, "So do I. Oh, never mind. It's all going to be fine. I'm fully qualified." Later in the story, the Doctor is once again going to face danger on his own, and he tells Romana and Adric to dematerialize in the TARDIS if he's not back soon. Romana refuses to let him go alone. The Doctor orders her to do as he says, but Romana talks him into her going along (and proceeds to order Adric around just as the Doctor tried to order her – with more success). Preventing Rorvik from attempting to blast through the mirrors in the gateway between N- and E-Space falls to Romana when Rorvik starts strangling the Doctor. The Doctor instructs Romana to drain the power. "I know," Romana retorts, sounding annoyed. "I've done it!"

After all this, it should come as little surprise that, once the TARDIS crew have saved the day, Romana informs the Doctor that she isn't returning to N-Space with him. The Doctor, however, is flabbergasted, and orders her inside the TARDIS. Smiling, she says, "No more orders, Doctor. Goodbye," and adds, "I've got to be my own Romana."

Romana heads off to help Biroc free enslaved Tharils throughout E-Space. K-9 tells Romana that he has all the necessary info for her to build her own TARDIS. So Romana ventures forth, with an entire universe to explore. She is her own Romana now. She's also her own version of the Doctor. There can be little doubt that, as the Doctor tells Adric, "She'll be superb."

Mouth on Legs

Tehani Wessely was a founding member of *Andromeda Spaceways Inflight Magazine* in 2001 and started her own boutique publishing house, FableCroft Publishing, in 2010. Now firmly entrenched in Australian speculative fiction and independent press, she also judges for several national literary awards and reads far more in one genre than is healthy. Tehani blames Neil Gaiman for her *Doctor Who* addiction, which is relatively recent and correlated to her desire to view *The Doctor's Wife*. Since becoming enamored with Matt Smith's portrayal of the Doctor, Tehani works hard to keep up with her friends in fandom, including blogging a series of conversational New *Who* reviews with Tansy Rayner Roberts and David McDonald. Tehani loves the idea that there is no wrong way to be a *Doctor Who* fan, and looks forward to many more years of exploring the history and future of the show and its affiliated media. In her spare moments, she works as Head of Library in a Canberra boys' school and enjoys spending time with her husband and four children. You can find Tehani online as @editor mum75 on Twitter, or at thebooknut.wordpress.com.

I was fated to see Tegan Jovanka through rose-colored glasses.[29] There is so much about her I relate to on a personal level – she's Australian, she's from a rural(ish) background, she's independent, she's forthright, she's in your face... Yeah, I was always going to love her.

I adored Tegan from the minute she opened her mouth on screen – her big smile, her obvious excitement at starting her new job, her assertive nature, all on display within seconds of appearing in the shot. Watching Tegan over the course of her time in the TARDIS, I saw more and more aspects of her that put me in mind of New *Who* companions, particularly Donna and Amy. Yet conventional fan wisdom would have it that Tegan was whiny, bumptious, unappreciative of the TARDIS experience and not very bright. Where does this perception come from, and is it time for a reassessment of Tegan's character?

Though I grew up with an awareness of Tom Baker, K-9 and Sarah Jane Smith, I was only drawn to revisit the classic series in *Doctor Who*'s 50th anniversary year. When I received the opportunity to write about Tegan, the outspoken Australian who accompanied the fifth Doctor

---

29 No pun intended! Though now I think about it...

through most of his journey, I wasn't sure I was up to the job – after all, I was such a new (in more than one sense) fan. Could I do Tegan, one of the longest serving companions of the entire series, the justice she deserved? In the end, I didn't have to think too hard about it – Tegan needed an Aussie to showcase her run, and I needed to visit her story. What a ride it's been...

My perspective on Tegan compares her with the New *Who* companions rather than her contemporaries. Other than some Sarah Jane memories more informed by *The Sarah Jane Adventures* and appearances with the tenth Doctor than the original context, my recent classic companion viewing includes only Adric, Nyssa, Turlough, and a tiny bit of Peri, Liz Shaw, Harry Sullivan and Grace Holloway. As I noted above, I loved Tegan from the start, so I find myself bewildered as to why she has received such a bad rap in fandom. The more I watched of her run, the more I found to like about her, and the more characteristics of New *Who* companions I identified. As far as I can see, Tegan is the template on which the new show's companions have been modelled!

And yet, in almost every blog post, fan article and information page I examined, even the positively framed ones, her character is called into question. She is irritating where Rose is confident; selfish where Martha is dedicated to her career; stroppy where Donna is direct; brash where Amy is assertive; stubborn where Clara is persistent. In my eyes, though, Tegan exhibits as much intelligence as Rose; as much resourcefulness as Martha; as much empathy as Donna; as much bravery as Amy; as much heart as Clara. So why, I wonder, does Tegan get such poor press?

Is it simply a matter of context? Does Tegan suffer from her close association with Nyssa, who is overtly intelligent, intrinsically kind and just ever so slightly bland? Is she interpreted only in terms of her first few stories, unable to be redeemed by her second and third seasons? Even there, I struggle to understand, because everything Tegan is, from her first minutes on screen, encapsulates her personality and strength, her bravery and kindness, and her capable nature.

We first meet Tegan in the fourth Doctor's final story, *Logopolis*. She is presented as an enthusiastic, efficient Aussie girl who quickly establishes herself as being independent and strong-willed, if (by her own admission) a little scattered. She reacts remarkably well to finding herself aboard the TARDIS, despite being lost within its corridors for no small amount of time.[30] Regardless of how strange the situation must be

---

30 Which was simply fascinating in light of *Journey to the Centre of the TARDIS*, in which Clara shows explores more of the Ship than we've seen since the show's return.

for her, she is quick to defy (with a bit of sass) the Master's invitation to scream, and this, as much as anything in her first story, establishes her courage and her unwillingness to be a victim. Later, in *Castrovalva*, she quickly establishes her resourcefulness by stealing an ambulance (with the newly regenerated Doctor inside) from under the nose of police, to facilitate their escape.

Throughout everything that happens in her first season with the fifth Doctor, Tegan maintains her resolve to return to her time and place on Earth. She is focussed on her career, determined to grab the opportunity it presents to her and run with it, which leads to several instances of distress and anger with the Doctor for not being able to get her home. Yet she still participates wholeheartedly in her adventures with the TARDIS team, revealing her loyalty to her friends and her innate empathy towards other beings along the way.

There's a perception that Tegan constantly harped on at the Doctor for his failure to get her back to her time and place, but this was only true of her first season – by *Time-Flight*, it's very clear that she is enjoying her adventures, and when confronted with Heathrow and a return to her own time, she willingly goes back to the Doctor... only to be accidentally left behind. When she finds the Doctor and Nyssa in *Arc of Infinity*, she leaps straight back into action and back into the fold. For two more seasons. Her longevity says something both about the character (yes, she really wanted to be there) and her place on the show – her run lasted longer than almost any other companions', demonstrating she had to be doing something right.

Given that both Steven Moffat and Mark Gatiss are old school fans, perhaps it's unsurprising that we recently had this little reference to Tegan in Gatiss' *The Crimson Horror*:

> **Clara:** You're making a habit of this, getting us lost.
> **The Doctor:** Sorry. It's much better than it used to be. Ooh, I once spent a hell of a long time trying to get a gobby Australian to Heathrow airport.
> **Clara:** What for?
> **The Doctor:** "Search me... Anyway..." (sound of screaming) "Brave heart, Clara.

While the "Brave heart" comment provides a little touch of nostalgia, it's the preceding lines that are disappointing. Dismissing Tegan as a "gobby Australian" plays right into that vitriolic fan-view of her that simply doesn't wash, and to indicate with "Search me" that he had no idea why Tegan initially felt so strongly about returning to her career does both Tegan *and* the Doctor a huge disservice.

I can't help but wonder if this negative image of Tegan has been played up over the years by discussions in fandom, as received fannish knowledge develops into caricature.

Seeing her through the lens of the New *Who* companions means all the aspects of Tegan that may have led to a "you either love her or you hate her" attitude among viewers of the time strike me as being made of awesome. Tegan is protective, resourceful, honest, tenacious, practical, outspoken and eminently sensible. She acts as the voice of reason, and although she can be a bit one-eyed (particularly in her early episodes), she's courageous to a fault. Tegan is the one who reins the Doctor in when he is behaving badly (shades of Donna, anyone?) and becomes the glue that holds the TARDIS team together. As early as *Castrovalva*, the Doctor identifies her as the "co-ordinator," letting her know he thinks she is vital to the crew and has skills that are necessary to the success of the plan.

While still playing the usual companion's role of the audience representative, Tegan also has her eyes wide open in her adventures and frequently offers a cautious position as opposed to her friends' willingness to jump into danger. Perhaps this too is something that counts against her in the popularity stakes – Tegan questions the Doctor (and that's just not done!), and her caution could possibly be interpreted on occasion as cowardice. One only has to consider Tegan's general nature, though, to be disabused of this idea. She might show restraint in the face of the unknown, but she will be front and center when it counts.

In many ways, the little things make Tegan stand out as a companion. For me, her broad Australian-ness in the early episodes was a delight – that overt ocker tone dimmed a little over time, but Tegan never lost touch with her roots. It was interesting (in the full sense of the word...) that she could purportedly speak an Australian Aboriginal language[31], and regardless of how likely that might be, it's still more evidence of Tegan's intelligence and empathic nature. I was delighted at the reference in *The Sarah Jane Adventures* to Tegan's work campaigning for the rights of Australian Aborigines; that just makes so much sense to me!

---

31 Setting aside the fact that any language so many thousands of years removed from its roots would have changed significantly, it would be a huge stroke of luck to come across the same Australian Aboriginal language you happened to know, as the Australian Aborigines had several hundred distinct dialects. Perhaps the TARDIS translation circuit played a role there...

Tegan's compassion is a major aspect of her character. Her evident pain over Adric's death (despite their frequent clashes), sadness over Nyssa's departure and distress over the plight of the victims in her stories demonstrates her deep-rooted empathy – this is particularly vivid in *Enlightenment*, where Tegan's concern for the human crews of ships being destroyed in the race clearly disturbs her greatly.

Janet Fielding, who played Tegan, suggested in a recent TV special that her character was:

> "... quite vociferous, and she was quite argumentative, and assertive, although not particularly smart... It's interesting that you can be one without the other. You can be assertive without being smart."[32]

Coming at the character with eyes wide open and lit by New *Who* love, I simply can't agree with that assessment – Tegan might not be Adric- or Nyssa-level smart, but she's certainly an intelligent woman. She refuses to accept matters blindly and questions the motives and ethics of those around her. I can't help but see this as a constructive character trait, one that helps keep her and her friends safe. She is often actively involved in solving the problem of the week (or even of the moment, as when she calmly slides open a door that Turlough and the Doctor have been struggling to push in *Warriors of the Deep*...), and if she sometimes needs rescuing, well, which character on the show (even the Doctor) doesn't? Sometimes, she actively participates in her own rescue (and that of others) – in *The Visitation*, she discovers the method of escape for both herself and Adric, and forces it to happen. Adric says, "Let me try, I'm stronger," and Tegan replies, "But not as determined!," and proceeds to get them out of a locked room.

Again and again, Tegan is a forerunner to the modern-era companions. She is one of very few classic companions to be shown as having an extended family. It's pretty much a given now, but it was rarely done in classic *Who* (only Ace comes close). Tegan is also firm in her self-belief as a career woman (see: Martha), and her knowledge that she can do just as much (and more) as the blokes in the show. She handles Adric and Turlough quite firmly, refusing to let them treat her with any less respect than they would the Doctor or other companions, and standing up for herself when anyone tries to suggest her instincts are wrong. It wouldn't sound out of place if any of the modern companions spoke

---

32 *The Doctors Revisited*: "The Fifth Doctor," BBC America, May 26th, 2013.

Tegan's lines.

A final point – one that cements Tegan's character as intelligent, thoughtful, kind-hearted and one of the most sensible companions of them all. In *Resurrection of the Daleks*, her last proper appearance on the show, Tegan decides to leave the TARDIS, finally tired of the death and sadness that comes with traveling with the Doctor. As she says, "It's stopped being fun." And in that, she proves exactly how smart she really is. We should all be so brave.

Tegan's run has not yet ended – still voiced by Janet Fielding, she continues to appear in Big Finish audio releases alongside the fifth Doctor, Adric, Nyssa and Turlough. Given Tegan's longevity as a companion, it still bemuses me that fandom at large could vilify her so much. Clearly she must have her advocates, though, to be such an enduring figure in the *Doctor Who* universe, and I look forward to hearing from those who – like me – think she's fabulous.

From "There's Nothing Only About Being a Girl" to "The Most Important Woman in the Whole of Creation": Feminism and the Female Companions

Linnea Dodson is a technical writer who has been in fannish culture since 1976. Her *Doctor Who* publications include the short story "God Send Me Well to Keep" in the *Short Trips* anthology *The Qualities of Leadership*, "Greatest Coulrophobia in the Galaxy" in *Outside In: 160 New Perspectives on 160 Classic Doctor Who Stories by 160 Writers* and "Conscious Colorblindness, Unconscious Racism" in *Doctor Who and Race*.

There's panic in the streets as an army of shop window dummies advances, shooting from their hands. Confused and disbelieving, a woman stands ready to defend her world beside the strange new Doctor she has just met. It's 1970, and *Spearhead from Space* is introducing both the third Doctor and Liz Shaw. It's 2005, and *Rose* is introducing both the ninth Doctor and Rose Tyler.

The same plot, the same intent – but what a difference 35 years makes! Liz worked with reel-to-reel computers and transistor radios; Rose grew up with micro-electronics. Liz used shillings and guineas; Rose knew only decimal currency. Most importantly, Rose was the beneficiary of social changes wrought by decades of feminist agitation and legislation that were just beginning in Liz's time. It's possible to trace the birth, growth and triumphs of English women's liberation simply by watching how the women in the TARDIS are presented and treated.

The Past is a Foreign Country: the 1960s

From the beginning, *Doctor Who* was meant to be a progressive show. Even in its first years, it included women as geniuses, professionals, soldiers and more – and that's not counting the BBC's first female producer behind the camera. And yet, these were also years when employment advertising was still divided into "men's jobs" and "women's work" (the latter garnering lower wages even for the same effort). Several Cambridge and Oxford colleges were closed to women. Unmarried women had difficulty getting access to contraceptives, and abortion was illegal. Although *The Feminine Mystique* was printed the same year as *Doctor Who* premiered, the concept of "women's lib" would not gain full focus until the next decade.

Which is why the power of *Doctor Who*'s initial set of women was undercut with "yes... but..." Yes, Verity Lambert was the BBC's first woman producer, but she was show creator Sydney Newman's third choice (two men turned him down). Yes, Barbara Wright's historical education was useful, but Ian was the action hero. Yes, Susan was a genius, but she was also the Doctor's ward – which in those days meant subordination to his will.

In the early 60s, no one inside the TARDIS or outside watching the show questioned that Susan's autocratic grandfather had the authority to make major life decisions for her regardless of what she wanted. Her time as a companion began and ended with her tearfully begging the Doctor not to do exactly what he was doing. In *An Unearthly Child*, Susan wanted to stay and pleaded for the release of her teachers, eventually throwing down a clear ultimatum: "I won't go, Grandfather. I won't leave the twentieth century. I'd rather leave the TARDIS and you." The Doctor's response was to snap "Now you're being sentimental and childish" as he swept them all away.

A year later, in the aftermath of *The Dalek Invasion of Earth*, just as Susan responded to an offer of marriage with "I can't stay, David. I don't belong to this time," the Doctor locked her out and left her. It was presented as a bittersweet romantic scene – the Doctor giving up the granddaughter he loved so she can be with the man she loved – but to modern eyes, can be read as nothing short of abusive. The Doctor's idea of "now, you are a woman" was not to give Susan the autonomy of an adult but to hand her over to another man – and then, as he abandoned her on a war-wasted world without her friends, her possessions or even a complete pair of shoes, command that "there must be no regrets, no tears, no anxieties"! Throughout this, Barbara and Ian never said anything, nor do they mention it later. For them, there was nothing wrong.

There's little to say from a feminist point of view about most of the rest of the companions of the 60s. Vicki and Victoria were wards and, like Susan, under the Doctor's authority; Polly and Dodo were adults who came and went without much note. (At least all four got to choose the time and manner of their leaving!)

There are two exceptions to the unexceptional, though: Sara Kingdom and Zoe.

Sydney Newman's other show, *The Avengers*, started climbing the ratings in 1962 when it introduced Cathy Gale, a cool, intellectual fighter who talked like a man (literally; *The Avengers'* scripts written for a male character weren't rewritten) and became an international hit with Emma Peel. Newman must have realized the power of women who combined brains, brawn and black leather. So it's surprising that *Doctor Who's* equivalent, soldier Sara Kingdom, didn't survive *The Daleks' Master Plan*. Zoe lasted longer, but her strength was undercut by her upbringing; she started out emotionally stunted. Her introduction in *The Wheel in Space* included a conversation on the subject, featuring the wistful, "My head's been pumped full of facts and figures... but, well, I want to feel things as well."

However, the world outside the TARDIS was changing. Between 1968 and 1969, English law began to seriously address women's rights. Abortion was legalized. The women of the Dagenham Ford Sewing Machinists Union went on strike when they discovered they were being paid less for the same work as the men (the strike was resolved when they accepted a gradual rise instead of full and immediate compensation).

Very small steps, but at least it meant that when a Time Lord stripped Zoe and Jamie of autonomy and memories, this time the Doctor and the audience saw it for what it was: a punishment they didn't deserve.

Nothing Only About Being a Girl: Staggering Towards Equality

In 1970, gender tensions exploded. In this year alone, the Equal Pay Act passed (prohibiting paying women less for the same work), the first meeting of the National Women's Liberation Movement was held at Ruskin College, feminists picketed the Miss World Contest at the Albert Hall, Lloyds of London hired its first female underwriters, and both *The Female Eunuch* and *Sexual Politics* were published. The next year, 4000 women marched through central London to demand equal rights.

Doctor Who tried to respond, with extremely mixed results. While the series *said* how accomplished the new female companions were, what it usually *showed* was women still being treated unequally.

Liz Shaw had the worst of this. Here was an incredibly brilliant, well-educated woman. (Technically too educated; no one could have actually become "an expert in meteorites, [with] degrees in medicine, physics and a dozen other subjects" and still be young enough to rock a miniskirt.) But the same man who gave her that praise also gave her casually sexist disrespect.

Part of it was so blatant that even the audience was supposed to realize that a line had been crossed. Liz's first scene in *Spearhead from Space* made it clear that she had been all but kidnapped by UNIT. The Brigadier ignored her objections – even when she outright asked, "How I feel doesn't matter?" However, some of it was so subtle, so normal for the time, that it takes looking back to realize exactly how badly she was treated. Liz was pulled away from her own important work; given substandard, mismatched equipment (the Brigadier apologized for that); and asked to believe things that outraged her scientific sensibilities. Yet the very man who did all of this scolded her for actually daring to object, as if she was expected to stay sweet and polite regardless. "Sometimes you can be very aggravating," the Brigadier chided, or "You could bring yourself to be less astringent." General Scobie saw fit to discuss her appearance with another man right in front of her. "Lucky fellow, Stewart, having a pretty face around the place." The Doctor wasn't much better; at the end of the adventure, he demanded Liz's continued support without asking her opinion, much less permission.

So it's not much of a surprise that Liz soon decamped, having apparently told him at one point, "What you need, Doctor, is someone to pass you your test tubes and to tell you how brilliant you are."

Out with the scientist, in with Jo Grant, a character both less accomplished and less likely to push back against sexism. (When asked about it in 1998 for *SFX* magazine #39, actress Katie Manning replied, "I don't think feminism started to be discussed in the news till many years later, did it? It wouldn't have been discussed around my era, certainly.") Jo was no woman's libber. She had flunked science and passed basic training – but her qualities as a soldier, spy, scientist or otherwise equal to the men around her were summed up by the Brigadier in *Terror of the Autons* as "Miss Grant was very keen to join us and she happens to have relatives in high places." Even the BBC's official website dubs her "ditzy." Yes, Jo had excellent emotional qualities: she was loyal, plucky, curious and brave. But in her first story, she only stays on because the

Doctor can't bring himself to hurt her by firing her, and her last story shows scenes of both the Doctor and Professor Jones (the man she is falling in love with) ignoring her, teasing her and occasionally shouting at her, all of which she quietly accepts. Jo's biggest contribution to the plot of *The Green Death* was accidentally knocking over fungal spores into the right petri dish. When it comes to liberation, the best that can be said for her is that when Jo left for love, it was her clear, uncontested choice (UNIT even threw her a party).

By 1973, it was impossible to not discuss feminism more substantially than *The Time Monster*'s single line "May God bless the good ship women's lib and all who sail in her." Five colleges in Oxford had opened to women. The London stock exchange had opened to women. Olga Korbet swept the Munich Olympics, inventing gymnastic moves never seen before, teaching the world that women could be incredible athletes. It was time for *Doctor Who* to seriously address a changing society. Enter Sarah Jane Smith, investigative journalist.

In many ways, Sarah Jane was introduced as a parody of feminism, making huffy speeches about equality that the people around her didn't take seriously (most notably complaining in *The Time Warrior* that unliberated medieval women were "living in the Middle Ages"). In *The Monster of Peladon*, the Doctor sent her to say stirring things about liberation to the new queen Thalira ("I'm only a girl." "There's nothing only about being a girl, your Majesty!"), but when Sarah Jane started teasing him at the end of the story, he dragged her into the TARDIS by her ear as if she was a willful child. In *The Ark in Space*, the Doctor rallied her in a moment of weakness by rattling off a series of gender-based insults until she was enraged into fighting back. (By the end of her run, Sarah Jane would no longer be making speeches about women's lib or being gender insulted – but her costumes became less professional and more childlike, finally ending up with the infamous striped Andy Pandy romper.)

Even so, Sarah Jane was a sea change. Even if she wasn't always effective, she fought back every single time, making the UNIT men and the viewers face the ingrained attitudes that Liz had suffered through. No companion after Sarah would have to swallow institutional sexism. It was one of the ways Sarah Jane rose above her clunky speeches and ridiculous costumes. Another compelling feature was that she was a woman any girl watching could realistically grow up to meet – or to be. She was smart and educated, but she didn't have an improbably long string of degrees. She wasn't from the past or a far-flung future (although she did spend a lot of 1975's *Pyramids of Mars* going on about how she came from 1980). She could shoot a rifle, but she wasn't a super soldier. She was brave and loyal and faced adversity with panache and humor. At times, she even acted as the conscience of the Doctor – it was her, not action man Harry, who tried to talk the Doctor out of his doubts during *Genesis of the Daleks*. She was the first companion the Doctor introduced as "my best friend."

In addition, Sarah Jane was living the woman's liberation ideal – she was doing the job of a man. Specifically, the job of two famous men: her introduction coincided with journalists Woodward and Bernstein breaking the Watergate scandal and ending the Nixon presidency. Between 1973 and 1976, an investigative reporter – even one in striped overalls – was to be reckoned with.

Sadly, Sarah Jane did not have the power to choose on her own when to leave. But this time, the parting shown in *The Hand of Fear* truly was bittersweet and has stayed so over the years. "Don't forget me," she asked. "Oh, Sarah," replied the man who saw Zoe's and Jamie's memories wiped, "Don't you forget me."

Neither one forgot. And no one knew then how predictive the Doctor's last words were: "Till we meet again, Sarah."

Back in the United Kingdom, feminism continued to rack up triumphs and break down barriers. Family planning was rolled into the NHS (making contraceptives free), the Sex Discrimination Act passed (ending the practice of gender-related job descriptions), the Employment Protection Act passed (now women couldn't be fired for becoming pregnant), the Domestic Violence Act passed (allowing women to file court orders against their abusers). Worldwide, the first International Year of the Woman was announced. Skater Dorothy Hamill and gymnast Nadia Comaneci continued the fame of female athletes, the latter being the first woman to achieve perfect scores in the Olympics.

To some degree, the *Doctor Who* producers overcompensated. They wanted the new companions to be strong women, but the setup of the show also required someone who needed the Doctor to explain things to them so the audience got exposition. For the next ten years, most companions fitted into a model where the strengths of each woman were counterbalanced by some deficiency – beyond her control, of course, it's not that she's flawed in any way, you understand – that only the Doctor could fix. It was the return of "yes, but..." with "so she needs the Doctor to..." tacked on.

Yes, Leela was a strong warrior, but she was also an uneducated savage, so she needed the Doctor to teach her about civilization. Yes, Romana was the Doctor's own kind and much smarter and better educated than he is (in *The Ribos Operation*, she gleefully revealed his lackluster academic history). But she was young and inexperienced, so she needed the Doctor to tutor her in the realities outside the classroom. (Romana's whole character changes, literally, to become more friendly and subordinate to the Doctor. After her regeneration, her wardrobe included a schoolgirl uniform and even a feminized version of his outfit.) Yes, Nyssa was a brilliant scientist, but she is the last survivor of Traken, so she needs the Doctor to watch over her. (At least in the Doctor's mind; in *Black Orchid*, Nyssa is the identical twin of a marriage-aged woman, but the Doctor pointedly makes her drink fruit juice like underaged Adric instead of allowing her alcohol like Tegan.) Tegan had a profession, but she became part of the TARDIS team by accident, so she needed the Doctor to get her back to her life in Heathrow.

Admittedly, Mel was there for the fun and had no "but... so she needed..." Peri, on the other hand, was a throwback to the worst objectification. She was introduced while stripped down to a tiny bikini, the sixth Doctor tried to throttle her, and, worst, she was left as Schrodinger's companion, either dead of vivisection or living happily ever after.

The Times, They are A-Changin':
Ace and Bambera, Heralds of a New Era

Non-fictional British women continued to break barriers. 1979: Margaret Thatcher, first woman Prime Minister. 1981: Lady Young, first woman leading the House of Lords. 1983: Mary Donaldson, first woman Lord Mayor of London. 1986: The Sex Discrimination Act is updated.

1987: Ace. In many ways, Ace was a fantasy character, combining castaway, chemist, bomber, delinquent and troubled soul. It's hard to argue the victim of a time storm and a carrier of the Curse of Fenric as having autonomy. Yet, she was never passive. This is a woman who took out Daleks with a baseball bat and a rocket launcher, plus mixed her own Nitro-9 explosives.

Ace was the companion the Doctor had plans for. She called him "Professor" from the beginning and he lived up to it. After 24 years of traveling with wards, friends, assistants and the occasional kidnappee, the Doctor was blatantly giving Ace on-the-job training as his apprentice, even moreso than Romana. *Remembrance of the Daleks* had a scene where the Doctor explained his perennial nemesis via the Socratic method. *Ghost Light* started with references to Ace's "Initiative Test."

Ace stepped up to the challenge and the girls watching loved her for it. Actress Sophie Aldred, looking back in the *Sydney Morning Herald* (March 12, 2013), said: "I used to get a lot of fan mail from girls, which was unusual at the time... Girls still say to me now 'She was my role model'."

This was the era of the Cartmel Masterplan, when the scripts were trying to hint at a dark backstory. That plan was interrupted, but not before Marc Platt began work on the idea that the Doctor would sponsor Ace to Prydon Academy to become a Time Lady in her own right. It was the ultimate equality the show could grant. The man who had abandoned his Time Lady granddaughter to a human woman's life now planned on elevating a human woman to Time Lady status.

On Earth, Brigadier Winifred Bambera also represented a powerful shift in perspectives on women's capabilities. She was more than just a commander who could, in a single day, lead her army troop, deal with alien incursion and best a medieval knight in hand-to-hand combat.

UNIT, for all its underlying sexism, had been surprisingly forward thinking – Corporal Bell was a recurring character, and *Spearhead from Space* showed a nameless woman duty officer 22 years before the gender integration of the Royal Army Corps. Brigadier Lethbridge-Stewart referred to an unnamed Prime Minister as "Madam" four years before Thatcher. But no current-day British woman had actually been shown in a position of military command until Bambera appeared.

But, by 1989, women (and minorities, another underserved demographic) had made enough gains in society that the idea of a woman of color leading a regiment wasn't outrageous. With little ceremony but much symbolism, Brigadier Lethbridge-Stewart and Brigadier Bambera met in *Battlefield*, the old white man relieved of command by the young black woman. (It would take another decade for Britain to have an actual woman brigadier, when Patricia Purves was promoted over four men.)

Then *Doctor Who* was cancelled.

Interim: Grace

Feminist-specific legislation slowed down drastically in the 90s. News of "the first woman to" practically disappeared, because so many barriers had already been broken. "Women's Lib" had become an antique and slightly cringeworthy phrase instead of a potent political rally cry. Yes, much ground had been gained by women. But...

While the 1996 TV movie was fortunately not typical *Doctor Who*,

Grace Holloway was a typical example of a role that was extremely popular at the time and still shows up today: a workaholic whose very dedication and skill are drawbacks. In Dr. Holloway's case, colleagues refer to her as "Amazing Grace" – a nickname that could as easily be sarcastic as respectful. Her boyfriend is furious that work comes first. Fans remember her as the first companion to be kissed by the Doctor and forget that the storyarc of this stereotype demands that the workaholic must either learn to balance work and love or, as Grace temporarily does, nobly sacrifice herself for a greater cause.

The Most Important Woman in the Whole of Creation: The Modern Companions

The twenty-first century did not start with space wheels and food cubes, as *Doctor Who* had predicted. It didn't start with the drastic social changes of the previous era either. Nevertheless the gaps between 1989, 1996 and 2005 still show a definable shift in presentation of women simply because New *Who* was written for a new generation – one which had grown up always having and taking for granted the rights won in previous decades. Just how drastic the changes were became immediately clear.

The disastrous movie had tried to dump 30-plus years of name-checking and exposition into the first few minutes, well before the casual or new viewer cared about the Doctor, the Master, Skaro, etc. In contrast, New *Who* started with a very understandable, relatable montage: here is your basic Londoner. She lives in a council flat with her mother. She has a job and a boyfriend. Her shop has a basement full of moving mannequins. Although the show had previously presented its adventures in the third person, now it was almost entirely from Rose's point of view; she was in all but two scenes and one of those was about her mother trying to contact her. (This wasn't just an introductory one-off, either. *Rose* was the first of several "Doctor light" episodes where the focus was on someone, often a woman, other than the titular hero.)

The story title flashed on the screen: *Rose*. In the entire run of classic *Who*, no recurring character was honored with an unadorned title; even stories titled *The... Doctors* had a qualifying number of incarnations. *Doctor Who* was no longer the Doctor's story; now the companion had center stage. This woman-centric focus – and in the ninth through eleventh Doctor eras, the Doctor always invited women first, although the women occasionally invited a man along later – meant that companions now fitted a specific set of criteria.

First, they're adults. The Doctor may interact with children, but by the time he sweeps anyone away long term in the TARDIS, she is old enough to make the informed choice to go. The era of the Doctor's ward is over – even the Doctor's daughter sprang from the DNA-duplicating machinery fully grown and able to argue military ethics with her horrified parent.

Second, they rarely think for a heartbeat that they have to prove anything, much less that they are an equal to a man. Even Donna's struggle with self-worth didn't come from feeling second best to men in a man's world, it came from being constantly ground down by her mother disapproving everything she did – or didn't – do. (It can even be argued that Donna's desperation to get married wasn't to check an item off the "things women ought to do" life list as much as it was to have someone else in her life who was supportive and loving like her grandfather and father.)

Third, the companions aren't notable mainly for a single aspect, as many of the old school companions could be. They all come well rounded with separate histories, hobbies and hopes. For instance, Rose didn't have to be The Athletic Fighter a la Leela to realistically swing in on a chain and save the Doctor in *Rose* – it was perfectly believable that a working class girl with middle class aspirations would look at all those famous female Olympians and see gymnastics as her ticket out. It was also perfectly believable that Donna could muster the resources and determination to educate herself from the dismissive, shallow, incurious Runaway Bride to eager and engaged Partners in Crime with the Doctor.

Fourth, they come with their own relationships. Classic *Who* companions were rarely shown with their families and lost contact once they entered the TARDIS. Some of the old school companions like Polly and Vicki didn't even have family names mentioned on screen. Now the entire audience is introduced to the complex family life of the new companions, usually before that companion meets the Doctor. (In the Davies era, these families inevitably included an opinionated mother who drove one or more plots herself.) The companions don't have to give up these ties, either. They're constantly being kept in touch with their parents (Rose, Martha, Donna, arguably River), lovers (Rose, Amy, River, Clara) or the children they teach or nanny (Clara again).

Finally, every one of the women who interacts with the Doctor has no hesitation to request, advise, demand or even punish him and he accepts this. "Stitch this!", snarled Jackie as she slapped an all-powerful alien upside the head (*Aliens of London*). Sarah Jane, who hadn't talked the Doctor into blowing up the Daleks, did talk him into stopping the Krillitanes (*School Reunion*) and reminded him that Time Lord or not, he can't hold onto the past. Martha didn't hesitate to let the Doctor know he wasn't respecting her and how badly he'd hurt her feelings (*Last of the Time Lords*). Donna warned him, "Find someone... because sometimes I think you need someone to stop you" in *The Runaway Bride* and ordered him to "just save someone" from the fires of Pompeii. The Doctor outright deferred to Amy, letting her make the determination of reality vs. dream in *Amy's Choice*.

But no discussion of women's treatment can avoid *Journey's End*. What started as a joyous celebration of the Whoniverse, pulling in every companion and family member of the Davies era plus the main players of both spin-offs, derailed into the violation of not one but two companions.

Rose had deliberately chosen not to follow her mother into the alternate universe during *Doomsday*; her alternate father dragged her there in a last-second rescue. Rose's opinion of this was to call it "the day I died." The audience would find out later that she spent much of her time trying to find a way to bridge the gap and get back. At *Journey's End*, Jackie wanted to return to her husband and new baby in the alternate universe, but Rose said directly, "I spent all that time trying to find you. I'm not going back now." She would change her mind only after the Doctor made his clone her new responsibility. (Side note: Rose's tenth Doctor fixation, after being asked to live "a fantastic life" in *The Parting of the Ways*, and even after she had seen her future by meeting Sarah Jane in *School Reunion*, was a fairly creepy and extremely unliberated plot point to saddle on the first of the new companions.)

But Rose eventually acquiesced. Donna agreed to nothing. For reasons unknown, the Doctor could not heal Donna from the metacrisis the way he pulled the TARDIS out of Rose before it killed her (*The Parting of the Ways*), so for the first time since the 60s, a begging, crying companion was stripped of *everything* she valued, including her memories and personal growth.

The circumstances and reactions, though, were directly opposite those of the 60s. The Doctor was not trying to decide which kind of life was best for Donna, he was trying to keep her alive, period. (Regardless, he is breaking English law; emergency services cannot forcibly treat anyone who is able to coherently refuse.) Even though he saved her, the characters within the show still treated it as a symbolic death. When the saddened Doctor returned the unconscious Donna to her home and tried to console her family with, "For one moment, one shining moment, she was the most important woman in the whole wide universe," they were not comforted. Wilf openly mourned the end of the woman his granddaughter had become. Sylvia snapped, "Mr. Smith is just leaving" – the polite person's way of saying, "Get out before I throw you out." The viewers certainly didn't see this as bittersweet or even acceptable behavior. Fan discussions included words like "abusive," "rape" and even "murder." *Io9* lists Donna's mindwipe second from the top in "10 Times the Doctor Acted Like a Total Bastard."

In 1964, saving romance was worth more than a woman's autonomy. By 2008, a woman's autonomy was more prized than life itself.

It Has Three Settings: Women as the Doctor

The twenty-first century has another new wrinkle – women who take over the Doctor's role. Not just potentially, as Ace was intended; or temporarily, as Rose did in *The Christmas Invasion*; but women who constantly function on screen as a version of the Doctor. River Song is the most obvious example: she is just as good (if not better) at time travel, delivering exposition and saving the day than the Doctor. She even complained in *The Time of Angels* that he doesn't fly the TARDIS correctly. "Use the stabilizers... It's not supposed to make that noise. You leave the brakes on." (If he does, the highly educated Romana did too – as well as the Rani and the Master – which is doubtful.)

But a better example is Sarah Jane. A perennially popular character, she had already been brought back for *The Five Doctors* and an ill-fated twentieth century spin-off, so she was a natural to bridge the gap between classic and New *Who*, returning in *School Reunion*.

Three decades had not changed Sarah Jane. The woman who had broken into UNIT in *The Time Warrior* took on Deffry Vale High School by letting herself through the front door with a recorder and through the back window with a crowbar. So it was more than a little surprising that she would wrap up the story with the declaration, "Time I stopped waiting for you, and found a life of my own."

That would come a year later. It could be argued that it was dismissive to make the "old girl" the leader of the children's show while Jack Harkness got the adult spin-off. But adult in this context also meant "low chance of winning/ high body count," whereas *The Sarah Jane Adventures* were the opposite. Sarah Jane was not going to be associated with angst and death! (With her UNIT background, she was also very unlikely to think herself "outside the government, beyond the police.")

The names of the equipment and the companions may have changed, but *The Sarah Jane Adventures* setup was identical to the third Doctor's Earthbound years. The main character had traveled extensively in time and space, but did not do so now. The main character was in touch with UNIT and aliens. There was a collection of off-world tat and technology. There was an extremely advanced alien device that provided power, exposition, communications and most of what else might be required by the plot. There were semi-independent companions whom the main character treated with openly parental concern.

And so it was that Sarah Jane Smith, who had entered at the beginning of women's lib as a stroppy "girl" who refused to make coffee, lived to see the cause she fought for be taken for granted, and went out as the living embodiment of one of feminism's most famous quotes:

Sarah Jane Smith had become the man she wanted to marry.

Companion Piece

Where in Eternity... is Josephine Grant Jones?

Joan Frances Turner grew up in a time when *Doctor Who* was only a sporadic, late-night Chicago public television rerun, almost always starring "that guy with the long scarf." She is the author of the novels *Dust, Frail* and *Grave*, and of the *Chicks Unravel Time* essay "I'm From the TARDIS, and I'm Here to Help You: Barbara Wright and the Limits of Intervention." Her favorite "covert Time Lords" include Sun Ra, the Chicken Man from *Lizard Music*, Orlando and Shelmerdine from *Orlando* and the Brother from *Brother From Another Planet*.

Jo Grant? Oh, poor old Jo, sandwiched between the brilliant scientist and the formidable journalist... she doesn't end up looking any good at all, does she? Hmph! That's what you think, is it? Well, pull up a chair, and let me tell you all about Jo Grant.

I mean, she had to pull rather hard on a few strings to get into UNIT in the first place – the whole world was changing, Aquarius rising and all that, Jo'd probably say, and she wanted a bit of excitement and the Brig needed someone to hand the Doctor his test tubes, tell him he's brilliant and not listen to a word he says otherwise. That was where he, and everyone else, thought Jo fitted in at the beginning.

She got treated as a tea girl, but that wasn't what she was hired as, and Jo knew it. She wasn't going to let anyone stop her from being a *proper* assistant even if she had to keep prodding and nagging the Doctor at first to let her help him.

She never did get around to much pass-the-test-tubes stuff with the Doctor, what with the Master causing all that trouble right off with the Nestenes and everything. They were actually going to leave Jo out of all that, if you can believe it, just because she'd done a bit of spying on the Master's factory without strictly waiting for orders – well, *someone* had to scout the place out and she *was* the Doctor's assistant, why shouldn't she have gone? – and got herself a little bit hypnotized, but unlike everyone else, at least she'd managed to *find* him. Still, she didn't point that out when she got told off – she never liked to cause a fuss upfront when she could just keep the peace and *then* go do what needed doing.

That's why whenever the Brig or whoever told her to keep her nose out of things, she'd smile and say, "Yes, you're quite right!" and wait until they'd left to go make herself really useful – well, technically she *was* following orders to stay put, in the immediate moment they told her to. And it's much easier asking forgiveness than permission, especially after she'd helped the Doctor get un-kidnapped again or something important like that.

Besides, the Doctor said it himself, the Brig needed to learn how to put the rules aside and cut through red tape. Jo was always a natural at that! The Doctor didn't exactly file forms in triplicate to get his TARDIS either, so even when he got all growly at her, she knew he understood. And he listened to her even when UNIT didn't, like when she saw the monster on the Axon ship and everyone else just got angry at her for going to the crash site and kept telling her it was all in her head. Seeing the Doctor handle UNIT the same way she did, smiling and saying what they wanted to hear and then doing just what he'd always meant to do anyway, it made her see they really were sympatico, deep down inside. Even if he could never get over her not quite passing those science A-levels with flying colors. She didn't lie, mind, she only ever said she *took* them.

By the way, speaking of that Nestene business, she should be proud the Master only managed to hypnotize her *once* – I don't doubt it was dead hard resisting him the second time. I imagine chanting all those nursery rhymes to shut him out felt like holding the ocean in a paper cup, but I could tell she was just so bloody *angry* with him for dragging her and the Doctor to the back of the interstellar beyond and trying to kill them and take the TARDIS, *again,* and *then* thinking she'd have forgotten all his old schemes in the bargain. Master of all time and space? One-trick bad penny, or whatever you call it, I'd say! Of course he still managed to shoot the Doctor and then they both got stranded on Spiridon almost like he'd planned it, but he never really got them because he was never as smart as he thought. At least she knows she can be a bit dim sometimes, and that she makes a lot of mistakes – but unlike *him,* she tries never to repeat one if she can help it!

The thing is that when Jo was with the Doctor, it's really not so much what she *did* that people remember, it's what they heard and saw. Do they not notice how all her escapology and lock-breaking came in a bit handy? She managed to rescue the Doctor when those Auton things were running about and the Master had captured him, and she helped him overpower the guards when Stangmoor Prison got overrun, and when they were on Uxarieus and that security fellow Winton and her were chained to that bomb thingy she got them both out of the cuffs, and when those twenty-second century freedom fighters had them tied up she got out of the ropes and got their dematerialization circuit (that did go a bit pear-shaped, accidentally traveling centuries out of her way, but she wasn't letting them take the Doctor hostage!), and she broke the Doctor out of that island prison when the Master was in it up to his neck with Sea Devils, and dug a tunnel out of that Ogron jail cell – but that's it, really, nothing much. I mean, it was just her job, being there for the appallingly dangerous stuff.

And even though she really was just so incredibly dim about science, especially the Doctor's kind of science, I suppose she did help a bit when his two selves were fighting about how to get out of that antimatter world, suggesting they just work together to open a door in the void. Really though, shouldn't he, I mean they, have thought of doing that *first?* I mean, astrophysics may be beyond Jo, but surely even she knew two is bigger than one by the time she could walk – the poor Doctor never *could* see the forest for the trees, sometimes. And she Time Rammed the TARDISes when the Doctor couldn't bring himself to do it, because it would've killed her – but not doing it would've killed everyone else, ever! Two is bigger than one, and two *billion* – or trillion – is a lot bigger than Jo. The Doctor might be a stone cold genius, everybody knows that, but he could lose all that maths and science in a hurry when he let himself go sentimental.

And that's the thing, you know, Jo does agree with the Doctor that science is the most important thing but really, you've still got to hold out for something bigger, something... well, magical. Jo wants to believe in magic, and maybe everything everywhere really does have a scientific explanation, like the Doctor said, but if you're never going to understand or get access to that explanation, not in a million years, what's wrong with calling it magic? Magic *or* science it's all part of the universe and that's bigger than all of us, now isn't it? Different cultures, different answers, but both sides are right. And Jo had to learn *fast* how to talk to people who didn't share her culture or language or anything else without seeming like she's barging in to "enlighten" everyone. Peladon was a crash course in that, her having to do heavy diplomatics with all kinds of higher-ups all because of mistaken identity. Just because it doesn't matter to *you* if you eat or reach for something with the wrong hand, or whatever, well, it's not all *about* you!

Anyway, science and magic. Well, when they were investigating those Daemons in Devil's End (speaking of how the Master just never knew when to quit), the Doctor might've thought Miss Hawthorne couldn't have seen the devil like she said, but they both knew she'd seen *something* and that it wasn't anything good. And he even said that Jo offering herself to Azal in his place was the right thing to do *because* it was irrational and illogical and inexplicable to a Daemon… unscientific, in other words. So if everything's down to science, no matter what it is, how could Azal not have found some scientific logic in what she did? So everything everywhere *can't* really be explained by science, now can it? Where's the science in the Doctor's daisiest daisy?

Jo never even *wanted* to visit other planets and galaxies, not at first – it's like she told the Doctor, she'd thought he was just making it up! And she knew she'd signed on for the dangerous stuff, but there are limits! Except that there aren't any limits, not really, that's what she found out pretty quickly. Anything's possible, and everything exists whether you could imagine it or not. Except that that isn't the most important thing, not in the end.

Jo loved working for UNIT, but surely, after a while, the whole military trip must just have begun to feel a bit… martial? Like how in Devil's End, the Doctor explains right out that without Azal and all his cronies directing human history, we might never have learned how to blow up our own planet, poison our own air and water – but then everyone just goes right back to their guns and bazookas without giving any of it a second thought. And when they fought the Sea Devils, that Secretary Walker going on about dogs of war and bombing everything, it's like he *wanted* to blow up a submarine and launch nuclear weapons, for fun.

And it wasn't just Earth. Peladon, all those guns on what was supposed to be a peaceful mission, and the king sentencing the Doctor to trial by combat when he knew, in his heart, it was wrong – for tradition! And that whole useless mess between Draconia and future Earthlings, and the whole Dalek war machine, the madness was everywhere! And nobody seemed to want to stop and *think* what they were doing to themselves! That couldn't have failed to open up Jo's eyes. A lot.

And then all over the universe, she saw everyone doing their best to poison themselves – the Daemons showing humans how to industrialize themselves into a stupor, and the horrible over-farming and strip-mining on Uxarieus and Solos, and the Daleks *deliberately* poisoning Spiridon with those terrible spores, like a smallpox blanket smothering the whole planet. And speaking of which, the way the so-called "primitive"

Uxarieans got treated by the mining company, and the Solons being used like lab rats and mutated until they were unrecognizable, and the Daleks slaughtering every indigenous person on Spiridon – it'd be nice, wouldn't it, if humans of today didn't see all that ourselves when we look in a mirror? But there you are.

And *seeing* the Earth's future after those twenty-second century rebels traveled back to our time, Shura and Boaz and all the rest, *knowing* what would happen if the peace conference failed, if humans didn't learn to work together and stop all this. Seeing what happened when the Daleks took advantage of our backbiting and disharmony, what they did to Spiridon and Earth and everywhere else they touched. That must have showed Jo she couldn't just wander about the universe gaping at things, there was so much work to do on Earth.

Imagine how she must have felt on Spiridon: she and the Doctor both stuck on an alien world, and she thought the Doctor was dying, and she was lost and terribly ill and really could have died light years from her home, her friends, from everyone including him. She'd done what she could in the moment, keeping that log of the Doctor's symptoms and what she saw outside the TARDIS, and searching for help, and then she couldn't get back to him and she was too sick from the spores to do much of anything for anyone. Before one of the Spiridons rescued her, she was lying there, knowing inside that she was dying, and trying to keep the Doctor in her head so she wouldn't die all alone. Perhaps, she remembered what he said at Devil's End, that science or not there's magic out there after all, or, later, "Jo, every choice we make changes the history of the world."

And all that stuff about the daisy too, maybe that's what she thought of. I'm pretty sure it's about how if you learn to look at things *as they are*, if you stop letting your own ideas of how things should be or how disappointing they can be get in the way, then there's so much beauty in the world that it just knocks you over. Everything you were missing before, like the colors of the mountain rocks he hadn't even noticed, because you'd just been seeing what you expected to see. Not what *is*. But once you try looking hard, really try (it takes practice), there it is. So much beauty. People always look at me funny when I tell them they're beautiful, like it's got to be a joke at their expense and the punchline's coming any second, and that's just *sad!* Because they *are*. Beautiful, I mean, not sad. Though there's so much sadness too. That's the other part of why you can't afford to look away, for even a second.

There's so much beauty in the smallest things, so much hidden magic even in what science can explain, and every choice we make affects all that. *Every choice we make.* Well, when Jo knew that, and knew how awful things could become – and already were – when people made the wrong choices, how could she just keep running around higgledy-piggledy with the Doctor?

She had to go home. She had to start trying to make the right choices for her own world. There's so much to see, and choose, and try and change, just on this one little planet.

Have you ever read *Gentlemen Prefer Blondes?* Well, that Lorelei knew what she wanted and was hell-bent on getting it, even though you could tell her best friend thought she was a bit stupid (stupid like a fox, she *got* everything she wanted in the end!), and even though she only wanted things like clothes and money – but what really stuck, in spite of that, was a line about how if a girl's got brains, she needs to do something with them besides think. Everyone always thinks that's another punchline, but really, think about it – it means you can't just *sit* there when you know something's wrong, or someone needs your help, or something you do is hurting someone you don't know on the other side of the world, pondering how deep and marvelous you are for knowing that. You've got to get out there and *act.* You've got to *move.* That's why even after Jo left the Doctor, she really never stopped running. She knew the Doctor didn't want her to leave – and she didn't want to say goodbye! – but she knew he understood. After all, what else has he ever done, for all his lives?

Jo wouldn't be the person she is if she hadn't met the Doctor, and the Doctor wouldn't be the person… people… *he* is, either, if he hadn't met her. That is how the world works, and the universe, now isn't it? Everything's interconnected, we are all together, goo goo ga joob.

So, Jo Grant? Standing between Liz Shaw and Sarah Jane Smith… Jo was never stupid, though she called herself dim. I hope Jo realized she wasn't stupid, and I hope she realized the Doctor *knew* she never was. Just like the Doctor being so very *himself* and yet a lot of different people with different faces, feelings, thoughts all at once.

I hope he meant what he said, and that he really is proud of her. I hope he knows there's a little bit of him, even now, in everything Jo thinks and does.

Well, except for how he *would* wear those flowing cape thingies around the most flammable laboratory materials. Safety first.

Companion Piece

Forever Playing Second Fiddle: How Sarah Jane and the Rest of Us are being Sold Short

Nina Allan's stories have been published in a wide variety of magazines and anthologies, including *Interzone, Albedo One, Best Horror of the Year* and *The Year's Best Fantasy and Science Fiction*. Her story of a future cosmonaut, "Angelus," won Ireland's Aeon Award in 2007, and her collection on the theme of time travel, *The Silver Wind*, was named by the British Science Fiction Association's critical journal Vector as one of their top ten reads of 2011. Her most recent collection, *Stardust*, was published in 2013 by PS Publishing, and her first novel *The Race* – featuring telepathic greyhounds and set in an alternate near future version of southern England – was released in 2014 by NewCon Press. Nina has been a *Doctor Who* fan since the age of six, and she once expressed an ambition to be the Master when she grew up. Her favorite adventure remains *Genesis of the Daleks*, although *The Family of Blood* gives it a close run for its money. She lives and writes in Hastings, East Sussex.

This isn't the essay I thought I was going to write.

Elisabeth Sladen made her first appearance as Sarah Jane Smith in December 1973, at the start of Season Eleven, in a four-part adventure called *The Time Warrior*. It wasn't just Sarah who was making her debut – *The Time Warrior* marked the Doctor's first on-screen encounter with the warlike Sontarans.

The Doctor first meets Sarah at UNIT HQ, where government scientists have been going missing in mysterious circumstances. Sarah has gained entry to UNIT by passing herself off as her aunt, the famous virologist Lavinia Smith. The Doctor is unconvinced, and Sarah is forced to admit that she is not a scientist, but a journalist. Her real name is Sarah Jane Smith, and she has borrowed her aunt's credentials in the hope of scooping a story for her paper.

There then follows the first real exchange between Sarah and the Doctor, which I think is worth repeating here in full:

Sarah: Are you going to give me away, Doctor?
The Doctor (*pauses and shakes his head*): No, I don't think so.
Sarah: Why not?
The Doctor: Well, you can make yourself useful. We need somebody around here to make the coffee.

The adventure proper then commences. Sarah and the Doctor use the TARDIS to travel backwards in time to the castle of Irongron, a medieval warlord. Linx, the eponymous Time Warrior, has turned Irongron's basement into a makeshift laboratory, where he is forcing the UNIT scientists to help him make repairs to his damaged spacecraft. Enlisting the help of Irongron's neighbors, the Doctor and Sarah eventually capture the castle, return the missing scientists to the twentieth century, and blow up Linx's hoard of weapons in a suitably large explosion. The case is closed. The Doctor and Sarah return to the TARDIS and take their leave.

The Time Warrior wasn't the first Doctor Who adventure I remember. That was *The Three Doctors*, broadcast a full 12 months earlier as the first adventure in Season Ten and featuring Katy Manning as the Doctor's companion, Jo Grant. I was six years old, and I found the idea of a television program entirely devoted to time travel and monsters utterly enthralling. I remember a lot of Season Ten pretty well actually, but it was with the arrival of Elisabeth Sladen as Sarah that my love affair with the series properly began.

I never found much to identify with in Jo Grant even as a six-year-old. As a character, she was altogether too bouncy, too silly, she was always dropping things, knocking things over, getting lost and liable to scream her head off at the first inkling of a monster. Right from the beginning, Sarah seemed different. She wasn't afraid to ask questions or answer back. She had a real job that she was passionate about. If anyone tried to tell her she couldn't do something, she protested vociferously. Sarah kicked serious ass. Or at least, that is the way I remembered it.

My memories of *The Time Warrior* were of an intense, rather brooding adventure. Dark doings in grimy dungeons, Sontarans lying in wait around every corner. It seemed to go on for ages. I was surprised to discover when I began researching this that it was a four-parter and not a six-parter, as memory insisted. By the time the TARDIS wheezed off into the ether, I felt as if I'd been on a long journey with these characters, and I was totally in love with Sarah Jane. Not in a romantic way, but in a Romantic way. I didn't just admire her, I wanted to be her.

I loved Jon Pertwee's Doctor, too. I enjoyed his irascible temperament, his sardonic putdowns, his headmasterly way of organizing people. I felt desperately sad when he regenerated at the end of *Planet of the Spiders*. I resented Tom Baker bitterly – a buffoon like this could never play the Doctor, surely? I felt I'd been cheated out of something I had grown to rely on.

Season Twelve kicked off in December with *Robot*, the first in what is now regarded as the "classic run" of Tom Baker adventures spanning the whole of Season Twelve and through to Season Fourteen. Of course I soon forgave the Doctor for turning into Tom Baker, and by the time he and Harry Sullivan and Sarah Jane found themselves marooned aboard Space Station Nerva, I had fully accepted him as "my" Doctor. It was Sarah who helped me most to bridge the gap. She was magnificent in *The Ark in Space* – crawling through the Wyrrn-infested service ducts armed only with a piece of electrical wire, appealing to the last vestiges of humanity in Wyrrn-Noah, risking her life to save the Ark and those aboard. It's difficult to adequately convey the love I felt for the show then, the influence it wielded over my inner life and the world of my developing imagination. Some adventures genuinely terrified me, others were just incredibly exciting. I still remember the hell of anticipation I endured between episodes three and four of *Genesis of the Daleks*, when Sarah loses her grip on the scaffolding in the Dalek rocket silo and hangs frozen in midair as the titles roll. And then there's that moment in *The Android Invasion*, when android-Sarah's faceplate swings open to reveal a pair of plastic eyeballs and a mass of computer chips. "You're not the real Sarah," the Doctor says. It still gives me the shivers.

Time seemed to pass more slowly then. When I look at the episode schedule and realize that Elisabeth Sladen was with the show for only three years, my heart breaks a little, because at the time it felt as if Sarah Jane would always be there and nothing would change. Sarah went through a great deal during those 18 adventures she shared with the Doctor. She was blinded, replicated, very nearly eviscerated, nearly trapped forever in a pyramid on Mars, forced to carry radioactive plutonium for the Daleks on Skaro. She even survived a second encounter with the Sontarans. And I adored every minute of it. Almost without realizing it, I was watching Sarah Jane grow from an inexperienced young reporter into a mature woman with a mind of her own and the courage to match. She became my role model, my alter ego, my friend.

When, in the closing moments of *The Hand of Fear*, the Doctor abandoned her in a suburban street with nothing more than a stuffed owl for company, I wept buckets. I couldn't take to Louise Jameson's Leela at all – I didn't see the point of her. It wasn't until September 1977 and *Horror of Fang Rock* that I began to relax my animosity even a little.

But time is a tricky substance, and even the longest memories are notoriously subjective and unreliable. When as a preparation for writing this article I sat down to watch *The Time Warrior*, it was in the knowledge that I hadn't seen it for 40 years. The prospect of revisiting such an important moment of my childhood was enthralling to me. I was going to see Sarah Jane as I had first seen her and I fully expected *The Time Warrior* to be amazing.

Only it wasn't. It really wasn't. And I'm not talking about the dodgy costumes or the bizarre arrangement of silver spheres that gets strapped to the Doctor's head in episode three. Special effects have always been low down on my list of priorities when it comes to film and TV, and so long as the script is well crafted and the acting convincing, I honestly don't care how obvious it is that the Sontaran spacecraft is actually constructed from cardboard boxes.

Which is why I was shocked to discover how poorly written it was. *The Time Warrior* proceeds at a glacial pace in what is mostly a series of infodumps. The few attempts to inject a sense of irony mostly fall flat. There is little on-screen chemistry between the characters, and the actors bark out their lines with the kind of faux-dramatic exaggeration you might find in a bad provincial production of *Richard III*. The story itself is pretty tame, and there is way too much to-ing and fro-ing between the rival castles. The drama feels insufficient for two episodes, let alone four.

It dragged, frankly. No wonder I remembered it as a six-parter.

More dismaying by far though is the way the personality of Sarah Jane Smith has been betrayed and subverted. Rather than being free to challenge the men who surround her, she is there mostly to provide a lively foil for the Doctor's superior knowledge. The reality she is forced to deal with is frighteningly regressive – and I don't just mean the Sontarans.

It is clear from the way she is presented that Sarah Jane Smith was originally intended to be a new kind of companion for the Doctor, a modern professional who would sweep away the still-lingering chauvinistic attitudes of the 1950s and steer the program towards a more enlightened attitude to women and their place in society. Sarah Jane is a journalist – a woman making her way in a profession previously dominated by men. She earns her living by asking questions, and from her first appearance on screen, it becomes obvious that she is not averse to taking risks in searching for answers. Neither does she make any secret of her feminist credentials. Her Aunt Lavinia is a famous scientist, as well as a seasoned campaigner for women's rights, and Sarah seems similarly determined not to let the men have all the action. She leaves us in no doubt during this first adventure as to the contempt she feels for the "typically masculine arrangement" that has dominated much of the series until now.

So far, so brilliant. But as so often when it comes to memory, I am left with the sense that nostalgia may in fact have warped our perceptions. Did we really see progress in action, or were we tricked by a series of half measures? Was the character of Sarah Jane Smith repeatedly hobbled by the (exclusively male) team of scriptwriters who brought her into being?

It would be unfair to ignore the fact that the very popularity of *Doctor Who* occasionally places it at something of a disadvantage. Most TV from the 60s and 70s is forgotten now, left to molder in the stacks where it belongs. The reprehensible social attitudes it displays are rarely exposed to wide public scrutiny – you don't see *Love Thy Neighbour* or *The Liver Birds* being aired on UK Gold, not even in the small hours. *Doctor Who* though is a worldwide phenomenon with a following of millions. Even the very earliest episodes are viewed and discussed on a regular basis. Fans search out lost footage and rare trivia with the fervor of treasure seekers.

It is impossible for *Doctor Who* to bury its mistakes.

Perhaps then it should not have come as such a shock to me, to be reminded that Sarah's first conversation with the Doctor consisted largely in him suggesting to her that she could be useful to him only in the provision of stimulating beverages. Such attitudes were typical of the time, even when as here there is an attempt to offset their effect by a token use of irony. Perhaps I was naive in supposing that as an alien of superior intelligence, the Doctor might have progressed beyond that, even if his hidebound colleagues at UNIT mostly hadn't.

But what *The Time Warrior* reveals most of all is that aside from the third Doctor's trademark irascibility and an annoying tendency not to detail the facts of a situation before the plot demands it, the show's scriptwriters made notably few attempts to create an alien character. What they offer us instead is an educated Englishman of a certain class who shares the attitudes of the Brigadier and the society that gave birth to him in pretty much every regard. The Doctor refers to the people of the Middle Ages as "just one step away from barbarism," incapable of utilizing future science except to blow themselves up with it. It's difficult now to separate these kind of beliefs from those of the Brig's colonial forebears, imparting superior wisdom and the "right way of life" to the "primitive" peoples at the further outposts of the British Empire. *The Time Warrior* is full of embarrassing stuff like this. The Doctor refers to Sarah throughout as a "young girl," even when her actions prove her as an independent and highly intelligent woman with considerable initiative. The script also sees to it that Sarah's competence as an investigative journalist is undermined more or less immediately when she jumps to the conclusion that it is the Doctor who is time-napping the scientists rather than Linx. When confronted with the evidence to the contrary, Sarah confesses that she "could have been wrong," to which the Doctor replies that this is "a generous admission – especially coming from one of the fair sex."

Yes, really. Sadly there's more.

Shortly after the coffee-making incident, we see Sarah observing the Doctor as he tinkers with some complicated-looking electrical equipment.

> **Sarah:** What's that?
> **The Doctor:** It's my alarm clock.
> **Sarah:** Oh, stop being so patronizing, Doctor. What is it really?
> **The Doctor:** It's a Rondium detector.

He then proceeds to blind Sarah with science, increasing the speed and density of his delivery as he goes, clearly indicating that he believes it is a waste of his time to try and explain something so complex to someone like her. Before you protest that this is what many specialists would do if confronted by an over-inquisitive layperson, compare his treatment of Sarah with his response to the Brigadier when he asks the Doctor what he has uncovered about the whereabouts of the missing scientists: "Someone's operating a matter transmitter. And the really odd thing is that there's a time transference, too. It's being operated from several centuries ago. Past and present mixed up."

Instead of the deliberate obfuscation that we saw him use on Sarah, here the Doctor provides a detailed and ready response to a reasonable question, all couched in a clear and plain English that even the blundering Brig can understand.

I find such a discrepancy difficult to deal with or justify.

When we look at the script on a line-by-line basis, what we find is that instead of the independent-minded, confrontational woman we were led to expect, the Sarah Jane of *The Time Warrior* is merely another variation on the "assistant as stooge" trope that the role of the Doctor's companion has been all along. Yes, Sarah is there to ask questions – but only so the Doctor can impart his wisdom or reveal the next stage of the plot to us through his answers. She is allowed to pursue her own investigation – but only as long as she grabs the wrong end of the stick and has to turn to the Doctor to sort things out. She is allowed to be a feminist – so long as she is a comedy, foot-stomping one, an effective counterpoint for the Doctor's witty one-liners.

Reviewing the show from this distance, it appears to me as if the show's male scriptwriters and editors suddenly came up with the idea that it would be a "good thing" to have a "new woman" aboard the TARDIS – a woman they then proceeded to undermine through the deployment of one establishment stereotype after another.

Things did seem to improve for a time after that. Tom Baker's version of the Doctor seemed more the maverick student than the hidebound professor, which allowed for Sarah Jane to form a closer and more inclusive bond with him. During the "classic run" from *Robot* to *The Hand of Fear*, there is the sense of the two of them getting into scrapes together. Sarah is given more to do and more to think. Sometimes she is allowed to voice a contrary opinion – few fans will have forgotten the "have I the right?" scene in *Genesis of the Daleks*.

Twenty years is a long time, and with the return of *Doctor Who* to our screens in 2005, the look and feel of the show was tangibly different. Billie Piper's Rose Tyler is easily my favorite of the companions since Sarah Jane, and the on-screen rapport she shared with Christopher Eccleston's ninth Doctor quickly became the cornerstone of the new series. Gone was the retrograde "kill all monsters" philosophy, replaced by a spirit of negotiation and understanding between alien races. The Doctor's human companions were more proactive. The special effects were a lot better, too. Some lessons have been learned, certainly, and with the program more popular than it has ever been, its future seems assured.

So is this a case of all's well that ends well? I'm not so sure. There are signs that certain of the show's bad habits are reasserting themselves and perhaps they never really went away. When Elisabeth Sladen made her triumphant return to the show in *School Reunion* in 2006, we see at once that Sarah Jane is now a mature woman, in control of her own life and still very much involved in solving mysteries. How in control is she really, though? In spite of Sarah's righteous anger at the way the Doctor abandoned her those many years before, the script still manages to convey the sense of a life wasted, of a woman who has spent much of the last 20 years awaiting the Doctor's return. This comes across way too much like waiting around at the end of the phone on a Friday night to me. The scriptwriters couldn't resist a bit of girl-on-girl cattiness between the older Sarah and the younger Rose, either.

The women who come after Rose – Martha, River, Amy – are all in thrall to the Doctor from the moment they meet him. The only one of the new companions who doesn't seem to have the hots for the Mad Man with a Box is Donna Noble – who is rewarded by having her mind wiped. She isn't strong enough to live with the memory of her Doctor-Donnaness, apparently. So much for freedom of choice and independent agency.

In *Journey to the Centre of the TARDIS*, the TARDIS has been illegally salvaged by a trio of space rag-and-bone men, the van Baalen brothers. The brothers' grab mechanism has caused critical damage to the TARDIS's engines. Emerging from the toppled blue box, Matt Smith's Doctor asks the discomfited brothers if they've seen Clara: "Girl, about so high – *feisty*."

If I never hear another woman described as feisty, it will be too soon.

The first time we met Clara was in September 2012, as Oswin Oswald in *Asylum of the Daleks*. At that point in time, she was an extraordinary genius: a computer hacker whose talent was such that the Daleks had preserved her life in order to convert her to their own corrupt ends. She saved the Doctor's life in *Asylum*, as well as the lives of Amy and Rory. Returned to us as Clara in 2013, she is just one more in the long line of pretty, sassy Doc-chicks, whose main purpose in the series, it seems, is to agonize over the nature of their relationship with the Doctor as well as providing some useful reversals, prompts and other plot stimuli along the way.

The only woman who's ever been allowed to be the Doctor's equal is the TARDIS herself. But as a machine she hasn't got much of a dress sense, so that's OK. She's also unpredictable and fickle, and just a tiny bit bitchy towards other women.

I read a disturbing statistic the other day: in all the time since the show was rebooted in 2005, only one woman writer, Helen Raynor, has scripted for *Doctor Who*. That was in 2008, 60 episodes ago, and no need to ask how many women wrote for the series before that. So far, there has not been a single woman writer on the team during the Moffat era.

To say this is a matter for concern is something of an understatement.

But one of *Doctor Who*'s key attributes – perhaps the attribute to which it most owes its longevity – is its inbuilt capacity for evolution. If change is overdue, it is equally clear that the show has within its DNA the ambition and imaginative reach necessary to implement it. None of us know what *Doctor Who* will look like a decade from now, but that's part of what keeps it exciting. That, and our own aspirations for the characters we cherish, our own secret hopes. Long may the conversation continue.

The Barbara Strain

Three-time Hugo Award winner **Lynne M. Thomas** is the co-editor-in-chief and publisher of *Uncanny Magazine* with her husband Michael Damian Thomas. The former editor-in-chief of *Apex Magazine* (from 2011 to 2013), she co-edited the Hugo Award-winning *Chicks Dig Time Lords*, as well as *Whedonistas* and *Chicks Dig Comics*. She moderates the Hugo-Award winning *SF Squeecast*, a monthly SF/F podcast, and contributes to the *Verity!* podcast. In her day job, she is the Curator of Rare Books and Special Collections at Northern Illinois University, where she is responsible for the papers of over 60 SF/F authors. You can learn more about her shenanigans at lynnemthomas.com.

Not Just a Screamer

One of the most famous shots in classic *Doctor Who* involves Barbara Wright screaming her head off while being menaced by a Dalek. This clip is often used as the basis for an argument that all of the Doctor's companions are just "screamers," followed by mentions of wobbly sets in an effort to discredit the show as silly. (These claims are often made by reviewers that have not watched much *Doctor Who* beyond carefully selected clips designed to bolster their arguments.)

In *Doctor Who* fan communities, we tend to classify the Doctor's companions (both classic and new series) into two distinct types: "screamers" (e.g.: Susan Foreman), or their polar opposite, "tomboys" (e.g.: Ace). Occasionally, "screamers" and "tomboys" are placed in opposition to highlight their differences, such as when Mel and Ace team up in *Dragonfire*. We follow them as they learn about life, the universe and everything, with the Doctor leading the way up and down countless corridors among the stars. Their youth and inexperience is emphasized as a major story point, and occasionally as a whole storyarc. We watch them grow up to become fully-fledged, knowledgeable people during their run on the series.

This essay is not about them.

The "screamer" and "tomboy" companions could not be *less* representative of Barbara Wright, and a subset of other companions that have followed her.

There's a third companion type that is often overlooked: those who don't accept the Doctor at face value. They point out when the Doctor makes questionable moral choices – when he lies, when he goes too far and when he has stopped being kind. They know that the universe, and the Doctor, is not always good. They try to do good themselves, when possible. In part, they are trying to balance out the darkness that they have seen and experienced. They save themselves, and care for others around them.

These companions are often grown women (as opposed to adolescents or young adults). They are not designed as a point of entry character for younger viewers, but as a counterpoint authority figure to contrast with the Doctor's eccentricity (as opposed to, say, the Brigadier, whose general default is "shoot it"). They often pay a hefty price for their hard-won knowledge of the universe, occasionally at the Doctor's own hand.

I'm referring to these companions as the Barbara Strain, because this type of companion begins in 1963, with Barbara Wright.

# # #

Barbara is not a young, innocent girl. She is a professional woman, with thoughts and opinions of her own. She spends much of her tenure comforting, nay, practically *parenting* Susan (*The Reign of Terror, Planet of Giants*), fending off sexual harassment and the threat of rape (*The Keys of Marinus, The Romans, The Chase*), and telling the Doctor to knock it off or that he's wrong (*The Edge of Destruction, The Aztecs*), all while making use of her cardigan as a defensive weapon (*The Space Museum, The Chase*). Barbara thinks for herself, and makes her own choices.

She considers herself responsible for her own person, as well as for the health and welfare of everyone around her: Ian and Susan, and later Vicki, and, of course, the Doctor. She pays a social price for speaking up when things are not going well, typically, a direct threat to her person.

The story-based peril for Barbara, both in Doylesian (metatextual) and Watsonian (in-story) terms, is to direct such behaviors towards *her* when she can, partially to protect Susan and Vicki, the designated young, innocent women, from similar threats. Thus we get Nero chasing Barbara rather than Vicki in *The Romans*, and Barbara ensuring that Susan gets sent to a seminary rather than married off against her will in *The Aztecs*. As the designated *adult* woman, it's Barbara's role to deal with sexually predatory men, and to protect Vicki and Susan from those without pure intentions, thereby saving Vicki's innocence for her romance with Troilus in *The Myth Makers*, and Susan's for David Campbell in *The Dalek Invasion of Earth*.

Barbara puts up with the sexist bullshit so that Susan and Vicki don't have to. It's not that Susan and Vicki don't encounter their own sexist bullshit, but the kind they deal with is more about infantilizing them. Barbara takes on the sexual threats in the series, so that Susan and Vicki have the opportunity to become fully realized, sexual adults in relatively healthy adult relationships.

While Barbara is not afraid to leverage her adulthood to protect those around her from unwanted sexual advances, that's not the only thing she does. She also problem-solves (*The Edge of Destruction*, *Planet of Giants*), caregives (*An Unearthly Child*: "The Forest of Fear"), tries to change whole societies (*The Aztecs*), and eventually takes out Daleks by bombing them and running them over with trucks (*The Dalek Invasion of Earth*).

Barbara does all this while consistently wearing sensible shoes and outfits, too. She's just *that* badass.

And she's not alone. Every decade of *Doctor Who* has companions that are part of the Barbara Strain.

The 1960s

Barbara is just the first in a long line of grown-up companions and guest stars that take on the mantle of "conscience" for the Doctor. They all understand Rule One, voiced by River Song for the first time on screen: the Doctor lies. (For our purposes, we include deliberately withholding crucial information in this rule).

Sara Kingdom is an interesting case, because she commands, she leads, she kicks ass, takes names, and wipes the floor with her enemies. She spends much of *The Daleks' Master Plan* ordering Steven to and fro. She does not expect the Doctor to always tell her the truth, and when he does lie about the taranium (this story's McGuffin), she takes it more or less in stride: as a trained security agent with military experience, she assumes she is given information on a need-to-know basis. She still dies attempting to save the Doctor and Steven, because it is the right thing to do.

Zoe Heriot is one of the youngest Barbara Strain companions, but she undoubtedly fits the profile. Many fans assume she's a screamer based on her youth and the infamous shot of her draped across the TARDIS console in *The Mind Robber*, but Zoe is a professionally trained librarian/

astrophysicist from the twenty-first century, and expects to be treated as such when she first meets the Doctor and Jamie. Zoe approaches traveling with the Doctor as another puzzle to solve. She nips aboard the TARDIS of her own volition after helping defeat the Cybermen. The Doctor's warnings about the dangers she'll face if she stays with him don't faze her.

The assumption that Zoe is less experienced or intelligent based on her age and appearance rankle her rather a bit. Her general response is to let her actions speak for themselves. She spends a fair amount of time explaining to Jamie what is actually going on, just as she completes problem solving for the Doctor (*The Krotons*). She's pretty sure that the Doctor is nearly as intelligent as she is (*The Dominators*). She shows compassion to Jamie when he literally loses his face, and defends the Doctor physically with her martial arts skills (*The Mind Robber*). She outwits computers routinely (*The Dominators, The Invasion, The Krotons*), and destroys a Cyberfleet with her calculator-like mathematical abilities (*The Invasion*). Zoe consistently shows bravery and resourcefulness when threatened by the Doctor's enemies. Her exit from the TARDIS is especially cruel, as the Time Lords selectively wipe her memory of her time with the Doctor at the end of *The War Games* (this is gradually undone throughout the Big Finish audio adventures, starting with *Fear of the Daleks* and ending with *Second Chances*).

The 1970s

Liz Shaw is a fantastic foil for Jon Pertwee's third Doctor. She knows her own mind, and applies scientific reasoning if and when she needs to change it. She is wryly amused, and rather snarky about the Doctor's patronizing attitude. I imagine she had to put up with similar nonsense in the course of getting several PhDs in the sciences (meteorites, physics, and medicine) and achieving a position at Cambridge in the 1970s, before being dragged down from said hard-won position and drafted as one of UNIT's scientific advisors.

Liz begins as appropriately skeptical of the existence of aliens, but is convinced otherwise during *Spearhead from Space* by the evidence before her. Her relationship with the Doctor, once they begin working together, is one of absolute mutual respect for each others' abilities. It is the Doctor who insists upon her staying to work with him after she deftly helps him defeat the Autons. She puts her scientific knowledge to work in *Doctor Who and the Silurians*, making possible the creation and mass-production of the vaccine that stops the Silurian virus from killing everyone. In *The Ambassadors of Death*, she is forced to help keep the Ambassadors alive, and builds a machine to communicate with them. She does her best to thwart the plans of the villains at every possible turn, while remaining compassionate to the plight of the alien Ambassadors. Liz's final adventure, *Inferno*, helps to demonstrate her competence and compassion by showing us her totalitarian alternate-universe version: cold, calculating and murderous.

Sadly, Liz only works with the Doctor for a year; she returns to Cambridge afterwards, noting to the Brigadier that the Doctor really just wants someone to hand him test tubes and tell him how brilliant he is, insinuating that her skills were perhaps being wasted. While the producers noted in later interviews that they did not feel that Liz was a successful character (supposedly, she was too intelligent to be the audience identifier), Liz Shaw was, to my mind, groundbreaking. She was a modern, well-educated adult woman, with a career and life all her own, projecting strength, intelligence and autonomy without ever being accused of, heaven forefend, a shrill, tinny sort of feminism.

It would be easy to write an entire essay about Sarah Jane Smith, a professional investigative journalist, with a robust career, who is decidedly a feminist, consistently stands up for herself, and encourages other women (such as the Queen of Peladon) to do the same. Most famously in *Genesis of the Daleks*, she urges the Doctor to destroy the Daleks in their infancy. While her morality is not the Doctor's, it is utterly human, and her humanity is the centerpiece of many adventures, including *The Brain of Morbius* and *The Masque of Mandragora.*

Sarah Jane is particularly interesting for the purposes of this essay, as her character develops over decades, as young and idealistic Sarah Jane becomes older, wiser Sarah Jane in the new series and *The Sarah Jane Adventures.* Sarah Jane understands firsthand that the Doctor lies, about many, many things (including his ability to drop her off where and when he claims he will).

She understands that intelligence and bravery are important, but she values and practices a radical kindness. I think that Sarah Jane tries to fulfill the promise that the Doctor showed her, but often failed to achieve, in her younger years. She spends much of her later life trying to be a kinder version of the Doctor on Earth, encouraging defaulting to compassion towards all aliens and firmly discouraging violence wherever possible. She mentors Maria and Rani, her son Luke and his friend Clyde to be self-aware, forthright and brave, and to trust in their abilities – while always trying to do good and, above all, be kind.

The 1980s

The 1980s are a loud decade, and the Barbara Strain companions for the 1980s reflect their time – not just in their outfits, but through their brash personalities. There are several fantastic examples of single-story characters that also fit the Barbara Strain mold (Dr. Todd from *Kinda* comes immediately to mind), but for this essay, I want to focus on Tegan and Mel.

Tegan Jovanka is just as loud as her outfits, describing herself as "a mouth on legs" (*Earthshock*). In *Logopolis*, she accidentally wanders into the TARDIS, and learns that the Master killed her aunt. She spends much of her time with the Doctor trying to return to her own time to begin her new job as a professional flight attendant, without much success. Even so, she has one of the longest companion runs, suggesting that despite her protests, she adapted quite well to traveling with the Doctor. Tegan is often our representative of Earth morality: Nyssa, Adric and Turlough all come from different planets, and Kamelion is an android; they don't have the same moral center as Tegan, and by extension, us.

After witnessing the Doctor's regeneration, she does everything in her power during *Castrovalva* to protect him while he's vulnerable. Tegan is passionate about justice and doing good, which can make her seem a bit prickly. When Tegan gets into trouble, or danger, it is usually because she is forging ahead to help the Doctor or someone in need. She takes her role seriously, battling the Mara to save her own sanity and the people around her in *Kinda* and *Snakedance*, feeling responsible for the Mara's initial arrival on Deva Loka through her unshielded mind.

Tegan is a good friend, too, especially to Nyssa. Theirs is a fantastic example of a functional, strong female friendship in media, which have, sadly, become all too rare. While their personalities are quite different, both women build each other up rather than bickering or tearing each other down. They work well as a team, trust one another and communicate consistently. Their friendship is core to *Castrovalva*, as together they bring the Doctor to safety in his Zero Room cabinet. In *Black Orchid*, Tegan is able to tell Anne from Nyssa, even when they are trying to pass for one another. There is never a moment when I doubt that Tegan has Nyssa's back just as much as the Doctor's, and when they finally do part, their affection for one another is clear.

In *The Visitation*, Tegan bravely refuses to tell the Terileptil anything when she is questioned, doing her best to protect the Doctor and Nyssa, and staring daggers at Adric when he blathers on about the TARDIS. She's the one that works on the escape route, and shoves Adric through it first, getting herself recaptured in the process.

Tegan is also *quite* clear that she's an adult, and will not allow the Doctor to treat her otherwise. In *Black Orchid*, when offered a beverage, she immediately requests a screwdriver. In the party scenes, she happily participates in the dancing, enjoying a good Charleston, and chatting sociably (unlike Adric, who sullenly grazes at the food table). In *The Five Doctors*, she makes it clear that she is not there to make tea, getting rather stroppy with the first Doctor when he suggests it, and forcing the fifth Doctor to rope Turlough into helping her. While she isn't always pleased with Adric's behavior (she finds him rather immature), she mourns his death deeply at the end of *Earthshock* and the beginning of *Time-Flight*, the story in which we see Tegan in professional mode. She not only directs passengers onto Concorde to return them to their own time, she is the person who volunteers to take on the dangerous job of getting the engines started using compressed air.

Accidentally left behind in *Time-Flight*, Tegan picks herself up, reclaims her life and starts again, until she runs into the Doctor and Nyssa a year later in Amsterdam while investigating the disappearance of her cousin in *Arc of Infinity*. While she is glad to be reunited with them, she is also just fine living her earthbound life without the Doctor. When Tegan finally leaves the TARDIS in *Resurrection of the Daleks*, she does so on her own terms, fed up with all of the death and destruction that has surrounded her during her time with the Doctor – one of the only companions to leave in such a manner.

Melanie Bush is generally classed as a screamer, but I would like to argue that she has earned a place in the Barbara Strain as well.

Mel is, ultimately, the most overt representative of humanity we have during this run of *Doctor Who*, when the Doctor is acting the least humanly. Uber-competent and relentlessly cheerful, a computer programmer with a photographic memory and a fondness for workouts, she is the moral center for two incarnations of the Doctor that are decidedly in need of same. Mel's friendliness makes her a much-needed counterpoint to Colin Baker's brusque sixth Doctor. Her genuineness and honesty contrasts with the initial buffoon act of Sylvester McCoy's seventh Doctor, and later, his decidedly manipulative turn.

Let's just dismiss the notion that a need to scream equates with ineffectiveness as a companion. Mel's scream is weaponized like Black Canary's: her vocal machinations in *Time and the Rani* and *Paradise Towers* paralyze Tetraps and Rezzies alike. At minimum, her enemies are stunned into giving her time to escape, and her scream makes her exceedingly easy for the Doctor to locate.

She is intrepid in her attempts to help the Doctor, and the people they encounter, to have better lives. She models radical trust for the Doctor in *Time and the Rani* and for all of the Paradise Towers residents. She teaches a Paradise Towers outcast, Pex, to be brave. She protests casual sexism in *Dragonfire*, and mourns her fellow space-bus passengers, the Navarinos, most keenly in *Delta and the Bannermen*. While her reasons for moving on to travel with Sabalom Glitz in *Dragonfire* are in contention (see my essay in *Chicks Unravel Time* for further theories), she clearly has done all she can for the Doctor when she leaves him.

The 1990s

There is not a ton of televised *Doctor Who* to be had in the 1990s, just the 1996 Fox television movie starring Paul McGann and Daphne Ashbrook. Dr. Grace Holloway is a cardiologist and opera lover – you can't get more grown-up than *that*. She spends the first half of the plot being incredulous and skeptical of the Doctor's behavior, right up until the point where she helps him save the world. Which just about makes up for accidentally killing his previous regeneration during surgery because *two hearts*. When the seventh Doctor dies on the operating table, her instinct is not to shy away from the problem: she roars "I want to see those X-RAYS. *Now*," to her staff, and *tries to figure out what happened*.

While it is occasionally still argued whether Grace "qualifies" as a companion, given that she helps the Doctor save the world, I think she should count. Grace is arguably one of the major prototypes for the new series companions as well. She has the distinction of being the first companion to say "no" when the Doctor proposes traveling in the TARDIS, as she has a life of her own on Earth. Grace is also the recipient of the Doctor's first on-screen kiss, which was rather controversial at the time. Whether overtly romantic, painted as a removal of TARDIS energy or just a genetic transfer to confuse Judoon, kissing – as we've seen in the new series – has become incorporated at least partially into the companion experience. Grace's self-assurance as a doctor, a companion, and a human are central to the story of the television movie, and place her squarely in the Barbara Strain of companions.

The New Series

Classic *Doctor Who* leans more towards companions who are orphans, have a complete lack of back story, or just don't discuss their pasts very much, so that we focus on the companion's adventure with the Doctor, and less on what they *feel* as a result of those experiences. Storytelling in television has changed over the past 50 years; genre audiences now expect more character arcs and development than was typical in classic series-era storytelling. (I'm looking pointedly at *Buffy the Vampire Slayer* and *Xena: Warrior Princess* here, along with later *Star Trek*.)

Russell T Davies-era *Doctor Who* in particular introduces and focuses upon companions with earthbound ties, using those ties to help the viewer parse the emotional impact of the companion's adventures. This leads to more characters that consistently challenge the Doctor's choices and values, as well as an acknowledgement that traveling with the Doctor is dangerous. It seems, sometimes, that the Barbara Strain is everywhere you look, and we also have our first male and non-human Barbara Strain companions.

Let's begin with Jackie Tyler, Rose's mom. She directly asks the most important question for any companion running off with the Doctor: "Is she safe?" This question is echoed across multiple seasons (and multiple mothers of companions), with the Doctor constantly being challenged on his propensity for whisking people off in time and space without so much as a by-your-leave. Jackie is the most reluctant of companions – she really only travels with the Doctor to be with Rose. Her reluctance is justified, as she is cyber-converted in one world, and exists in her parallel universe version in another. Her question is not only relevant, she gets the most direct answer possible through her own adventures with the Doctor. And that answer is "no."

Martha Jones is educated, professional and knows her own mind. She is very clear that the Doctor must earn that title, just as she did (*Smith and Jones*). She insists that the Doctor explain what's going on when she doesn't understand (*Gridlock*) and points out that she cannot just swan about time and space as though she owns the place (*The Shakespeare Code*). She keeps the Doctor safe when he doesn't know who he is (*Human Nature / Family of Blood*). She saves the world, and the Doctor, by walking the earth and telling a single story (*The Sound of Drums / Last of the Time Lords*). Her decision to leave the Doctor and the TARDIS behind is hers (*Last of the Time Lords*), and hers alone, and she moves on with her life, even working with UNIT and attempting to get Torchwood to be workable (no small feat). She calls the Doctor consistently on his poor ethical choices, and reminds him repeatedly that he cannot just go haring off to do what he likes when there are lives at stake. Martha Jones is nothing but badass, from beginning to end, a perfect example of a

Barbara Strain companion in the modern era.

Donna Noble has been around the block, luv. She may not know what she wants to be when she grows up, as the choices being presented are rather limited, but she does know that she doesn't need a skinny thing like the Doctor to make her life more awesome. She is intelligent and resourceful, even if her career has been a bit lacking according to her mum's metric. Nonetheless, she leverages her "supertemp" skills to aid in saving the world. She investigates for herself, draws her own conclusions, and is always more concerned about the people *affected* by a given problem than solving the puzzle of the problem itself. *Partners in Crime* illustrates this beautifully, as Donna follows the *people* who are hurt by Adipose Industries, while the Doctor focuses on the Adipose themselves, without worrying much about the folks being hurt. Donna is, above all, truly and thoroughly *human* in the best possible manner: she is kind and intelligent, but she is flawed, fallible and willing to learn and change. She stops the Doctor from lashing out when he loses his fondness for humanity. Her magnificence, fuelled by her deep empathy for others (like the Ood that sing of her still) is forcibly stripped from her in her final story, which makes her ending among the most tragic for Barbara Strain companions. She is punished by the Doctor's own hand when she becomes her most Doctorial, in the cruelest way possible: removing her memories, and her growth as a person from her mind.

River Song has had a bumpy road, but she's always traveled it with style, panache and a devil-may-care attitude. She understands, fundamentally, that you can always trust the Doctor to be true... to himself. She declares: Rule one: the Doctor lies. River, like her timeline, is complicated (I'm *still* not sure I understand it entirely). Yes, she became an archaeologist to keep track of the Doctor, choosing to structure her entire existence around him once she determined that museum-based messaging was an easy way to grab his attention. River may also be the least merciful of the Barbara Strain companions – Barbara may have killed Daleks, but River makes them *beg for mercy* before gleefully destroying them.

Given that she is part of the TARDIS as Rory and Amy's daughter (baby timehead!), it's not surprising that River would want to keep tabs on her childhood home and the Doctor. She is happy to check in with the Doctor periodically and remind him about how he's rubbish at piloting the TARDIS. And dating. And being married to her. Nonetheless, she spends a goodly amount of time off having her own adventures, thank you, turning up when she thinks the Doctor needs her most, or wants her least (often both). Above all, she *loves* to keep him off balance. (I suspect it's her way of getting back at him about the lying.)

If River is the least merciful of the Barbara Strain companions, Rory Williams may be the *most* merciful. Rory, bless him, is our only male companion in the Barbara Strain. His role in the series is often treated as feminized. He is mocked for being a "non-alpha" type male, from his chosen profession of nursing to the fact that he is often the most reluctant of adventurers. He travels mostly because he would rather be with Amy than without her. And yet, Rory is a fantastic example of an alternative construction of masculinity (just as the Doctor tends to be). Rory is no nonsense and intelligent, but above all, he is compassionate in a way that the Doctor often forgets to be. Rory understands that intelligence alone is not enough to make the world a better place, just as his dad taught him. A good life is one that helps others, even if it's only watering the plants as a favor to your loved ones. It is Rory who reminds Amy and the Doctor that their choices and adventures can have devastating effects on others. Rory is the model of a loving husband, involved parent and truly compassionate, all-around great human being, which is dead sexy, if you ask me. Especially when wearing Roman armor.

From our most merciful to our most snarky Barbara Strain companion, Madame Vastra takes great delight in telling contemporary Victorians the absolute truth of who she is and where she's from, and watching their reactions. She may not be human (Silurians are superior, anyhow, in her opinion), but with her human partner Jenny and her friend/butler/dogsbody/bodyguard Strax (everyone's favorite bumbling Sontaran), she does her best to keep the Doctor engaged in the human world, and caring about humanity until Clara comes along. She has lived a long, interesting life, and has grown from a warrior to a problem-solver, with wit, style and a firm sense of humor about herself, her situation, and the response of her chosen home to her choices. This makes her an excellent choice to deflate the Doctor's ego when he gets beyond himself, just as she can run interference for him to keep him from being overwhelmed. She is, above all, a good friend to the Doctor, loving him flaws and all, just as she loves Jenny and Strax. Theirs is a strange family, but a family it is, with Vastra as the matriarch, and the Doctor is always welcome within it.

But What Does It All Mean?

When you build a robust universe with 50 years of history, you have a lot of different character types surrounding your iconic lead character.

In the case of the Barbara Strain companions, you have a collective group of *grownups*. They are not typically young by the standards of their time. They are not naive. They have had relatively full lives before haring off to travel in the TARDIS.

Which means that they have, more than our screamer or tomboy ingénues, experienced some loss. They have failed before, often in grand or glorious ways that hurt other people. They have paid hard prices for their experiences. They're old enough to know they're not invincible, and they make very different choices as a result. The Barbara Strain companions are far less likely to respond "okay, Doctor, whatever you like" when he's about to do something callous, foolhardy, or with great cost to others that he's not considering because he's distracted by the bigger picture.

The Barbara Strain companions have learned that to live a truly good life, while it is certainly important to be smart and brave, it's also important to be kind, because kindness is where the true core of our humanity lies. The Barbara Strain, again and again, reminds (and sometimes forces) the Doctor to be kind, for all of our sakes.

All hail the battle cardigan.

The Curious Case of Miss Victoria Waterfield

Jennifer Adams Kelley has devoted far too much of her adult life to *Doctor Who*. After finding the show as a high school senior (months after Lennon's assassination), she dove into fandom – attending cons, costuming, filmmaking, writing unpublishable fanfic. When the show entered hiatus hut, she upped her game by joining convention committees. She has finally found a splish of notoriety by writing several essays deemed worthy of publication. In real life, she wonders what to do with herself once her daughter (in uterus during the TV Movie) goes off to university in the fall of 2015.

You've fallen for the line – nearly everyone has. Victoria Waterfield, if you believe conventional fannish wisdom, spent her 41 episodes screaming, fainting and generally wilting. Conventional wisdom, however, has it wrong. Yes, Victoria screams, faints and wilts, but that's just one side of her character: she also shows herself to be determined, courageous and, most of all, curious when encountering extraordinary new situations and new people during her TARDIS travels.

Victoria's first extant appearance, in episode two of *The Evil of the Daleks*, finds her imprisoned by the Daleks. She likes to feed the birds outside her window instead of herself, and her guard Dalek won't stand for it. He weighs her, ordering her to eat or be force-fed. Victoria doesn't simper during this encounter: she faces the Dalek with head held high, agreeing to the Dalek's orders succinctly and with enough pause (not hesitation) before speaking to imply she has a bit of backbone. She breaks down into tears only after the Dalek leaves, crying for her situation more than for being afraid of a rusty old pepperpot. This scene sets up her character nicely for her first full story as a companion.

The Tomb of the Cybermen starts with the Doctor and Jamie bringing Victoria into the TARDIS. She isn't frightened or overwhelmed by the ship – she merely comments that time travel is silly and decides that the Doctor must be really old to have "perfected" it. After meeting up with the archaeological party who decide to go investigate the insides of the tomb, Victoria and Kaftan, being female, get ordered to stay behind in the main room. "Rubbish!" Victoria replies. "We can make a party!" And they do: she and Kaftan go exploring themselves; Victoria finds a Cybermat and puts it in her bag. She also gets trapped in a sarcophagus by Kaftan – mostly because she's curious about it and steps inside. Would the Doctor really do any less?

Throughout the story, yes, she screams... maybe once an episode, and mostly because she's startled. She's clearly aware of how she reacts, and how to use it to her advantage: one time she fake-screams in order to distract Kaftan so the latter can be captured. She doesn't scream when held at gunpoint. She doesn't scream when people die. All right, she *does* scream when the Cybermats advance, but, well... they're in a group and she knows by that point what they can do.

The fact that she's occasionally frightened, though, tends to over-shadow the rest of her traits: she spends more time being curious than scared. She wants to go with the boys to find out what's down the hatch, she inspects equipment lying around the tomb, and she won't be put off from exploring. She's also sure of what's proper and what's not, whether it be the length of skirts, the place of threats against her person, or the amount of sleep someone as old as the Doctor should have. She handles a Cybermat solo, shooting it with a gun, but she also goes to get help when needed, in the case of *Tomb* by fetching Captain Hopper after failing to open the shut hatch door (leading to where the Doctor and Jamie have gone with others) herself.

The Tomb of the Cybermen isn't the only story where Victoria shows more substantive qualities than "being scared." In episode two of *The Abominable Snowmen*, Victoria opts to go look for the Doctor instead of returning to the safety of the TARDIS. She gets indignant with Professor Travers when he insists on being taken to the cave where Yeti have been spotted – "you don't want to go there," she decrees, believing she knows best. In *The Ice Warriors*, she asks all sorts of questions of the titular characters, countering their suspicions with saying, "I'm curious, that's all." In *The Enemy of the World*, she's cautious about but interested in the hovercraft, challenges Bruce when he declares her and Jamie to be killers, uses a well-aimed serving cart to slow down chasing guards and becomes indignant when she thinks she's pointing out to Salamander all the wrongs he's done. In *The Web of Fear*, her screaming does attract soldiers' attention... but she screams only because she's startled by walking into some cobwebs.

Victoria isn't dumb either. She has amazing scientific understanding, considering her age and the era in which she originated. Her father clearly taught her the basics of chemistry, sound waves and climatology. (She even says so in *The Ice Warriors*, which is one big Victoria-knows-science fest until she gets banished from the story in the beginning of episode six.)

So... curious, cautious, indignant, assured of her own beliefs, intelligent. Scared, sometimes; screams, sometimes. Do these qualities differ so greatly from any other female companion prior to Leela? No. What makes Victoria different? Why has her character been reduced to "a screamer" more so than any other companion?

One reason, I'd argue: her age is overlooked.

Victoria is young... a teenager, really, and, judging by her hair and dress in *The Evil of the Daleks*, a teenager who hasn't "come out" yet. (Novels have placed her age at a plausible 15.) She gets hungry easily, bored easily, fussy easily and worried easily. Even the aliens she encounters notice her age: both the Ice Warriors and the Great Intelligence refer to her as "a child." Whenever she moans about being captured, she wants to be with the missing others more than wanting to just escape.

None of Victoria's behavior is extraordinary – because it's not of the fainting/screaming/crying 24/7, conventional fannish wisdom holds that it is. But lack of exposure meant this fannish wisdom prevailed.

Until 1992, when *The Tomb of the Cybermen* came out on VHS, no one had *seen* a Victoria story unless they happened to have caught it when it originally aired in the late 1960s. For those fans lucky enough, they were likely to have been rather young at the time, thus not into girl characters. They remembered the Doctor being clever, Jamie being brave... and Victoria screaming. The novelizations didn't do much to negate this collective fandom memory – really, fans read the novelizations for plot, not character. Those fortunate to view the telesnaps fan episode reconstructions heard a lot of screaming, but didn't get much nuance in body language or facial expression (episode three of the recent *Web of Fear* release provides a nice example). Fan commentators had no way of knowing Victoria's description was wrong... so they kept repeating this perceived description until it became an assumed fact.

Even the release of *Tomb* did little to dissuade this assumed fact. Fan (and professional) commentary focused on the story, not so much the cast. The release of selected *Ice Warriors* and *Web of Fear* episodes prior to the series' return did nothing for Victoria. The return of all of *The Enemy of the World* and the vast majority of *The Web of Fear* in 2013 also distracted from Victoria's characterization because of all the "OMG Troughton!" feels.

So... Victoria is capable, but young, and not necessarily deserving of the "screamer" tag. What purpose, then, does she serve?

Perhaps moreso than any other companion, Victoria's biggest purpose in her stories is to inspire "her boys" (not that she would ever use that Pondian phrase to describe her companions) to protect, comfort and rescue her. She's very young, a Victorian orphan out of time. Her need, and desire, to be protected is understandable given her background, but it does emphasize her fears and diminish her other qualities. Victoria is a rare companion: she's not looking for a way to escape, she wants to be rescued. That's where Jamie comes in.

The Doctor assigns Jamie to take care of Victoria almost from the first moment the trio steps into the TARDIS together. Declaring Victoria's hoop skirts impractical for their adventures, he tells Jamie to take her to the wardrobe to find something else. Further along in *Tomb*, the Doctor requests that Jamie look after Victoria again... and Jamie honors that request throughout Victoria's time in the TARDIS.

Whether it's wandering the mountains of Tibet, the Underground tunnels in London, or places in between, Jamie stays by Victoria's side whenever possible. He makes sure she has a hand to hold, a shoulder to cry on and a lap to sit on whenever she needs it. He also protects her... or tries to, at least. And if she's captured? He obsesses over rescuing her. In *The Ice Warriors*, this leads to temporary paralysis when he's sonically stunned by a Warrior. In *The Web of Fear*, Jamie ignores Colonel Lethbridge-Stewart's direct order to go find her.

Is Jamie doing all of this protecting etc. because the Doctor has asked him to? No, he has great affection for Victoria. Granted, at first he was into the eye candy aspects – he thought the portrait of Victoria's mother in *The Evil of the Daleks* was pretty attractive, and as late as *The Ice Warriors*, Jamie was suggesting that Victoria should wear really, *really* short skirts. ("We will now change the subject, please," Victoria replies.) Still, their overall relationship exists on a sibling level. Jamie acts as the older, protective brother, Victoria the little sister, with both knowing how the Doctor operates. They share conspiratorial eyerolls and "Here we go again" comments whenever the Doctor chooses to plunge into situations the two humans know probably won't work out well.

Nothing extraordinary, right?

Go ahead, watch *The Tomb of the Cybermen* or *The Enemy of the World*, pay attention to what Victoria does, and be prepared to approve. She is brave, clever, opinionated and cute – everything she needs to be a fantastic classic series companion.

"Where Do I Fit In?": The Tale of Perpugilliam Brown

Stephanie Lai is a queer Australian of Chinese-descent (and a left-handed archer); she likes penguins, infrastructure and Asian steampunk, and is occasionally paid to train people in surviving our oncoming dystopic climate change future. She has done so in Perth, Beijing and Melbourne. Stephanie writes non-fiction and science fiction, particularly looking at South East Asian identity issues. She blogs about social justice, media, fandom and drop bears at *No Award* (no-award.net); being a Chinese vegan (with lots of recipes and things) at *Vegan About Town* (veganabouttown. blogspot.com); and everything else at her Tumblr, *A Penguin of Very Little Brain* (yiduiqie.tumblr.com). Stephanie loves it when people come say hi.

Introduced in 1984, and companion to two Doctors, Peri begins her story in fits and starts, sometimes confused but never unsure. She continues in this vein, poking around, asking questions and generally making a nuisance of herself right up until her possessed-or-married-off end. Though she is often held back by those who think they know better, she never lets it stop her. And she would want you to know it.

Maligned as eye candy / sex appeal, a character "for the dads," Peri was frequently subjected to the gross, rapey desires of the villains of the week. Ostensibly the one through whom the audience related, Peri tried to learn more about the places she was visiting – and as a botany student at university, and an experienced visitor to archeological dig sites, she had the skills necessary – but despite her best efforts, she was ultimately prevented from doing so not just by the bad guys, but by our old friend, the Doctor.

"I get the picture, mud baths for everyone." (Peri, *The Caves of Androzani*)

Peri arrives on the TARDIS with part of a university degree and a whole lot of curiosity, and she doesn't let the opportunity go to waste. She works out for herself that Gallifreyans control their TARDIS via symbiosis; that Kamelion is a robot; that a device on his chest has prematurely aged a resistance fighter on Thoros Beta. She makes these deductions based on nothing but throwaway comments, often while panicking in unfamiliar situations. In *The Caves of Androzani*, she asks a question, and when the Doctor explains, she gets it right away, interrupting his answer before he can finish it. "I get the picture, mud baths for everyone," she says, demonstrating that she has understood not only the explanation but also what the Doctor has left unsaid, that they may be in danger.

Peri's conclusions are not just practical but also philosophical. The Doctor is surprised when Peri suggests that perhaps the Time Lords, on Space Station Chimera, had no other way through than to enact violence upon the scientists, having concluded that the end justifies the means: "isn't that always the excuse for something really bad?" She deduces that they have landed on Earth in *The Mysterious Planet*; and in *The Caves of Androzani*, Peri notices the "glass" (fused silica) as she is admiring the planet, her tone and attitude reminiscent perhaps of being on a dig, before making a clever sarcastic comment about it all.

As Peri and Six climb into the depths of Space Station Chimera, Peri's planning and observational skills outshine Six's (and not for the first time). "How will we get out again?" she asks; Six replies that there will be service ducts, which hardly helps with the planning (a theme, with Six). In her very first visit to the TARDIS, she doesn't understand what's going on but she knows enough to understand that "Howard" shouldn't be doing whatever it is that he's doing; later, she calls for Kamelion to thwart the Master's hold. After learning that the Doctor wears the celery because he's allergic to certain things, she later offers Six celery to help him recover from a dizzy spell.

These are not the actions of a woman who is unlearned, who is stupid; a woman who can do nothing but stand around and scream and show off her breasts to best effect (though she does that, and this is fine). She is a university student, and she has presumably been on more than one dig with her stepfather.

And she wants to learn more. As Sharaz Jek rants on Androzani Minor, she is the first to ask what his demands actually are. Although Peri has been criticized as the stereotypical companion asking, "What's that, Doctor?", her questions are frequently logical. She wants to know how Six knows he's talking to a computer on the Space Station Chimera; she wants to know (quite reasonably) who the Sontarans are; she wants to know how the Doctor, as both Six and Two, can be in the same point of space and time (she even asks this twice).

Peri asks questions not only because she wants to learn, but as a way of pointing out things she already knows, without shaking the foundations of patriarchy. On Thoros Beta, Yrcanos declares that he believes the resistance fighters require, and are waiting for, a great leader (him). "Do these resistance fighters know that?" she asks, causing him to question his own plans.

The Doctor is not unaware of this companion's intelligence. Though at times condescending and dismissive of Peri, he acknowledges her contribution to their adventures together. When she deduces that perhaps someone is setting up the Time Lords in *The Two Doctors*, with which he concurs, he admits, "Sometimes, young Peri, you make amazingly shrewd remarks." He can be dismissive of her reasoning, implying she comes across this answer by accident, but for all that, he is encouraging her making deductions. In *The Mysterious Planet*, he remarks that he knew, as a student, that Peri would "soon realize the truth without any prompting from me."

Peri is not merely intelligent; she has more rounded qualities also, all on display in *The Two Doctors*. She is pragmatic! Six tells Peri of the death of the universe. "How long will it take?" she asks. When he tells her centuries, she shrugs and chooses to check on the injured Jamie. Yes, her actions say, it's awful – but there are more immediate concerns. She can herd cats! When the two Doctors are squabbling over directions, she takes charge, selecting their direction and demanding they follow her. She is empathetic! When Oscar is dying, she sits with him, offering him support and comfort as he fades away.

"I thought I heard something, but you kept speaking." (Six, *The Two Doctors*)

We are introduced to Peri in *Planet of Fire*, as her stepfather mansplains at her. "Howard, do you have to talk to me like I'm the Albuquerque Women's League or something," she says, as he tells her something she already knows. Later, after lying to her and gaining her trust, Howard maroons her on his boat, ensuring that she will miss her flight to Morocco and undermining the plans she has made for herself.

As a person, Peri is deeply damaged. *Planet of Fire* sees her tossing in her sleep, as she yells "please don't leave me alone ... please don't turn out the light!" In a story so steeped in Howard, Howard's influence over her bodily autonomy, and her obviously well-established weariness with his patronizing attitudes towards her, the assumption here is – at its least horrifying – an antagonistic and worrying relationship with her stepfather; at worst, it's abuse.

This impression is certainly not helped by the early sexual harass-ment and potential abuse she experiences at the hands of Jek, both in and out of the Doctor's presence. This obvious misogyny reflects poorly on many of the men – and, sometimes, the women – around her, and she struggles to find sympathetic allies.

But Peri's most significant barrier to contributing is often the Doctor himself.

Peri's comfort and concerns are secondary to him. In *The Mysterious Planet*, the Doctor and Peri are walking in a light drizzle, the Doctor holding his umbrella above both of them. He takes great delight in twirl-ing the rainbow colored umbrella, creating a whirl of colors and inadver-tently exposing Peri to the bracing dampness, whilst conveniently keep-ing himself covered. Peri is forced to move the umbrella back to cover her. It's something of a metaphor for their relationship.

When the Doctor notes that the death of the universe is going to take centuries in *The Two Doctors*, as noted above, Peri shrugs and goes to check on Jamie. After she leaves, Six becomes maudlin, and notes that she "can't understand" – dismissing her productive and pragmatic take on the situation in favor of wallowing in uselessness.

At the end of *The Two Doctors*, it is the Doctor who decides that "they" are to become vegetarians, at no moment stopping to ask Peri how she has dealt with being trussed up in preparation for cooking. Perhaps her reaction would be to eat more meat! But we shall never know, because the Doctor, on behalf of the audience, didn't care enough to ask her.

In *The Mark of the Rani*, she talks about the hedgerows of England, and their upcoming disappearance; never is this more relevant than now, and for once it is a subject she knows more about than the Doctor! But he strides ahead, dismissing her.

Upon Thoros Beta, Peri notes the speed of the tide going out, specu-lating it's to do with the giant moon looming on the horizon. In classic style, Six dismisses her theory, claiming it's mechanical; and when she asks why someone would want to control the tide, replies, "Why wouldn't they?" As always, Peri is the counterpoint to the Doctor's carelessness for anything that's not clever enough for his interest.

The Doctor's lack of consideration for Peri might stem from any number of sources, but its result is the same. She ends her journey with him just as she came in: dismissed, curious, and leaping in to the fray as best as her knowledge and skills will allow her. And what does this say of the audience, with Peri as our stand in; of the roles of the Doctor's companions, who are so often women?

"I am interested, I just don't like being lectured, that's all." (Peri, *Planet of Fire*)

Peri is not unaware of her situation. In *Mindwarp*, she comments that she wants out, and her skepticism and distrust of the Doctor becomes clear. When they narrowly avoid running into Sil, previously encountered in *Vengeance on Varos*, she notes her unawareness of the danger in the situation is "only because you didn't tell me, Doctor."

As we move into Peri's later stories, this awareness only deepens. She acknowledges in *The Mark of the Rani* that she hasn't "been safe since I first found myself in the TARDIS," and in *The Mysterious Planet*, she snaps at the Doctor when he patronizes her. Yet, even as her situation remains untenable, still Peri continues to learn and grow, despite the Doctor's ridicule.

As a companion, Peri has all she needs to act as a foil and a keeper to the Doctor. She has an attention to detail and a need to plan that is in perfect contrast to the Doctor's "leap in and see what happens" tomfoolery. She is focused and determined in ways the Doctor is not. She is empathetic where he is not, often highlighted in the ways she smooths over the Doctor's behavior with a thank you or a sorry. Most notably, it is Peri who gets them past the dog and guard in *Mark of the Rani*, with a comment that makes the Doctor seem harmless.

But in the end, Peri is never able to overcome the barriers to her development. In her final story, Peri is undermined and dismissed, even as she soldiers on to learn more and understand everything that's going on and struggles to have her knowledge and insight heard. On Ravolox, it is Peri who first notes that the planet seems familiar (and she is right, though the Doctor once again dismisses her). On this planet, Six gives his usual mixed signals of both declaring "that girl can't obey an order," and then trusting her to accurately and successfully complete tasks.

And despite the potential unreliability of the narrative, our last glimpse of Peri is as yet another pawn of the patriarchy: her body modified to accommodate Lord Kiv, a mouthpiece for his words and a vessel for his spirit. The key to the happenings on this planet, what happens to her and how the Doctor apparently treats her, are in large part because the Valeyard is not wrong – this is how the Doctor regularly treats her, this is how concerned with her wellbeing and autonomy he usually is.

Maybe Peri really is Yrcanos' queen, teaching Yrcanos and their warriors about the benefits of retreat, exchanging the idea of love, and learning how to charge forward without a glance back. Maybe she's talking about ambush, arguing that if it is a woman's way of fighting, that doesn't make it bad. Maybe she's asking the right questions and making the right plans. She's a much better cultural ambassador than the Doctor ever has been, and when Krontep is filled with warriors whose strength lies in a lack of fear and a knowledge of planning, we'll know why and we'll acknowledge that it was Peri who made it so.

My Doctor: Harry Sullivan

Sarah McDermott is a copywriter who lives in London and pines for the North. When she isn't preoccupied with television, she spends her time worrying about the rent and reading about recent history. She can be found on Twitter @most_illegible.

For a New *Who* fan, diving into the Tom Baker era confirms many vague images of the classic series have been assimilated into popular culture: there's the scarf, the robot dog, the bag of jelly babies. It's easy to find fans of the fourth Doctor and his most popular companions: fellow Gallifreyan Romana, Sevateem warrior Leela and Sarah Jane Smith, the reporter-next-door who dressed like Andy Pandy (a cultural reference almost as mysterious to the millennial generation as classic *Who* itself).

But one companion is generally dismissed or forgotten about entirely. His name is Harry Sullivan, and his reputation is unfairly tarnished. Companions – especially in the classic series – sometimes get overshadowed by the Doctor, which is a shame, but also in the job description.

Harry, however, takes the tradition a step further and is overshadowed by *almost everyone he meets*. Even so, there's more to him than meets the eye. And one of the perks of growing up without a Doctor is that you can make your own rules. Harry Sullivan isn't as impressive as *the* Doctor, but he's still *my* Doctor.

# # #

It doesn't help that Harry takes a while to make an impression – but he's introduced in the same scene as the new Doctor, and who can compete with that? Harry is summoned to UNIT HQ, where a freshly transformed Tom Baker is still in the throes of regeneration. While the Doctor shamelessly hogs the attention of Sarah Jane, the Brigadier and the audience, Harry gets a few perfunctory lines and a blink-and-you'll-miss-it close-up. The audience would be forgiven for assuming he's a bit player given some dialogue out of misplaced pity. But, on the off chance that someone might be paying attention, we're informed that this dashing young medic is Surgeon Lieutenant Harry Sullivan. He's a naval doctor and the closest thing that UNIT has to medical expertise. The Doctor will later claim that Harry is only qualified to work on sailors – but there's nothing *only* about working on sailors.

Poor Harry never quite finds his place aboard the TARDIS; his fellow travelers are a well-established double act. By the time Harry arrives, Sarah has been in league with the Doctor for five adventures. After he moves on, she'll stick around for another seven, and even then she'll pop back every so often and star in her own spin-offs. Sarah and the Doctor are thick as thieves. They spend a lot of time hugging, laughing and worrying about each other. As for Harry? Well, it's different with Harry...

It's not that the Doctor and Sarah don't like Harry. They do. It's just that Harry inspires as much frustration as affection. And, the Doctor isn't exactly easy to get along with. In his first story, Harry is tasked with babysitting the newly regenerated Doctor and, still in military mode, conducts a brisk check-up. But his manful attempt to exert authority goes awry, leading to Harry finding himself tied up in a cupboard with a skipping rope. The Doctor, it transpires, takes orders poorly. Luckily, Harry takes orders in good spirit and executes them with middling success, so everyone's happier once the Doctor has established a proper pecking order.

Unfortunately for Harry, there's a more fundamental tension. The Doctor doesn't suffer fools gladly, and Harry is a man who veers towards the foolish end of the spectrum. He may only stick around for six adventures, but that's long enough for the Doctor to heap so much scorn on him, the insults almost end up defining him as a character. During Harry's brief tenure, he's on the receiving end of an unprecedented stream of Time Lord grumpiness – he has more than a little in common with Mickey Smith, who had more than his fair share of insults from the Eccleston Doctor.

In fact, the Doctor's reactions to Harry's mishaps are often more memorable than the mishaps themselves. It may be difficult to recall the details of how Harry started the rock fall that knocked out the Doctor in *Revenge of the Cybermen*, but the aftermath is unforgettable: the Doctor wakes up, recaps Harry's chain of disasters – including nearly setting off a booby-trapped harness – and bellows the immortal line: "Harry Sullivan is an imbecile!" The walls of the mine tremble, and Harry goes down in companion history as a snappy but unflattering sound bite.

Actually, one suspects that part of the Doctor's frustration is that Harry is more similar to him than he's comfortable admitting. Harry's cheerful Bertie Wooster mannerisms and gentlemanly ways are starting to seem dated in the 1970s he lives in, so in many ways he's a perfect candidate to be transported to another time and place. He and the Doctor share a healthy contempt for bullies and a passionate regard for human life. They also both love cricket, although it's probably a stretch to suggest that the fifth Doctor donned his Edwardian cricketing getup in a sort of temporal shout-out to Harry. One thing that can't be denied is that the Doctor, loath as he may be to admit it, is just as prone to slapstick as his hapless companion. Upon hearing, in *The Sontaran Experiment*, that Harry's fallen down a hole and can't get out, the Doctor grumbles that this sort of behavior is absolutely typical of Harry and wonders out loud why the man can't look where he's going. Or he would do, but his rant is cut short when he trips and falls into the exact same trap.

Harry fares better with Sarah, forging a protective bond in a short space of time. Companions have to stick together, after all, and Harry's so relentlessly well-meaning that it's hard to take exception to him. They're on hand to rescue each other from danger and provide a friendly body to cling to. It's telling that aliens use Harry's likeness to terrorize Sarah on more than one occasion – the sight of Harry Sullivan jabbing a pitchfork in your direction is all the more alarming if you're emotionally attached to him. But their relationship isn't without its own pressures, which can be summed up in two words: old girl. It's the nickname Harry bestows on Sarah Jane, but it's also far more than that. At times, it feels more like an uncontrollable verbal tic.

When they first meet, Sarah dismisses Harry as woefully old-fashioned, and never really backs down on the issue. To be judged old-fashioned in 1974 is quite something. It's an age in which Sarah is seen as a female chauvinist for choosing to wear trousers and taking objection when she's dismissed as "only" a girl. Sarah never warms to "old girl," which might make for uncomfortable viewing if she weren't perfectly capable of telling Harry where he can stick his unwanted pet names. "Call me old girl again," she drawls as Harry dusts her off after a stint in a cryogenic chamber, "and I'll spit in your eye." Harry takes it on the chin (which is admittedly quite easy when your chin is as prominent as his). But while Harry's attitude to the so-called fairer sex is a touch condescending, it's never enough to dent their friendship. He's happy to let Sarah get on with the alpha companioning and she's happy to have him around to squabble with.

Harry doesn't last long in the TARDIS, and everyone knows the official reason why: Tom Baker's rippling abs. Harry's character was originally conceived as a kind of latter day Ian Chesterton – a younger man who could run around and get into the kind of exciting scrapes that an older Time Lord may not be able to tackle. But while the fifty-something William Hartnell needed backup in the shape of a macho, becardiganed science teacher, Tom "Rambo" Baker proved more than capable of doing his own stunts. So Harry was left at a loose end. And while he was occasionally called upon to get his hands dirty, he wound up more likely to bumble than rumble. In practice, the character had more in common with sweet, simple Jamie McCrimmon. But at least Jamie had the excuse of being stranded centuries in the future. Harry manages to achieve the same effect with no timey-wimey meddling on anyone's part.

Perhaps it's understandable that Harry doesn't get the same recognition that his TARDIS contemporaries do. With Sarah Jane on hand to ask the questions and Tom "Action Jackson" Baker's fists at the ready, Harry can sometimes feel like a spare part. Whenever there's an important discussion to be had, Harry has the good sense to step back and let the grown-ups talk. He's a man who knows his own limitations, and while that's a quality to be applauded when you have as many limitations as Harry, it leaves him with less to do. Which is a shame, because like all good companions, Harry is infinitely curious. Sadly, this makes him twice as dangerous as he is useful.

Harry's personal weakness is technology. The man just loves pressing buttons. He's so fascinated by the time ring in *Revenge of the Cybermen* that he asks to take it home with him. And, in fact, Harry's love affair with an unmarked TARDIS switch is what lands him in the future (*The Ark in Space*) to begin with.

It's surprising that a man with Harry's archaic sensibilities is so delighted by futuristic gizmos. But then, Harry's full of contradictions. He's a perfect gentleman, but he can't open his mouth without offending somebody. He's a man of medicine working for the military. And he throws himself into his adventures with the Doctor, but emotionally he's anchored to the Earth. Even when cast into the depths of space, Harry dreams of the day he'll be able to buy himself out of the Navy and set up a small country practice. Of course, in his dream, the practice is funded entirely by stolen alien gold and Harry gets to use an impractical-sounding solid gold stethoscope. But the neighbors won't need to know that little detail, and they won't ask questions when the local cricket team gets a load of Harry's overarm.

The real tragedy of Harry Sullivan is one of unfulfilled potential. He may have only lasted six stories, but he's surrounded by some of the most memorable and beloved aspects of *Doctor Who*. Flanked by The Best Doctor Ever (As Elected By Readers Of *Doctor Who Magazine*) Tom Baker and A Robot Dog's Best Friend Sarah Jane Smith, Harry's in intimidating company. He runs up against Daleks and Cybermen, reports in to the Brigadier, wields the sonic screwdriver and even gets to drive Bessie, but somehow he's overshadowed. He's adjacent to greatness, but never quite on the same level.

Genesis of the Daleks is touted as one of the greatest *Doctor Who* stories ever, essential viewing for fans of the show and unsubtle allegory alike, but fans of Harry Sullivan are likely to be left unsatisfied. His main contribution is to get his foot stuck in one of the oversized clams that loiter outside the Kaled bunker. The Doctor frees Harry by breaking off a stalagmite with his bare hands and wrenching the monster open, establishing his dominance as the true action star of the series. Even Harry's dismayed by his own clumsiness, and plaintively wonders why he's the one who always puts his foot in it.

Which isn't to say you should steer clear of *Genesis*. Who doesn't want to see Harry get stuck in a giant clam? The troubling Freudian implications alone are worth the price of the box set. We also get a glimpse of pure heroism from Harry. The Doctor missteps, accidentally triggering a landmine, and Harry risks his life to get him off it in one piece.

Despite this, *Genesis* isn't the best introduction to Harry. He copes admirably with the grimmer side of space adventure, but he's no fun in the hands of writer Terry Nation. To truly understand Harry, look no further than *The Ark in Space*. Written by Robert Holmes (who is beloved for his chatty, character-driven stories), it's a breath of fresh air in the early Baker stories. Unburdened by the weight of the show's history, it more than earns its place in the pantheon of classic stories with its nimble dialogue, moderately scary monsters and innovative use of green bubble wrap.

It also gets the best out of Harry, who's positively delighted to be out in space and spends most of his time oohing and aahing over mysterious banks of switches, transmat beams and other futuristic gizmos. We witness the first of his serious blunders as he accidentally traps Sarah Jane in an airless room. Landing Sarah in a cryogenic chamber is a pretty bad slip-up for the first time out, but we also see his bedside manner in action as he sets to work defrosting her. Harry finds his voice with the help of Holmes's ear for dialogue and, much to Sarah's chagrin, we get the first onslaught of "old girl"s. Oh, and he performs an alien autopsy on a giant space insect. And all the while, he dashes off throwaway bits of backstory and, in a truly thrilling moment, casually quotes the first law of the sea. (That's "gremlins can get into anything, old girl," in case you're curious.)

The Ark in Space is where we see Harry at his most laudable, albeit perhaps not his most medically competent. But then, this is Harry Sullivan we're talking about. He's not above making the odd sniffy remark about Sarah Jane's tibias, but if he can name the bones of the hand, he keeps it to himself. Harry's medical knowledge is mostly put to use in the time-honored tradition of sci-fi doctors: he declares auxiliary characters dead. Occasionally, as in this adventure, he'll get a bit over-zealous and then find out they weren't dead after all. Embarrassing, sure, but what's a little malpractice between friends?

Harry spends most of *The Ark in Space* running barefoot through a space station. A space station that's crawling with giant green space slugs, no less. Everyone goes on about the female companions' unsuitable footwear – from Jo Grant's go-go boots to River Song's high heels – but does Harry get any credit when he accepts the risk of getting alien slug goo all over his toes? None in the slightest. Just as Harry Sullivan is the unsung hero of his era, his little piggies are the unsung heroes of the Nerva Beacon. Although, speaking of heroism, Harry gets a fair bit of action in: ducking daringly behind a table with Tom "Big Daddy" Baker, demonstrating his bowling skills and boldly shooting an alien slug at point blank range with the assistance of only two other humans. You go, Harry. Show that slow-moving mollusk who's boss.

But for a more tantalizing glimpse of the action hero that Harry could have been, look no further than *The Sontaran Experiment*. Yes, that's the one where he falls down a hole, but we do get to see some feats of strength along with the stumbling. Tom "Atlas" Baker may possess the strength of a dozen men, but Harry can scale a cliff like nobody's business. Later, we'll see him swoop in to rescue Sarah when a Sontaran kidnaps her. It's not actually the most well thought-out rescue – Harry brandishes a metal bar, never actually confronts his enemy head-on, and he's ultimately thwarted by a force field – but it's the thought that counts. He even takes time out to considerately mop a dying prisoner's brow (without going so far as to unchain him or offer much in the way of medical assistance) and, at the story's climax, infiltrate the Sontaran spacecraft. All in a day's work for hero-doctor Harry Sullivan. He doesn't even get himself kidnapped in the process! No mean feat, considering how much time Harry spends in various alien jails.

In fact, as capable as Harry is of playing the square-jawed hero, he plays the damsel in distress just as well. Let's face it: Harry kidnaps easily. When the Doctor ties him up and leaves him in a cupboard in *Robot*, he seems to silently accept that being kidnapped is something he's probably going to have to deal with on a regular basis if he keeps spending time with the Doctor. Later in the same story, Harry gets himself kidnapped when he infiltrates the sinister Think Tank research facility. In *Terror of the Zygons*, getting kidnapped is probably the most useful thing Harry can do, if only because it gives him the opportunity to chat to the Zygons, who decide to explain their plans and methodology to him in great detail.

He spends some time at Davros's pleasure in *Genesis of the Daleks*, but it's not until *Revenge of the Cybermen* that he lands in a prison so ill-conceived that even he can break out of it. When he escorts an ailing Sarah Jane to the asteroid Voga in *Revenge*, he attracts the locals' attention by helping himself to some of the gold he sees lying around. Sarah and Harry are packed off to the alien clink, but luckily it turns out that the Vogans are as impractical with their gold as Harry is in his gold-stethoscope-filled fantasies. Everything on that asteroid's made of gold. They treat it as though it's MFD or fiber wood. Unfortunately for the Vogans, it dawns on Harry that gold is about as sensible a restraint as MDF, and he and Sarah make short work of their chains. Jabba the Hutt, take heed.

Traveling with the Doctor means accepting the risk of kidnap, but Harry sometimes seems to actively court it. After his final story as a regular, Harry makes a last appearance a short while later in *The Android Invasion*. When the Doctor and Sarah Jane visit the small town of Devesham, they find themselves surrounded by enemies with familiar faces. They soon discover that their old UNIT friends have turned against them and are – spoiler alert – androids designed to destroy all life on Earth. Happily, the Doctor is able to find the real Harry Sullivan at the end of the story. He's been kidnapped and tied up on an alien spaceship, which was no doubt a familiar and soothing experience for him. This is the kind of character continuity that *Doctor Who* doesn't get enough credit for.

Harry may never learn how to avoid being kidnapped, but he picks up a trick or two during his time with the Doctor. First and foremost, he learns to trust the Doctor with his life, but not with his work schedule.

After returning to Earth and helping solve a final mystery near Loch Ness, Harry leaves with as little fanfare as he arrived. It's not the emotional goodbye that many companions get, but Harry's stiff upper-lip and a dedication to duty are poignant and admirable in their own way. It's just a shame he only has one line in the entire scene. But then, what else can be expected of the Baker era's unsung hero?

Still, Harry has the last laugh. He bids goodbye to the Doctor for the eminently sensible reason that he's due back at UNIT HQ and needs to catch a train back to London. The Doctor offers him a lift back in the TARDIS, but Harry, who already knows the first rule of the sea, has now learned the first rule of traveling with the Doctor: don't expect him to take the shortest route. Sure enough, the Doctor and Sarah hop in the TARDIS and immediately vindicate Harry by getting sidetracked by about 30,000 years. Maybe the boy's not such an imbecile after all.

Donna: Noble by Name and Noble by Nature

Karen Miller writes speculative fiction. Mostly of the epic historical kind, but she's also written *Star Wars* and *Stargate* novels and under the pen-name K.E. Mills writes the Rogue Agent series, about a wizard with special skills who works for his government under unusual circumstances. She lives in Sydney, travels as often as she can, and when she's not glued to the computer writing a book or researching history for a book, she can be found having fun at her local theatre, swimming laps at the pool, walking the dogs, reading or watching great films and TV dramas, or lazily socializing with friends.

> "You're not special, you're not powerful, you're not connected, you're not clever, you're not important!"

So says the tenth Doctor to Donna Noble as they take a breather on top of a London building in *The Runaway Bride*.

As it turns out, he couldn't have been more mistaken. By the time Donna Noble's adventures with the Doctor ended, she'd saved the universe – and him, too. More than once.

The Runaway Bride was the first episode of *Doctor Who* I ever saw. For whatever reason, the show never appealed to me growing up. Then, when it was rebooted, my vague childhood memories kept me from watching it, despite the impassioned urgings of friends who thought I'd really love Russell T Davies's reimagined version. After much nagging, I decided I'd watch one episode, hate it, and so hush up my nagging friends.

Instead, as the credits rolled on *The Runaway Bride*, I was online ordering the first two seasons on DVD – still wiping the tears from my eyes. Worse, after devouring those two box sets, I started counting down the days and hours for each new episode as it arrived on TV.

Donna Noble was a large part of my conversion from nose-in-air naysayer to an unabashed *Doctor Who* fan.

When Donna meets the Doctor, they're both having one of the worst days of their lives. He's just lost his great love, Rose Tyler, and she's been plucked out of a church moments before marrying the man of her dreams. Both Donna and the Doctor are people adept at wearing masks. Because of the lives they've lived and the challenges they've faced, they're in the habit of covering up the depth of their feelings, even going so far as to pretend they don't have feelings at all, sometimes. And yet...

In *The Runaway Bride*, both characters have lost their masks. They're emotionally raw – the Doctor because of grief, Donna initially because her big day is being ruined, then as she finds out she's the target of aliens, followed by her family and friends and fiancé holding the wedding reception without her, and ending with the man of her dreams being revealed as a cruel-spirited, murderous nightmare. It's their mutually recognized misery, and the sympathy arising from it, that allows them to bond quickly – and on a much deeper level than might ordinarily be the case for either of them. Especially the Doctor, so bruised from losing Rose.

And the bond only strengthens as the mystery unfolds. In the middle of all the Christmas and wedding mayhem, brash, boisterous Donna is also revealed as a woman of courage and keen insight. At the reception, one of her greatest qualities is showcased: her ability to keep the Doctor focused on the needs of ordinary people, even as universe-and-mind-bending events unfold around her. After the Christmas tree attacks, she points out that people are hurt and tells him, "You're a doctor. You can help." He dismisses her then, it's true, but the seed is planted. Later, when he makes the Huon Particle connection and is getting carried away by the implications, completely oblivious to how awful the situation is for her, she slaps him and demands, "Are you enjoying this?" His dismay is quite amusing, but she's made her point. She's forced him to stop and think about the real human consequences of his current adventure. He's not unkind, he's thoughtless. Understanding that, she points it out. And what lingers is the impression that here is a woman who'll go toe to toe with him without fear or favor. Later events show that this feisty confrontation wasn't a one-off.

After Rose's unconditional love, and her eager willingness to leave Earth and humanity and family behind without ever looking back, Donna's unassailable allegiance to humanity and her family – combined with her bluntly unimpressed and uncompromising response to the Doctor's mad enthusiasms – come as something of a shock. For all his wonderful qualities, the Doctor is arrogant. He certainly doesn't take kindly to being challenged, second-guessed or crossed – as Prime Minister Harriet Jones learned the hard way. But outspoken Donna has made a deep impression on him. So deep that as the dust settles, he asks her, in his typically oblique fashion, to be his next companion.

The obvious question, of course, is why? Donna's loud, she's bossy, she's argumentative, she's obstinate, she's contrary. You couldn't find a greater contrast to Rose. But that's not why the Doctor is drawn to her. It isn't simply a case of slotting the first available not-Rose into the empty space where Rose used to be. And it's not just because he can't face an empty TARDIS, so any old random passing person will do. It's Donna herself. Donna, whose refusal to crumble in the face of Lance's betrayal, who stood shoulder to shoulder with him to stare down a ferocious and unimaginable alien threat, who even in the midst of that insanity was able to conquer her own fear and reach him – save him – that wins her his genuine respect and admiration.

As slightly as he knows her by the end of *The Runaway Bride*, the Doctor knows enough to recognize that here is a gutsy, magnificent woman, strong enough and fearless enough to take him on. To tell him the truths that he doesn't want to hear. Which answers the question, why her?

And then, because she's Donna, she turns him down!

It's maybe only in that moment, after that off-handed and maybe even impulsive offer, that he realizes he really meant it. So he tries to convince her. And because she's Donna, she stands her ground – but not without remaining true to herself to the very end.

"Promise me one thing," she says. "Find someone." And when he denies that he needs anyone, she replies: "Yes, you do. 'Cause sometimes I think you need someone to stop you."

Which is piercingly insightful of her... and true. But he's not ready to admit that yet.

So she turns him down and they go their separate ways, the Doctor and Donna Noble. He meets Martha Jones, medical student, and together they survive a plasmavore and a platoon of Judoon on the moon. Martha is brilliant and inquisitive and courageous. He likes her immediately – and she falls head over heels for him. It's destined to be an unrequited love. And even though Martha knows that, knows she's going to get her heart broken, she sticks with the Doctor. Because he's everything to her and she loves him to bits.

But sticking with him costs her. Martha's life is turned upside down and inside out and when it's all over, she's not the same person. Worse, she can't ever go back. She's got scars now. She's battle-hardened. She's still a doctor, but she's a doctor with a gun, who has seen things and done things that will forever set her apart from the rest of humanity, save for a select few fellow veterans.

As for the Doctor, by the time Martha walks away from him, he's added a few more scars to his collection. For one brief, terrible moment he wasn't alone. He wasn't the last Time Lord any more. But his brother-Time Lord died in his arms, mad and vengeful, and he was alone again in the most terribly permanent way. Perhaps even harder to bear, the knowledge of what knowing him, loving him, traveling with him, has done to Martha.

Re-enter Donna Noble.

"You look older," she tells the Doctor. "Still alone?" He tells her about Martha. Later, when she notices that he's changed, she gives Martha the credit. "She fancied me," the Doctor confides. Donna rolls her eyes. "Mad Martha, that one. Blind Martha. Charity Martha."

And there she is. Donna Noble. Still brash and outspoken. Still calling it like she sees it, no holds barred. On the surface, the same woman who blinked into the TARDIS wearing her wedding dress without pockets.

Except... since *The Runaway Bride*, things haven't quite worked out the way she dreamed. She tried to live a life less ordinary, but life refused to co-operate with her. It kept tripping her up. She started to regret not going with the Doctor when she had the chance. She had seen and done extraordinary things too, things that mean she can no longer look at the world in the same boring old way. She wants to do more than type 100 words a minute. And at some point those regrets turned into action. She starts looking for the Doctor... which leads her to Adipose Industries and the mystery of the disappearing fat. A mystery which has also piqued the Doctor's interest.

As they fight to thwart the infant Adipose's nanny and her nefarious plan, and defeat is staring them in the face, Donna demands: "Doctor, tell me, what do you need?" The answer is twofold, yet simple. The Doctor needs Donna. She gives him the extra necklace she'd cleverly purloined – and she gives him the kind of companionship he can't get from anyone else. They're a perfect match.

But in the end, he hesitates. The guilt he feels for half-destroying Martha's life is too close, too painful. He can't forgive himself for hurting her and he's terrified he'll do the same to Donna. He tries to put Donna off the idea of traveling with him. But Donna's made up her mind. She's outgrown her humdrum, suburban London life. She doesn't want an intergalactic romance, thank you very much. She wants the stars – and the Doctor can give them to her.

So fate and time and destiny collide. It's the Doctor and Donna, shoulder to shoulder again, fighting for humanity again. The Doctor-Donna. Running hand in hand towards a future neither of them ever imagined.

One of the most profound things they experience together happens in Pompeii. There, Donna runs headlong into what it means to be a Time Lord. What it means to have the power to change every bad thing that has ever happened anywhere, and yet be powerless. She learns how it feels to hold thousands of lives in your hand and be forced to let them slip through your fingers so that history might remain unaltered, as it should be. Being Donna, her first instinct is to fight for humanity, for the innocent victims of the imminent volcanic eruption, and not back down – even in the face of a Time Lord who refuses to be swayed by an impassioned plea for mercy.

"Listen," she says to the Doctor, "I dunno what sort of kids you've been flying around with in outer space, but you're not telling me to shut up!"

She's right, of course. From the human perspective, the only possible course of action is to warn the town of the impending cataclysm. It's just a shame, for her and for Pompeii, that the Doctor isn't human.

Up until that point, even though she's seen behind his mask, Donna doesn't truly understand the Doctor. The TARDIS and time travel and aliens, it's all exciting and challenging and scary and wonderful, yes – but until Pompeii, she has no idea of the burden he bears by being a Time Lord. Pompeii is Donna's crucible. It's where she must shoulder the burden of a Time Lord. Make the impossible choice. Pompeii, or the whole world. One small, ancient town, or the Earth's entire future. Donna's not a Time Lord. She's human. Such a terrible choice would likely destroy anyone else. But because she's Donna Noble, she can make that terrible choice. The right choice, a Time Lord's choice. She chooses the future. And because she's Donna Noble she puts her hand over the Doctor's hand so that he doesn't have to end Pompeii alone.

Has anyone ever given the Doctor a greater gift?

But she doesn't stop giving. After that eloquent, compassionate gesture, she finds a way to salvage something from all the death and destruction. For herself, yes, but also for him. Because she knows that the loss of Pompeii and all those lives is tearing him apart too. So even though it's against the rules, she begs him to save that one family, just four people. For her. And for him. And he saves them, because he knows he needs it as much as she does.

So Pompeii changes Donna. You might even say it paved the way for her final transformation, the creation of the most unique being in all of time: a woman who's part human and part Time Lord. Perhaps she could encompass the Doctor's intellect as well as she did, for as long as she did, because of what she experienced in Pompeii. Because, from that fateful day on, she carried a Time Lord's burden on her shoulders and in her heart.

Leaving Pompeii behind, Donna and the Doctor romp off for more adventures. They help save the enslaved Ood, and in doing so, Donna learns more of what it means to be a Time Lord. She can bear the Ood's singing only for a few moments. Discovering that the Doctor hears it all the time, without respite, gives her yet another insight into his strength and courage. But not even that understanding means she will ever stop taking the piss.

It seems clear Donna realizes early on that she can do him a huge favor by never taking him too dreadfully seriously. So as they fight the Sontarans' attempt to turn Earth into a clone world, she makes sure to tease him, string him along, distract him with gentle mockery. By never succumbing to hero-worship, by remaining her outspoken and contrary self, Donna gives the Doctor strength. She gives him a safe place to stand, to be himself, to trust that he can trust her to stop him when he needs to be stopped, when he starts taking himself too seriously or forgets there are people in the middle of his mysteries. When the Doctor's daughter is created, from his tissue sample she stands with the girl, refusing to let the Doctor dismiss her, making him acknowledge that no matter how Jenny came into being, she is his offspring and he owes her that recognition.

Again and always, Donna fights for humanity. On the planet Midnight, her strength is shown yet again. She sticks to her guns, doing what she wants to do, not letting the Doctor distract her from relaxing in her own way. And then, after his ordeal in the tourist car, she's there for him to lean on, so he can let his guard down and share his true feelings. It's another of the gifts she's able to give to him.

And all the while, she keeps on insisting she's nothing special, she's just a temp from Chiswick. Never clearly seeing herself. Never trusting in her own strength the way the Doctor does. Even as aliens bend time and space around her, trying to contain her, trying to derail the future that depends on her, Donna still believes she's just an ordinary human.

"But why me?" she asks, bewildered, as Davros's terrible end game plays out. "Because you're special," the human Doctor tells her. "I keep telling you, I'm not!" she insists. "No, you are," he says. And then the penny drops. "Oh, you really don't believe that, do you?"

No. She really doesn't. Perhaps because her mother spends so much time nagging and criticizing, finding fault and tearing down instead of building up. Perhaps because of her faux-friend Nerys, who smiles in Donna's face while stabbing her in the back. Perhaps because, until the Doctor, only her grandfather ever saw the pure gold beneath the brass.

But she is special. And essential. Without Donna Noble, Davros and his reborn Dalek empire would have destroyed the universe. It's the utterly unique combination of Time Lord knowledge and fearlessly outspoken, irreverent, passionate, feisty, here's mud in your eye Chiswick temp that was able to defeat the greatest threat countless worlds had ever faced.

Which leads us to an interesting question. It's the human Doctor who makes the call to destroy Davros and his reborn Daleks. To, in the words of the wholly Time Lord Doctor, commit genocide. And he decides to act because he understands that even though the reality bomb is no more, the Daleks have the will and the power to slaughter billions if given the chance. If they're not stopped now, they never will be stopped.

So he takes it upon himself to stop them, no matter the cost. Just as the very human Harriet Jones made the choice to stop the Sycorax, because she knew – even if the Doctor couldn't imagine it, would never believe – that just because he declared Earth was defended that didn't mean it always would be. He might be a Time Lord, but he's not boss of the universe.

Donna says it. The human Doctor has the capacity to think outside the box, to think tricky, to think devious, to think like the enemy, in ways the purely Gallifreyan Doctor can't – or can't let himself. That little dash of human makes all the difference. Maybe it's because the human Doctor only has one heart. One life. When you've only got one of something, you fight harder and dirtier to protect it. To be human is to have no redundancies. To be human means it's now or never. Use it or lose it. Do or die.

The human Doctor sees the Daleks and realizes: it's us or them.

That's what Donna gives him. She gives him the part of herself that so passionately believes the helpless must be fought for, even if it means breaking the rules. That protecting the innocent from the wicked is the right thing to do. That standing up for those who can't stand for themselves, no matter the personal cost, is a duty that mustn't be shirked.

The Gallifreyan Time Lord would have let the Daleks live, arrogantly confident that he'd be able to stop them the next time they tried to kill the universe. The human Time Lord – the Doctor-Donna – isn't about to take that chance.

And so the universe is saved. Earth is returned to its rightful place orbiting the sun. Rose and the human Doctor get their happily ever after in the parallel world. And Donna, the unimportant temp from Chiswick who changed so many lives? Who was deemed such a threat that aliens tried to alter history to make sure she wouldn't beat them? Who stopped all the stars from going out?

Well... she dies.

Not physically. When all's said and done, there is still a Donna Noble living in Chiswick, but it's not the one who saved a universe. For any Donna to live, that Donna had to die. And the Doctor had to kill her, so he could save her life.

In the end, Donna's story is a tragedy of epic proportions. But it's so often the way of things, isn't it? The one who fights hardest is the one who in victory loses the most, who is denied the reward of a job well done. Who must lose his or her life so that others might live. In the end, Donna's nobility shines brighter than any star that she saved.

"I just want you to know," the Doctor tells Donna's mother and grandfather, "there are worlds out there safe in the sky, because of her. And there are people living in the light and singing songs of Donna Noble a thousand million light years away. They will never forget her, while she can never remember. And for one moment, one shining moment, she was the most important woman in the whole wide universe."

Yes, Doctor. She was. And we're all of us better people for having known her.

Companion Piece

Rewriting History with Sticky Notes: Narrative, Agency and Bernice Summerfield

Like the subject of her essay, **Emma Ward** is prone to one-liners, statement earrings, being the place pop culture references go to die, and suspecting it all of being Braxiatel's fault, although rumors that her first draft consisted entirely of the words "Benny/Jason OTP 5EVA" written over and over in increasingly large typeface are scurrilous calumnies all. She is currently engaged in a complex dance of avoidance with a novel she describes as "post-post-Singularity gothic lesbian YA on a space station," assuming her day job doesn't kill her first. She lives in western Massachusetts and would like to thank Elyssa Santos-Abrams for, well, everything, basically.

> "Virtual post-it note: make sure I review that entry at a later date, to see whether it is ironically post-modern to a degree that could be described as criminal within the boundaries of the law or my Collection contract."
>
> —Bernice Summerfield,
> *The Greatest Shop in the Galaxy* by Paul Ebbs

Doctor Who has long been concerned not only with the telling of stories, but with the ways in which stories are told. The televised series' interest in playing with and examining narrative tropes was established as early as 1968's *The Mind Robber*. With its characters stranded in a Land of Fiction where the laws of reality are secondary to those of plot, the story displays a distinctly postmodern sensibility concerning the function and protocols of narrative. However, the tropes it uses are largely those of classic fairytales and fantastic literature. It would take the accumulation of another 20 years of *Doctor Who* canon before the New Adventures novels could begin to play with the tropes of the *Doctor Who* universe itself.

A number of adjectives could safely be applied to the New Adventures; "self-referential" would be one of the more neutral ones. This is hardly surprising, considering that a significant number of the staff writers had participated in *Doctor Who* fandom before making the transition into professional writing for the series. Fanwork, and specifically fanwriting, is a highly referential and metatextual craft: the telling of unlicensed, unauthorized stories which, while requiring knowledge of a given source text, are created by observers positioned outside the official production of the text. Even those fanwriters dedicated to emulating canon as closely as possible are to some degree engaged in commentary upon their source text as well as addition to it. The lasting innovation of the New Adventures was the canonization of this attitude to the *Doctor Who* universe.

Self-referential fiction needs a self-referential hero, and one was provided in the form of Bernice Summerfield, the New Adventures' first and most successful original companion. From her inception, Benny was intended as a deliberate commentary upon and change in direction from the archetypal companion-ingénue. Comparatively mature at 30 in order to further the New Adventures mandate of "adult" storytelling, she was also vocally skeptical about the Doctor and – conveniently – a 26th-century citizen fascinated with mid-20th-century pop culture and folklore, a fascination which positioned her as an outside observer to the very science-fiction tropes *Doctor Who* relied on.

While her career in the early New Adventures was variably successful, Benny proved a viable enough character that, following Virgin Books' loss of the *Doctor Who* license after the release of the 1996 TV movie, the series was revamped to center around her. The first Bernice Summerfield New Adventure, *Oh No It Isn't!*, continues in the tradition of engagement with every genre trope available. It contrives to pitch Benny into a computer-projected world governed by the conventions of traditional British pantomime, in which the rules of the universe are derived from mildly smutty jokes and Benny demonstrates her genre-savviness by crashing the program with a promise to marry *all* the male characters competing for her hand. Coming in the wake of the Doctor-led New Adventures, *Oh No It Isn't!*'s positioning of Benny as the controlling force in her own narrative is, in its own way, a startlingly clear prefiguration of the trajectory in store for her character. It is also a direct refutation of the 61 New Adventures that preceded it.

The *Doctor Who* New Adventures' central narrative and thematic obsession is with the Doctor's influence over the lives and stories of his companions. The series was overtly intended to expand on script editor Andrew Cartmel's agenda of presenting the Doctor as a more mysterious and dangerous being than had henceforth been the case. To this end,

Doctor Who canon began its first sustained period of questioning the benignity of the Doctor's attitude towards and power over the lesser mortals with whom he comes in contact.

As the series progressed, this became a point of fanatical interest, perhaps exemplified in Nigel Robinson's *Birthright*, the seventeenth installment in the series. *Birthright* is simultaneously an atypical and an extremely representative New Adventure. In it, the fascination with the Doctor as a manipulative, potentially malign force spanning all space-time is taken to its logical extreme; while his influence and that of the TARDIS are in evidence throughout, the Doctor himself almost never appears on page. Without putting in more than six pages' worth of an appearance, he manages to force Benny to strand herself in Edwardian London, provide her with lodgings, funds and allies, and position her perfectly to defeat the alien threat of the month.

In fact, every character in *Birthright* the novel, including the alien invaders themselves, is positioned as a chess piece in a long game between the absent Doctor and an uncharismatic fellow Time Lord – with more than a slight implication that the other player, Muldwych, is himself a future incarnation of the Doctor. There is something intensely and unpleasantly circular about the entire novel; its plot loops in on itself, dragging the rather palely drawn characters along with it. Benny, the ostensible protagonist, is given little agency and nothing much actually to do; the absent Doctor moves her along from one scene to the next without much concern for either her autonomy or her feelings. Her description of the Doctor as "*medicus ex machina*" has rarely been more accurate, and the reader's uncertainty as to what we are intended to take away from the text rarely more acute.

In fact, when taken as a whole, the New Adventures make up a notably inconsistent and thematically imbalanced experiment in long-form storytelling – perhaps understandably, considering that the series was produced at the pace of one book per month, without necessarily a great deal of consultation between the writers. Certain themes are run into the ground; in particular, the Doctor's untrustworthiness and manipulative nature are so stressed that one suspects the idea was new and startling to every writer who worked on the series. His behavior is frequently challenged ringingly in one volume, only for everything to be reset to status quo in the next. In-text explanations for this cycle of outrage and acceptance – not to mention the question of why any companion willingly travels with the Doctor more than once – suggest outright mind control, making for uncomfortable reading at best.

Other elements of the series are inconsistent at best; entirely symptomatic of this is the fact that, in an essay on the subject of Bernice Summerfield, it has taken me approximately a thousand words to say anything much about her character as described in the New Adventures. A survey of the books leaves one with the impression that in their context, "Bernice Summerfield" is primarily a highly contested set of signifiers. A small core of personality traits – or at least quirks – can generally be found in common; most portrayals of Benny can accurately be described as argumentative, intellectual, humanist, neurotic, hard-drinking, defensive, romantic and compassionate, but the expression and narrative significance of these traits varies heavily from one installment to the next.

It can safely said that, after 50 years of *Doctor Who*, every writer currently at work on the series is writing a separate, deeply personal take on the Doctor. A comparable process seems to have taken place with Benny within months. Paul Cornell, who created the character, has a tendency to speak about her as though she were a real person whose life he was chronicling; other writers seem to have been largely uninterested in her, reducing her to an assemblage of stereotyped personality traits; others still seem to have gone busily to work deconstructing her as well as the Doctor.

Lance Parkin's work in *Just War* is an exemplar of this latter tendency. Easily among the strongest of the New Adventures, and a high point in *Doctor Who* canon overall, it places Benny in captivity in Nazi-occupied Guernsey and engages in a genuine, serious examination of the morality of time travel. Benny's ironic detachment and tendency to move through historical tragedies without ultimately being greatly affected by them is called into question alongside the Doctor's treatment of other sentient beings as game counters, and the resulting characterization is some of the richest available.

It is possible, in this context, to speak of "Parkin's Benny" – or "Cornell's Benny," "[Kate] Orman's Benny," "[Jim] Mortimore's Benny," to name only a few – much as one would discuss theatrical performances by different actors, in different productions, of the same role. A comparison with the various incarnations of the Doctor almost begs to be made, with one signal difference: the Doctors are deliberately portrayed as distinct individuals, with a literal actor's performance to anchor each one and render it coherent. Without this advantage, Benny in the New Adventures is at the mercy of her writers as much as that of the Doctor, and this discontinuity largely continues over the course of her 23 post-

Doctor novels.

It is these three signal characteristics of the New Adventures – the Doctor's manipulative nature, the failure to build to a narrative and thematic arc larger than the sum of its parts, and the relative sketchiness of Benny's character – that I believe are being addressed and rewritten by the Big Finish Bernice Summerfield audio series in its central, overarching plot. Significantly, after Big Finish Productions acquired rights to the character of Bernice Summerfield, the new series opened with audio adaptations of five of the New Adventures. While a pragmatically sound move in and of itself, providing a bridge for readers of the New Adventures to transition into listeners of the audios, the decision to adapt, and *which* books to adapt, was also an important one in terms of characterization and theme.

Three of the books in question, including *Oh No It Isn't!*, were from the post-Doctor era; however, the other two, *Birthright* and *Just War*, had originally featured the Doctor. *Just War* in either format is a superb piece of writing (and, in the case of the audio, performance) which does not change significantly in theme by being adapted. It performs the same work in the audio series as it does in the New Adventures, that of putting Benny in extremis and engaging with the moral issues inherent in her space-and-time-hopping lifestyle.

Birthright, however, changes theme entirely in adaptation; while the plot remains largely unaltered, the removal of the Doctor entirely reworks the context in which said plot takes place. Benny's place in the narrative is literally rewritten, becoming far more active and important. The central conflict is no longer "the Doctor vs. himself," but "Bernice Summerfield vs. the universe"; moreover, with the removal of her Doctor-created safety net, Benny is forced to actively work to establish herself in the past timeline. While the storyline does not become fundamentally more interesting (it is difficult to accuse any work in which the ravaged alien world turns out to be a far-future Earth of *radical* originality), it becomes fundamentally more of a story.

Moreover, the choice of *Oh No It Isn't!* as the inaugural entry in the Big Finish series was an equally important one. As mentioned before, it is an extremely self-referential and genre-aware story – a story, literally, about stories – and Benny's eventual triumph derives from her ability to hack the protocols of the narrative she finds herself trapped in. It functions, therefore, as a keynote for the series: while the character of Bernice Summerfield might stand very well on her own, the Big Finish Bernice Summerfield series was going to be heavily referential and metatextual, concerned with the conventions of narrative in general and *Doctor Who* in particular. In fact, I argue that the central project of the audio series has been the rewriting – literally, in some instances – of the *Doctor Who* New Adventures, the repositioning of Benny as active protagonist, and the extended deconstruction of one of the New Adventures' core tropes: the Time Lord as omnipotent, inevitable, undefeatable chessmaster.

Taken together, the adapted Big Finish audios become a mission statement for the direction in which Benny's story is being taken. By choosing or rewriting texts in which she appears to advantage or displays significant depth of character, and displaying a concern with genre and plot conventions, the creative team perform their own act of reframing canon: the "rescuing" of an under- or misused character and their subsequent re-envisioning as a central figure. (This is, of course, a familiar fanwork strategy; it is worth noting that members of the original Big Finish production team had previously been involved in producing unlicensed *Doctor Who* fan films.) It becomes possible to speak of a single, coherent, three-dimensional "Big Finish Benny" – perhaps more aptly "Bowerman's Benny," as Lisa Bowerman's voice performance provides an important creative throughline of the series – as it never does with the New Adventures.

Following the initial run of adaptations, the original stories that make up the remainder of the series begin to focus on continuity and consequences. Benny is provided with a steady job, a family and a new home base on the museum-planetoid known as the Braxiatel Collection. The setting brings with it a regular cast of characters, including Irving Braxiatel, the proprietor of the Collection and – I argue – a rewriting of the New Adventures Doctor.

From his introduction in the New Adventures, Braxiatel's character was an echo of the Doctor's: first established as a Time Lord himself, with a penchant for cross-temporal interference and interaction with his own past and present selves, he is in fact heavily implied to be the Doctor's brother. In the Big Finish audio series, he is introduced as a mysterious, eccentric, but kindly benefactor before slowly being revealed as malevolent, manipulative and power-mad, with a tendency to rewrite history to his own ends – a trajectory exactly mirroring the Doctor's in the transition from television to print.

With this revelation, however, he is firmly established as the series' *antagonist*; rather than an inevitable force of nature, as the New Adventures tended to portray the Doctor, he becomes an opponent who should and *can* be bested. His attempts to use Benny and her new extended family for his own ends are occasionally successful, but invariably presented as a challenge rather than an inevitability; where in the New Adventures the Doctor's companions displayed a worrying tendency to shrug and accept his problematic behavior, the struggle of Benny and her allies *against* Braxiatel becomes the overarching plot of the series. Moreover, both he and Benny are proven to be skilled manipulators of genre tropes for their own ends, as is perhaps best demonstrated in a pair of diametrically-opposed but confusingly titled audios: *The Worst Thing in the World* and *The End of the World*.

On a strict plot level, *The Worst Thing in the World* is deliberately and stately frivolous; coming in the middle of a determinedly serious plotline, it contains the line of dialogue "I think we could all do with a fun adventure that doesn't really relate to anything else," which is exactly indicative of the degree of parody and metatextuality involved. It is set on a planetoid known as the Drome, wholly devoted to the production of video entertainment and ruled over by a crazed sentient supercomputer which acquires the ability to influence human behavior; in context, the parallel with the Braxiatel Collection under the control of Braxiatel is inevitable and obvious. Benny and her ex-husband Jason arrive on the Drome to investigate a series of catastrophes which prove to be caused by the computer's forcing the inhabitants to play out various clichéd genre storylines (including, of course, a zero-budget SF drama clearly inspired by *Doctor Who* itself).

However, Benny proves to be equally adept at manipulating genre conventions. Faced with the computer's frantic genre-switching, she ultimately seizes control for herself not through violence or action, but by performing a final genre switch of her own: performing an upbeat eleventh-hour musical number and transforming a rampaging horde of zombies into the chorus. In addition to being sublimely funny, the scene is highly metafictional, establishing Benny as a master of controlling her own narrative; in the inescapable chess metaphor of the New Adventures, she has been promoted from pawn to queen.

However, the full extent of Braxiatel's control over reality is revealed in *The End of the World*, which performs the masterful feat of pulling together contradictory threads of both the Big Finish audios and the New Adventures into one coherent plot; in it, Benny's ex-husband Jason, previously often portrayed as a bit of a buffoon, sets out to unravel Braxiatel's editing of both Benny's timeline and Jason's own memories. *The End of the World* draws heavily on the New Adventures, reproducing a scene from the novel *Death and Diplomacy* almost verbatim and dealing largely with a plotline previously thought to have been retconned out of existence – that of the future timeline shown in the New Adventures (shortly before their divorce by editorial fiat) in which he and Benny were happily married with two children, neither of whom is the son she bears over the course of the Big Finish series. Braxiatel's manipulation of the timeline – pulling characters out of their proper times, reworking their history, even excising them completely from reality – is directly analogous both to the Doctor's behavior and that of the writers of a long-running science fiction series; he has assumed editorial power over reality and is honestly offended when his "characters" object to manipulation. Needless to say, *The End of the World* ends with Braxiatel facilitating Jason's death.

However, Benny's subsequent escape from Braxiatel's control marks a significant albeit easy-to-overlook departure from the model of Time Lord/ human interaction established across the entire *Doctor Who* range. It is not only in the New Adventures that the Doctor's problematic effect on the future lives of his companions is explored. Even in the comparatively optimistic *School Reunion* episode of the revived series, it is implied that former companions – including those who left the Doctor's company under comparatively peaceful circumstances, which is by no means all of them – have experienced long-lasting difficulty readjusting to mundane life, and the succession of recent companions who have been mind-wiped, trapped in alternate universes or set adrift in time make the Doctor's company seem dangerous to a breathtaking degree.

When looking at the *Doctor Who* universe from a high-level perspective, in fact, it is difficult *not* to see Bernice Summerfield as "the one who got away" – not only from the Doctor or from Braxiatel, but from the traditional companion narrative itself and even from her own writers. The peculiar thing about Paul Cornell's above-mentioned tendency to speak of her as an autonomous human being is how natural it seems. Even in the patchwork characterization of the New Adventures as a whole, one frequently has the sense that what one is facing is not one inconsistently written character, but several variously-accurate and -motivated depictions of the same actual person.

Ruling out a quasi-mystical interpretation of this phenomenon, one is left with the conclusion that it is intimately connected to the history of the character and her creators' backgrounds in fan culture: this plurality of variant and sometimes entirely contradictory definitions of a single character, resulting in a sort of *gestalt* impression that a sort of ur-character, a Platonic ideal character as complex as an actual person, exists on some level of reality and can be described, is one of the defining characteristics of fandom.

Unlike even certain other companions, Benny arrived at this state of holographic dimensionality remarkably early in her career; it is notoriously difficult to pinpoint what makes a successful fictional character, but in this case – although hesitant to make a firm statement – I would point to the very self-referential nature of her character design as a potential answer.

It is important to remember that Benny was designed as a character who would be unimpressed by the Doctor, and that the Doctor's power over reality is always, if not always explicitly, parallel to that of his writers – his power over time and space giving him an unimaginable degree of control over the fates of individuals. Like the writers, he can decide who lives and who dies (in this author's opinion, the tenth Doctor episode *The Fires of Pompeii* provides the most visually stunning imagery connected to this fact), and can move easily from one point in the universe to another, stepping in and out of various characters' storylines with ease. The difference between the Doctor and Braxiatel, in the end, is frequently a matter of textual perspective and nothing else; any Time Lord, by virtue of their established abilities, *automatically* becomes possessed of authorial powers over reality. A recurring line in the revived series is "Time can be *rewritten*."

From this perspective, the reason for Benny's power as a character becomes obvious; immersed in a self-referential fictional universe which is constantly being re-envisioned, she is both aware of the rewriting and distinctly unimpressed by it. Like the protagonists of far more explicitly metafictional texts, she knows someone else is writing her world into existence, and she does not approve of their plotting; her determination to seize control of her own story makes her as metatextual a character as any Time Lord, and one with whose goals, in the end, it is far easier to sympathize.

Companion Piece

Scientists, Not Office Boys: Zoe and Liz, Science-Heroes

By day, **Anna Livingston** designs interfaces for web and mobile applications, and is the co-author of two books about web design. By night, she's the lead moderator for *A Teaspoon and an Open Mind* (www.whofic.com), a fanfiction archive with over 38,000 stories about *Doctor Who* and related series and media. Livingston is also a fanfic author herself, having written more than 90 stories for both Classic and New *Who* that range from family-friendly fare to "Dear God, I hope no one from the show ever sees this." Livingston lives near Boston, Massachusetts with two difficult cats and a tall man with curly brown hair, a long scarf and a great smile.

There are many types of hero, but *Doctor Who*'s model has always been the science-hero: the protagonist who relies on wits instead of weaponry to save the day. Brute force may be involved, but only as part of a broader plan based on intelligence, rationality and a dash of intuition or educated guesswork. The science-hero[33] is nerd fantasy: for once, the smartest person in the room is the winner, and the most popular or physically powerful people are lesser beings by comparison.

And more often than not, the science-hero is exactly that: a hero, not a heroine.

There's no reason for science-heroes to be male other than that they unfortunately reflect society's vision of a scientist. Traditionally, science, technology, engineering and math (STEM) fields have been a man's domain. With 2013 statistics showing that fewer than one in ten engineers employed in the UK are women[34], and numbers from 1971 not even one in 20[35], it's hardly unexpected that most of the scientists in

---

33 Although this essay was not inspired by the *TV Tropes* page on science-heroes, the site provides a good overview and examples of the archetype (including the Doctor himself): tvtropes.org/ pmwiki/ pmwiki.php/ Main/ ScienceHero.

34 Daniels, E. "The Chronic Shortage of Girls in Science is a Threat to Economic Growth," *The Evening Standard*. March 13, 2013; retrieved May 1, 2013.

35 Mitchell, B. (1988). British Historical Statistics. Retrieved August 4, 2013, from Google Books. Statistics based on census results for women in professional and technical services in England, Wales and Scotland, not the entire United Kingdom. (Note that because this occupation group inexplicably includes artists as well, the actual ratio of women in STEM fields in 1971 may be closer to one in 25.)

Doctor Who would be male as well. Male science-heroes represented what the show's writers and producers would have considered normal in daily life.

Yet given the real-world numbers of women in STEM fields, *Doctor Who* has been surprisingly egalitarian in bringing on female companions with scientific backgrounds. In some cases, their backgrounds didn't always figure heavily in their storylines, but we still got Nyssa the bio-electronics specialist, Peri the botanist, Martha and Grace the physicians, and Mel the computer whiz.

And we also got two female, full-on science-heroes: Zoe Heriot, and Liz Shaw.

In the 1960s and 1970s, there was little incentive to produce a female character like this, and yet in *Doctor Who*, we're given two such companions in a row. Both Zoe and Liz seem designed to balance the scales, albeit in different ways: Zoe kills computers with her brain, while Jamie handles the head-bashing; Liz and the Doctor form Team Science, arguing for rationality and exploration when Team Military would rather order five rounds rapid or a box of explosives.

Depending on Science, Not Superstition

Zoe first appears in *The Wheel in Space* as the titular Wheel's astrophysicist/astrometrician, a set of hardcore scientific disciplines if there ever were any. She's young and straight out of "parapsychology" training, which taught her science and math, but hindered her emotional development. In that sense, she matches the stereotype of the scientist as purely rational – but rather than being a coldly mathematical creature who finds feelings only get in her way, Zoe is acutely aware of her shortcomings in this range. Accused by communications officer Leo of being "a little robot... all brain and no heart," a frustrated Zoe later exclaims, "I don't want to be thought of as a robot!... I want to feel things as well!"

By contrast, meteorite expert and polymath Dr. Liz Shaw is mature and completely comfortable with her knowledge and position. Summoned to UNIT headquarters in *Spearhead from Space*, she's not happy about undergoing a search or being taken away from her research, nor with the Brigadier's suggestions that recent meteorite sightings may be something more sinister than chunks of space debris falling to Earth. Liz has a scientist's confidence that the meteorites' presence must have a rational explanation, and that UNIT's claims of twice repelling alien attacks are unlikely at best. She openly mocks the Brigadier for believing a man like the Doctor could exist, much less travel in time and space.

But the Doctor, unlike the Brigadier, quickly wins Liz over with charm, ready speculation about the real nature and purpose of the meteorites, and a unified front against military oversight, snapping at the Brig: "Go away, and let Miss Shaw and I get on with our work." Science is what's important; bureaucracy is not.

In their initial stories, Zoe and Liz both face threats to their homes. *The Wheel in Space* is classic Troughton-era "base under siege" – with the Cybermen picking off the Wheel crew one by one – while *Spearhead from Space* brings the action to Earth, where the Autons have already set up shop in a doll factory and are building strength for a global invasion.

Each woman confronts these threats in her characteristic way. Zoe relies purely on science and logic, but is tripped up when she discovers the latter isn't a universal solution. Realizing that there's nothing she can do to help the Wheel's over-confident commander, Jarvis, out of his fugue state, she doesn't know how to proceed. Her entire belief system has been shaken, like a fundamentalist suddenly grasping that the world is far more complicated than a narrow view of religion can support.

Liz, on the other hand, is almost completely in her element throughout *Spearhead from Space*. While she's never faced an alien enemy before, she remains calm and rational, patiently applying scientific principles to unravel the questions she and the Doctor face, and only becoming rattled in a creepy sequence in a wax museum populated by Autons. Even when the Doctor is literally wrestling with the Nestene Consciousness, Liz fights through her fear, focusing on readjusting an electroshock weapon to save him from death by tentacle.

Like the Doctor, Zoe and Liz's primary weapon is their intelligence. Companions are often allowed to save the day, and occasionally allowed to come up with solutions the Doctor himself would never have thought of, but rarely do they get to consistently show off an intellect as (or nearly as) bright as his own. "The Doctor's almost as clever as I am!" exclaims Zoe in *The Krotons*, and the Krotons' tests prove she may well be right; even the Doctor admits with exasperation, "Zoe is something of a genius. It can be very irritating at times." Zoe's mighty brain comes especially in handy in *The Invasion*, where she gleefully tricks a computer into tying itself in logical knots, then later analyzes a space fleet's flying pattern in mere seconds to determine how to take out 90% of them with a single missile.

Liz, too, relies almost exclusively on her ability to think her way out of trouble. Clever and determined, she's not above playing politics to get what she wants, extorting her way into the Silurian caves by threatening to tell the Brigadier the Doctor is planning another illicit underground trip. This same determination serves her well in *The Ambassadors of Death*, in which she evades her kidnappers by car, on foot and very nearly in water. Best of all, the scripts have the Doctor acknowledge Liz's intelligence and competence. The Doctor sharply tells the Silurians that he cannot help them without Liz: "Miss Shaw is a scientist. If I am to do what you want, I shall need her help." And by the end of *The Ambassadors of Death*, the Doctor is willing to entirely cede his role as interstellar diplomat to his assistant, telling the Brigadier, "Here's Miss Shaw. She's much more practical than I am."

Science-Hero Evolution

Where Zoe is sunny and cheerful, Liz is wry and sarcastic; where Zoe screams in terror when confronted by mortal peril, Liz has a cooler head, even when facing the unfamiliar. "[Liz] seems like a very grown-up woman to be hanging around the Doctor," said Steven Moffat. "Somehow, he usually attracts the more irresponsible people."[36]

But there's more to life than simply being the smartest woman in the room, and Zoe, younger and less settled in her life than Liz, still needs to learn to push herself beyond her facts and logic.

It's this desire to broaden every one of her horizons that leads Zoe to stow away on the TARDIS – her first step beyond mere scientist and towards science-hero. In *The Dominators*, Zoe's initial outing in the TARDIS, we see what happens when scientists devote themselves purely to facts, setting aside inquisitiveness and imagination: university researchers surveying radiation's effects on a test site blithely accept not just that all radiation has suddenly disappeared after 172 years, but also that the Doctor, Jamie and Zoe – who otherwise look ordinary – are in reality the very first outer space travelers to arrive on Dulkis. Zoe's natural curiosity immediately brands her as different from her peers, and iconoclastic fabulist Cully takes notice: "This girl's got an inquiring mind," he says, taunting the survey team. "She can't possibly come from Dulkis."

When Zoe visits the Land of Fiction in *The Mind Robber*, we see that she can be emotional and uncertain of herself, even terrified by a realm where imagination takes physical form, running counter to the logic she's always relied on. But some of her greatest emotional development comes in *The Invasion* – in which she meets photographer Isobel Watkins, arguably her first real female friend. Zoe was professional and

---

36 *The Doctors Revisited*: "The Third Doctor," BBC America, March 31, 2013.

companionable with her female colleagues on the Wheel, but only with Isobel do we see her having pure, unstructured fun, playing dress-up and modeling for her new friend. As satisfying as it is to see Zoe pushing her brain to its limits, it's just as satisfying to see her grow into the parts of herself she'd completely ignored before now.

Zoe's character continues to evolve in the Big Finish audio *Fear of the Daleks*. While the plot hinges on Zoe's brainpower, which uniquely qualifies her to serve as a programmable assassin, what's most remarkable is a brief but critical emotional moment at the very end. A visit to the Wheel's counselor isn't the cure for Zoe's nightmares about the Daleks; instead, what staves them off is a soothing psychic message from the Doctor – a trigger for the heart, not for the mind.

Similarly, a far-future Zoe re-visiting the Land of Fiction in the audio *Legend of the Cybermen* no longer fears how imagination can work against her, instead saving the Land from the Cybermen by blending fictional characters in a wildly creative crossover narrative that would make any fanfic author proud.

By the time Zoe, Jamie and the Doctor are finally forced to go their separate ways in *The War Games*, Zoe has pushed herself far beyond her initial wonkishness: she's now an independent leader who has explored captured territory on her own, remained cool and confident that her mental abilities will never fail her, and even bested a comic strip character in hand-to-hand combat. She is a hero in her own right.

Her successor arrives on the scene fully formed as a capable adult with an established career, and curiously lacks a key personality trait that's often part of the companion role: Liz Shaw has no dissatisfaction with her life, other than annoyance at the Brigadier tearing her away from her research. It's not that life with the Doctor offers no benefits – the prospect of new knowledge excites and inspires Liz as it would any good scientist – but rather that she's neither running away from or towards something, nor is she trying to fulfill a missing need in her life. Zoe's youth and inexperience lead her to seek out adventure; Liz tells the Brigadier quite bluntly that she's got a lab of her own to manage, and isn't interested in what she considers flights of fancy.

Liz's arc from pure scientist to science-hero happens across the course of *Spearhead from Space*, perhaps because Liz is further along in her career than Zoe – or, at least, was never exposed to education via brainwashing – and is used to taking charge of things on her own. She has little patience for sexism, engaging in epic eye-rolling when the Brigadier describes her as "not just a pretty face," and in *Doctor Who and the Silurians,* snapping "I am a scientist, not an office boy" when the Brig pulls her away from her work to help him answer the phones. Anything that interferes with Liz's scientific pursuit of the truth, whether it's pig-headed male ignorance, kidnapping or accidentally being ditched by the Doctor when he disappears into *Inferno's* parallel dimension, is simply another hurdle she knows she's capable of jumping, and which she soars over every time.

Liz is no less capable once she leaves UNIT, abandoning her science-heroism for pure science back in her lab at Cambridge, where she consults on a colleague's time-travel research in Big Finish's *Sentinels of the New Dawn.* She misses her more active career: "Academia is my natural home," she says, "but life seemed uneventful after my time with the Doctor." Still, after a quick jaunt to 2014 – where she and the Doctor encounter a megalomaniac cult, are attacked by a genetically engineered creature, save the world from a potential Ebola outbreak and wind up the day with a helicopter chase – Liz has had enough adventure (as would most of us!), and makes peace with her decision to leave her science-hero life behind.

Turning Science-Heroes Into Science-Naïfs

As solidly as the stories establish that Zoe and Liz are serious scientists, they also sometimes undermine both women, because part of the companion's role is to translate Doctor-to-human, asking occasionally obvious questions so that the script can deliver necessary exposition. As Caroline John (who played Liz) said, "I love all these [laboratory scenes], because it shows that I was a scientist, and that I wasn't just feeble-minded... though I do remember trying to find 70 different ways to say 'What are we going to do now, Doctor?'"[37]

Asking that particular question doesn't by definition undermine a scientist character; science is an ongoing process of discovery, and that means asking questions when you don't know the answer. But when a male scientist asks a question, he may be perceived as inquisitive; standards are much less forgiving for female characters, who will instead come across as unqualified. And when a female scientist character fails to understand something most people – particularly other scientists – would understand, the end result is unfortunately sexist, disappointing characterization.

Thus Zoe, trapped by a terrible pun in a giant glass jar with a paper lid, stands inside it, screaming for Jamie and the Doctor to help her in

---

37 *Spearhead from Space* DVD commentary track.

The Mind Robber, when she could easily have torn her way out herself. In fact, she seems fairly undone by the Land of Fiction, knowing that willpower and closed eyes alone will save her from a unicorn and minotaur, but so emotional she can hardly concentrate to do it. In *The Space Pirates*, she's unaware of what a candle is – as if writer Robert Holmes assumed that despite candles being a technology so useful they've survived thousands of years, somehow in the relatively near future of Zoe's time, humankind would completely forget not just how candles work, but what they are entirely. It's a moment clearly designed to demonstrate Zoe's naiveté, but there's a difference between that and "idiot plot."

Similarly, Liz, for all her higher degrees, doesn't recognize a globe depicting Pangaea, a moment deeply insulting to the credibility of a character smart enough to be UNIT's scientific advisor. Worse still is when she and the Doctor explore the underground caves in *Doctor Who and the Silurians* and discover an obvious passageway – to which Liz says, "It's a doorway!", and the Doctor responds, "Well, anyone can see that."

But what's most frustrating is the constant reference to "Miss Shaw," while all the male scientists are called by their title, "Doctor." (In the *Spearhead from Space* commentary, John herself introduces her character as "Doctor Elizabeth Shaw.") The only way I can reconcile what otherwise appears to be blatantly disrespectful sexism is to subscribe to the theory that Liz was not merely a medical doctor, but a surgeon, in which case British tradition holds that her title would revert to "Miss."[38]

In fact, the BBC seemed to view Liz's intelligence as a threat to the program, precisely because it made her stating the obvious so difficult.[39] It hardly mattered that the show's premise meant the Doctor would always be the smartest man in the room; a companion who couldn't believably fail to understand what was going on wasn't fulfilling her role. She had to be bright enough to attract the Doctor's attention, but dumb enough to ask the questions the script demanded – as if it were too challenging for scriptwriters to come up with situations that would show off a companion's intelligence while allowing for narrative progression the audience could follow. Apparently, there was a glass ceiling for companions: hyperintelligent astrophysicists with eidetic memory are acceptable, provided they're sufficiently youthful and naive; hyper-

38 Halliday, M. (2012). "Seven to Doomsday." In L. M. Myles & D. Stanish (Ed.), *Chicks Unravel Time* (p. 209). Illinois: Mad Norwegian Press.
39 BBC (n.d.). *BBC – Doctor Who Classic Episode Guide – Season 7*. Retrieved May 10, 2013, from www.bbc.co.uk/doctorwho/classic/episodeguide/season7.shtml

intelligent Earthbound scientists with labs of their own in Cambridge and occasional flashes of gullibility were so dangerously smart, they had to be removed from the program.

The Final Bend of a Hero's Arc

All companions eventually leave the Doctor, but neither Zoe's nor Liz's ending sits right, albeit for different reasons. Zoe, after withstanding the war games both on the battlefield and within Central Control, is forcibly separated from the Doctor by the Time Lords, as is Jamie. There's barely time for a heart-rending goodbye before the Time Lords do something even worse than punishing the Doctor by sending his companions home: they wipe Zoe's memory of every adventure she's experienced save her first one on the Wheel, completely negating her character development.[40]

If the Time Lords hadn't removed Zoe from the Doctor, resetting her memory in the process, how might she have continued to grow and change? Surviving an environment as hostile and harrowing as that of *The War Games* would either give someone the confidence to believe they can handle anything on their own, or leave them cringing with PTSD – and given the type of danger Team TARDIS faced on a regular basis, Zoe was more likely to have the former reaction than the latter.

Perhaps she'd have eventually returned to the Wheel, newly equipped with empathy and a broader understanding of the diversity of the universe, and would have moved into a leadership role. But the Wheel's hermetically sealed existence might have been too confining for someone who'd traveled in time and space – would Zoe instead have wanted to continue traveling, using her mighty brain to solve problems wherever she went? Ultimately, that's the scenario that feels most satisfying to me as a viewer: an older Zoe, possibly the chief science officer on an exploratory vessel, bringing wisdom and compassion to her work.

Liz's ending, however, is far more disappointing than Zoe's, because we never even get to see it on screen – instead, it's mentioned offhandedly in *Terror of the Autons*, with the Brigadier saying that Liz left because the Doctor only needed someone to pass him test tubes and tell him how brilliant he is. While no scientist of Liz's stature could be comfortable doing that, there are only two instances where the Doctor treats her as little more than a bottle-washer, and both of these – his patronizing refusal to explain "dimensional transcendentalism," and his

---

40 Donna Noble would later suffer a similar fate, though as a character who'd progressed even further than Zoe, her reset was that much more galling.

equally patronizing use of her to steal his TARDIS key back from the Brig – take place practically the moment he meets Liz. Once he realizes that she's a highly qualified scientist, he relies on her implicitly both inside and outside the lab. Liz helps him build the device that neutralizes the Nestene Consciousness; she runs slide samples and proposes a possible cure for a deadly Silurian virus; she identifies critical warnings in computer output that hubristic Dr. Stahlman ignores. And, most important, the Doctor trusts Liz to help him fix the TARDIS.

What rings most false about Liz's departure is that it's nearly impossible to believe that a meteorite expert and scientific genius wouldn't be interested in continuing to repair an actual spacecraft – and not just any spacecraft, but one that can travel in time, and which relies on technology far beyond that available on Earth. Even without the immediate promise of being able to journey to far-off worlds, working on the TARDIS offered an unparalleled learning opportunity. A woman who'd already pursued multiple higher degrees clearly has a continual thirst for knowledge; what held Liz back here was not a character flaw, but a flaw in the writing, and in Barry Letts and Terrance Dicks's vision of what the companion should be.

So where would Liz have wound up, if she could have continued on past Season Seven? With no obvious ties to Earth beyond her own lab, perhaps she'd have had a similar ending to Nyssa's: discovering a unique chance to use her scientific abilities to help others, even if it meant leaving her friends behind to spend the rest of her days on an unfamiliar world. The unofficial spinoff *P.R.O.B.E.* supplied another possible option, promoting Liz to head of a team investigating paranormal incidents. But the career path Russell T Davies posited in his *Sarah Jane Adventures* story *Death of the Doctor* rings truest to me: Liz continues her scientific research on UNIT's moonbase, that much closer to the stars she never got to see with the Doctor.

In the end, though, even if neither Zoe nor Liz got the type of ending this science geek hoped they would, it's still satisfying to see two such women on screen, heroically waving the flag of science and logic, often in the face of men who dismiss them. It's both remarkable and disappointing that in the new series – airing more than 40 years after Zoe and Liz first graced the television – only one companion (Martha) has trained in any sort of science. With women increasingly entering STEM fields worldwide, it's more important than ever to provide them with not just real-world role models, but fictional, aspirational ones as well.

Someday, perhaps. On the moonbase, or a wheel in space.

The Uses of Turlough

Anne Goldsmith had an inauspicious introduction to *Doctor Who* when she was terrified by episode four of *The Seeds of Doom* at a vulnerable age. For the next 12 years, she fled the room whenever she heard the theme song. Fortunately, she recovered from her phobia just enough to peek out from behind the couch when the ABC repeated the entire series starting in 2004. Several hundred TV episodes, audios, books and comics later, she has now celebrated her tenth year as a fan.

> **Turlough:** I thought I would learn more if I stayed with you. It's true.
> **The Doctor:** Of course.
> **Turlough:** I mean it.
> **The Doctor:** I believe you. I'm just a little doubtful about how resolute you'll remain.
> **Turlough:** Time will tell.
> **The Doctor:** Yes, indeed. Aboard the TARDIS it always does.
>
> —*Warriors of the Deep*

The Doctor isn't the only one with doubts about Turlough. At first glance, one might even wonder what he's doing in the TARDIS. He joins the crew under false pretences and – once those have been resolved – seems to stay on board more to avoid school than because he actually enjoys the excitement. On an out-of-story level, it's not always clear what he provides that Tegan doesn't already have, other than a lot of contradictions. Those contradictions, though, are what make the character so fascinating...

Coming Up Short...

Turlough is a murderous schemer who can't follow through and kill anybody. He hates his school, yet constantly wears its uniform until his last appearance.[41] He asks the Doctor to take him home at the end of *Enlightenment*, then changes his mind for no clear reason, and *then* turns out to be actively avoiding his own people. He holds a rank in the Trion

---

41 Given the sartorial state of the rest of the crew during this era, it's tempting to conclude that the Doctor has misplaced the wardrobe room.

army, but seems inexperienced with weapons and uncomfortable with violence. Never mind the fact that he looks rather mature for a schoolboy and occasionally wears a wedding ring when Mark Strickson forgets to take it off.

Turlough enters the story inauspiciously in *Mawdryn Undead*, by stealing and wrecking the Brigadier's antique car, then pinning the blame on his unfortunate friend Hippo. He proceeds to make a deal with the Black Guardian, thereby becoming the most rubbish villain of Season Twenty.[42] As an evil minion, he mainly has intense conversations with a lump of quartz and/or the studio ceiling. His one attempt at killing the Doctor involves trying to brain him with an unconvincing rock. (Even if he'd managed it, Turlough would presumably have needed to beat the Doctor to death eight more times to achieve anything permanent.) All things considered, he appears only slightly more dangerous than the Myrka.

Trying to murder the driver, however, is certainly an unusual motivation for entering the TARDIS. One might wonder why the Doctor is so keen to have Turlough along, until the end of *Enlightenment* arrives and the Doctor suggests that he knew that something was up the whole time. (He'd have to be very blond indeed not to notice that Turlough knows far more about temporal mechanics than your average schoolboy.) It seems that, as is often the case, the Doctor keeps Turlough around for his benefit rather than his own.

While teenage boys who hated their school uniforms were probably a fair proportion of the show's viewers in the 1980s, it's hard to imagine Turlough as a successful audience identification figure. While he's hardly the only companion with an interesting backstory that never gets explored properly, it's unusual that we don't even find out what the story *is* until he's leaving. In *Planet of Fire*, it turns out that Turlough has a long-lost brother, two dead parents, a prison tattoo and a first name. After the last-minute reveal, his homeworld's culture and background remain largely unexplored, leaving his context opaque. He often complains about Earth and humans, but we don't learn much about his own species or their culture that to understand what makes them different.

Turlough can ask, "What's that, Doctor?" with the best of them, but he's not as well-suited as Earth girl Tegan to being expositioned *at*. He's capable of serving the other basic narrative purpose of the companion – to wander off and get into trouble – but again, not as well as Tegan,

---

42 Since this is a year that includes the Master using a singing robot to stop King John signing the Magna Carta, this is saying something.

since he frequently gives the impression that he'd rather stay in the TARDIS where it's safe. He can run up and down corridors, crawl through ventilation shafts and get captured like a pro, but Tegan does all of that in high heels and a short skirt.[43]

Into the bargain, Turlough is untrustworthy and a self-confessed coward. While most of *us* might indeed have a slobbering breakdown when confronted with evil giant woodlice, companions are usually brave in the face of danger despite a bit of initial screaming. The Doctor and Tegan never seem to shake off the feeling that Turlough can't be depended on in a crisis. Even in *Planet of Fire*, the Doctor chastises him for holding back information about Trion and warns him that if he conceals anything that helps the Master, their friendship will end.

This also leaves him poorly qualified for the action hero role that male companions have traditionally taken on. (Although he does handle a gun in *Warriors from the Deep*, bluffs some colonists with a "deadly" hat rack during *Frontios* and *successfully* brains someone with a rock in *The Awakening*.) From Ian Chesterton to Jack Harkness, and even to Eternal Centurion Rory, it's been a male companion's job to punch the villains when the Doctor can't or won't. Turlough is more likely to cower away from a monster than to get into a fight with it, and with the young and athletic Peter Davison around, there's little need for someone else to do the rough stuff anyway.[44] It's emblematic of his character that in *The Five Doctors*, Turlough stays in the TARDIS with Susan and her twisted ankle while Tegan and Sarah Jane boldly journey to the Tower of Rassilon.

So if he doesn't work as a villain or an identification figure, and is redundant as a narrative device and an action hero, what *is* Turlough good for?

... And Yet, the Whole is More than the Sum of Its Parts

Firstly, the production staff had every motivation to replace Adric. Producer John Nathan-Turner felt that his initial "Artful Dodger" character concept had gone astray in the execution, and decided it was time for another go at an unreliable companion. Eric Saward, as script editor, was reportedly keen on the idea.[45]

43 Turlough frequently appears to be borrowing Tegan's eye make-up, but doesn't seem to have swiped any of her footwear or clothing. At least, not on camera.

44 Not that Davison's Doctor actually commits many violent acts, other than shooting some Daleks and playing a brutal game of cricket.

45 *A Brief History of Time (Travel)* provides a summary of the behind-the-scenes events that resulted in Turlough's creation in its background to *Mawdryn Undead* at

Secondly, Turlough has intriguing qualities that his fellow travelers lack. Given that he spends almost his entire run in a school uniform, is manacled to a wall more than once and eventually gets his trousers off, it's tempting to conclude that demographics other than the "dads" were being catered to.[46] (You can tell that *Enlightenment* is the first *Doctor Who* story written by a woman, because Strickson ends up crawling on the carpet in front of a dominatrix who then handcuffs him and bosses him around.) The relevant scene in *Planet of Fire* was reportedly included to appeal to female viewers, and generations of fangirls – and not a few fanboys, for that matter – have rightly declared him a Ginger Love God.[47]

Above all, though, the purpose of a companion is to provide a contrast to the Doctor. If the Doctor is a grumpy old man, they have to be young and compassionate. If he's a schemer, they have to wade in with a baseball bat and a backpack full of Nitro-9. If he's a jaded war veteran, they have to give him a fresh perspective on the universe. Even that most Doctor-ish of companions, Romana, is a young woman of a mere 140, just starting her journey, while he's the old hand who's seen it all before. The "dad" demographic aside, this is the basic reason why most *Doctor Who* companions are female; it's the most straightforward way to distinguish them from the main character.

Turlough certainly provides a contrast, both with the Doctor and his fellow companions. On a visual level, he's dressed in dark, somber shades while Tegan is colorful and the Doctor perpetually beige. Nathan-Turner also had Strickson dye his naturally blond hair to further distinguish him from Davison.[48] Where Tegan is brash and argumentative but true of heart, Turlough is accommodating but untrustworthy. Where Nyssa is sweetness and light, he's darkness and deceit. Moreover,

www.shannonsullivan.com/drwho/serials/6f.html. Among other things, it reveals that Turlough was originally meant to be trapped in the belly of a giant space whale rather than an English public school. He would probably have preferred the whale.

46 Proverbially, scantily clad companions such as Leela and Peri were intended to hold the interest of the adult male audience. Whether the dads of the 1980s were actually into leotards and matching shorts remains under-researched.

47 According to interviews with Mark Strickson (for example, with the Doctor Who Fanclub of New Zealand, handily available at doctorwho.org.nz/archive/tsv21/markstrickson.html), the production crew kept getting letters pointing out that the female companions were always showing off their legs, and demanding some equality. John Nathan-Turner finally persuaded Strickson to get his trousers off by arranging for Turlough to go swimming in his last story.

48 After originally suggesting he play the part bald. Fortunately, Strickson demanded more money to shave his head and make-up designer Sheelagh Wells found another solution. Strickson's pillowcases suffered for his art.

Turlough's reactions to danger are generally far more realistic than the Doctor's. Even by his high personal standards, courage seems to come easily to his fifth incarnation. Turlough is certainly capable of heroism, but it's not something he seeks out.

The Doctor is an idealist, always searching for a better way – even if the fifth Doctor is not lucky enough to find one, especially in Season Twenty-One. Often he's positioned as the only decent man in a dark universe, although with Nyssa and Tegan around, he's not the only person with a strong moral compass. Turlough, however, initially allies himself with the Black Guardian, and is always ready to do whatever it takes to save his own skin. While he's not eager to harm others, Turlough is generally careful to preserve his own life first. The heroics of his fellow travelers exasperate him. "What is it about Earth people that makes them think that a futile gesture is a noble one?" he asks rhetorically in *Warriors of the Deep*. For all the darkness that surrounds the TARDIS during this era, Turlough is the only series regular who represents the narrative universe's increasing cynicism.

He refers to himself as a coward more than once, but underlying that is a grim pragmatism. He drags Tegan away when the Doctor seems to have drowned (awfully quickly – maybe people drown faster on Trion?) in *Warriors of the Deep*. Yet when the base staff shut the Doctor and Tegan in with the Myrka, he wrestles a gun away from his captors and threaten them.[49] He has no enthusiasm for heroically sacrificing himself in *Resurrection of the Daleks* when the prison-guards want to blow up the space station, and suggests killing the Dalek troops between them and the time corridor. (In the same story, unlike Tegan, he has no apparent problem with the Doctor's plan to kill Davros.) In *Planet of Fire*, he's even willing to hurt Kamelion to keep his past a secret from the Doctor. Where the Doctor currently has a pleasant, open face seems unusually straightforward and Tegan is mouthy and brash, Turlough has a "mind like a corkscrew." Captain Wrack has trouble reading Turlough's mind because he's so devious, and the Doctor also notes that he can never tell what this particular companion is thinking. His enigmatic background and shifting allegiances only serve to make him more ambiguous.

Turlough's other job is to add dry humor to the proceedings. Davison's Doctor has a reputation for being "the nice one," which is not

---

49 Despite holding the rank of Junior Ensign Commander in the Trion army, he seems semi-competent at best, which makes one wonder if he's ever held a gun before. On the other hand, he's hardly the only soldier in *Doctor Who* history to point a laser rifle at his allies and his own face.

entirely justified – he can be surprisingly snarky, especially on audio – but unlike the Doctor, Turlough has no compunction about unleashing the full strength of his sarcasm even at dark moments. (Susan in *The Five Doctors*: "What are we going to do now?" Turlough: "Die, it seems.") Turlough can say the things the Doctor can't, and he's more frightened of monsters and better focused on staying alive. In an era where it was unthinkable for the Doctor to be presented as a sex symbol, Turlough can wear tiny shorts.

# # #

By the time he leaves, Turlough has learned from the Doctor and become a little more like him. In *Planet of Fire*, he's still hiding his past, but he saves Peri from drowning, helps rescue the people of Sarn and ultimately returns home – the Doctor believes – "a bit of a hero." From the Doctor's point of view, his decision to keep Turlough around so he'd become a better person by association seems to have paid off. Turlough even gets to star in his own novel and save two planets in *Turlough and the Earthlink Dilemma* (1986). His character and back-story have also been further explored in Big Finish audios such as *Kiss of Death*.[50]

While it's impossible to fault Mark Strickson for moving on because he felt the part was underwritten and going nowhere (he was hardly the first or last companion-actor to do so), there's a lot that does work about Turlough. His contradictions and unexplored facets give his character texture. Moreover, his natural cowardice and dubious ethics make his moments of heroism stand out all the more. It would hardly be worth noticing if Nyssa refused Enlightenment or the Doctor pulled somebody out of the ocean (unless he took off his stripey trousers before diving in). When Tegan marches into the Tractator tunnels on Frontios without a second thought, it's what we expect of her. When Turlough does it, it's hard not to cheer.

In an era where character development was still an afterthought, Turlough managed to have a character arc almost by accident. From an audience point of view, he's engaging precisely because he's so flawed – and never likely to be mistaken for the Doctor.

---

50 If they're in need of ideas, Nick Briggs should totally call me.

Amy's Choice: *Doctor Who* Companions and the Nightmare of Domesticity

Una McCormack is a creative writing lecturer and a *New York Times* best-selling author. She has written two *Doctor Who* novels featuring the eleventh Doctor for BBC Books: *The King's Dragon* and *The Way through the Woods*. Her *Doctor Who* short fiction and journalism have been published in *Doctor Who Magazine*, and her audio dramas *Gallifrey: Evolution*, *Bernice Summerfield: Good Night, Sweet Ladies* and *Doctor Who: An Eye for Murder* have been produced by Big Finish. She lives in Cambridge with her partner, Matthew, and their daughter, Verity.

What's a Girl to Do?

I want to read (and watch) stories about girls – real girls – growing, learning, living, loving, grieving, finding their own way in the world through their wits, intelligence, and, yes, charm. You can find them in novels (particularly in children's and young adult novels), but when it comes to film and television, such stories are in short supply. Stories about girls are, in the main, stories about service: facilitating the adventures of other people. They trace the trajectory from girlhood to inevitable marriage and motherhood – perhaps with variations on the theme, but the same theme nonetheless. Eventually a girl must put away her childish dreams and come home. Inevitably, the story ends with the wedding. The door to adventure closes behind her, back in the domestic space, and the adventure continues elsewhere – without her.

The late Joanna Russ, in her essay "What Can a Heroine Do?," examines the paucity of stories for women and girls. What myths, she asks, what plots and actions are available to a woman protagonist? Her answer is "Very few":

"The tone may range from grave to gay, from the tragedy of *Anna Karenina* to the comedy of *Emma*, but the myth is always the same: innumerable versions of Falling In Love, on courtship, on marriage, on the failure of courtship and marriage. How She Got Married. How She Did Not Get Married (always tragic). How She Fell In Love and Committed Adultery. How She Saved Her Marriage But Just Barely. How She Loved a Vile Seducer And Eloped. How She Loved a Vile Seducer, Eloped, And Died in Childbirth [p. 84]."

The space is domestic: the woman exists in relationship to the protagonist – who is male. So what, Russ asks, can a girl do? What can a heroine do? What space is there for her in narrative to grow, to learn, to find her own way in the world on her own terms?

The role of companion in *Doctor Who* is ancillary, in the fullest sense of the word: she is there to be the handmaiden to the Time Lord, to ask him questions, to facilitate his adventure. She does not, on the whole, have these adventures on her own terms. It seems (if the debates during the run-up to the casting of the twelfth Doctor were anything to go by) that many people still have a long way to come before they are able even to imagine a woman as the kingpin of the narrative of *Doctor Who*.

So what's a (*Doctor Who*) girl to do? What *can* she do?

No Place Like Home
The private and domestic space is necessarily an ambivalent place in *Doctor Who*. Since the 1960s, the program has been in the business of serving up small slices of nightmare to the nation's children in the comfort of their own homes. Many have their own particular memory of something that gave them a scare and a sleepless night, whether Daleks, Cybermen or Monoids; giant robots, giant ants, giant maggots, giant spiders and, of course, giant Bertie Bassetts. Week after week, on a Saturday night, the show led us through the uncanny valley that lay between the football results and *The Generation Game*.

The storytelling too replicates – or, at least, tried to echo – something of the nature of dream: chases, relentless pursuit down endless corridors, implacable enemies immune to reason or the power of argument. Week after week, year after year, companions walked through the door of the TARDIS and were transported to worlds containing multiple horrors, terrors and fears. They traveled with a sense of wonder, but also in the hope that they would one day return safely home – to London of the 1960s, Croydon of the 1970s or even Heathrow of the 1980s.

The new series has once again successfully delivered up nightmares old and new – dusting down the Daleks and the Cybermen, and giving us new monsters such as Weeping Angels who can send you to the past in the blink of an eye, or gas-masked children who demand to know again and again, "Are you my mummy?" The storytelling has remained broadly familiar: the chases and pursuits, the running down corridors and countdowns to disaster. And the home has explicitly become the site of nightmare in episodes such as *Night Terrors* and *Closing Time*: the events of which notably unfold when the mother isn't there.

There's also been a new dimension to the storytelling. *Doctor Who*, since its revival, has focused more than ever before on the home life of the Doctor's companions. These days, when you enter the TARDIS, the relatives follow close behind you – mothers, fathers, brothers, sisters, grandfathers and boyfriends. For many, this has brought the program perilously close to soap, burdening the narrative with emotional "journeys" at the expense of the rational problem-solving that is, presumably, more "properly" the subject matter of science fiction.

For me, this extra narrative dimension has given us some of the show's most memorable characters and poignant storylines: the redoubtable Jackie Tyler, reunited beyond death with her beloved husband Pete; Rory's dad Brian, waiting at home and watering the plants, hoping to hear from his lost son and daughter-in-law, gone forever in the past; or Donna's granddad Wilfred Mott, for whom the tenth Doctor gives up his life. More significantly, the interruption of the private, domestic sphere into what had previously been the Doctor's playground has radical potential. The personal, after all, is political, and bringing the domestic into play is precisely what could enable the boundary between public and private spheres to be dissolved. Whatever we may fantasize, home life – the feminine sphere – exists, supporting dilettante adventurers or career-minded young people in their endeavors, no matter how much we might try to wish it away, or pretend it isn't there. Opening up this space alongside the space where the Doctor travels could well be a radical move: recognition that adventure doesn't really take place in a vacuum or a vortex. It is dependent upon quieter, private spaces.

Always the Bridesmaid, Always the Bride

In general, however, this promise hasn't been delivered upon. These close relationships are exactly what the new companions are trying to escape. Again and again, the revived show gives us a vision of the domestic which emphasizes its deadly qualities: the boredom of day-to-day life, of having to get up and go out to work, of evenings spent slumped in front of the television in the company of nagging parents and unsatisfactory boyfriends. Rose Tyler sprints away from the Powell estate and a lifetime of chips and poorly paid employment to go adventuring in the TARDIS. Donna Noble meets the Doctor during her wedding from hell and the events of that day fill her with a wanderlust that's only satisfied when she too goes traveling with the Doctor.

With both of these companions, we're left in no doubt that, given the choice, being with the Doctor in the TARDIS is what they would happily do for the rest of their lives. Who wouldn't, after all, want to spend a lifetime running down corridors, being chased by monsters, and bringing down totalitarian regimes? That choice, however, turns out not to be theirs to make. Because, ultimately, the Doctor has different ideas – and both of these companions are, in the end, put back in the box. They're sent home. Rose is dispatched to another dimension with all her family and the unsatisfactory boyfriend. And in one of the cruelest ends for a fictional character I've ever seen, Donna has all memory of her life-enhancing experiences with the Doctor removed in order to save her life. The last we see of Donna is, inevitably, back in her wedding dress, nagging her family – back where she started. We see a foreshadowing of these narrative trajectories in *School Reunion*, when Sarah Jane Smith tells us about the hole left when the Doctor departed and the adventure went away.[51]

By setting up this narrative tension between the nightmare of domesticity and the dream of escape to a more fulfilling life, the program is likely to deliver some very ambivalent endings for its female characters. Adventure is something you can do for a while, it seems to say, but then – inevitably, relentlessly – the wedding day will arrive, after which it's best to put these things out of your mind, or else the pain of remembering this life without limits might kill you.

The Girl Who Wanted Everything – and Got It

All of this is what makes Amelia Pond so refreshing. Like Donna, we meet Amy as she's about to embark on married life. Amy goes into the TARDIS the night before her wedding day, leaving the white dress hanging on the back of her bedroom door. The choice between childhood dreams of escape and the adult world of domesticity is specifically dramatized in *Amy's Choice*, in which the mysterious Dream Lord asks a

---

51 Martha Jones is a slightly different case, in that although she too initially runs into the TARDIS to escape from the mess her parents are making of their divorce, ultimately she chooses to go home. But as her name implies, she too is a handmaiden, the disciple to the Doctor's Messiah, traveling the world to preach the good news about him. She serves her purpose in the Doctor's story – and then leaves.

heavily pregnant Amy to choose between two potential ways of being: a wandering life with the Doctor so dangerous it will kill you, or a settled life with Rory so boring it sends you to sleep in seconds. Amy is given a choice between two irreconcilable nightmares. When Rory is killed (only ever a temporary state for Rory), Amy – rather than choosing one of these – instead rejects life without Rory, thereby waking from her dream and keeping her options open for a while longer. This choice – anywhere as long as Rory's there, with the Doctor as a bonus – is one that we see repeated again and again.

The wedding, moreover, is emphatically not the end of Amy's story – Amy does indeed marry Rory in *The Big Bang*, but immediately drags him after her into the TARDIS to carry on adventuring. Summoning the Doctor – her childhood friend, the symbol of her desires for freedom and adventure – to her wedding reception is a most Amy-like refusal to obey cultural injunctions to put away childish things and settle down. Amy intends to have it all, and the Ponds' domestic life is shown to carry on alongside their adventures – home for a while, then the Doctor turns up and takes them away, bringing them back to the same party months after they slipped off.

Their marriage and, more importantly, their family life is set not in opposition to life with the Doctor, but is crucially shaped by their interaction with him. Their daughter, Melody, becomes the Doctor's wife – the Doctor is their son-in-law. From the devastation of the events of *A Good Man Goes to War*, they somehow construct a loving form of family life with the daughter (first, unknowingly, as Mels, and later with River herself, drinking wine in the garden with her mum in *The Wedding of River Song*). They recommit after a break-up arising from grief over the loss of their child (and the loss of future children), and, later, they adopt – and send their son to Brian, his grandfather, to pass on the message that they lived happily and well.

Within the marriage itself, Amy seems to dominate. But Rory is a condition of her existence: he steadily supports her through numerous careers – as model, as writer, as adventurer in time and space – and this holds true whatever the timeline. Amy remains consistent across the multiverse: fierce, loyal and the boss of Rory – but always his essential other half, as we see most heartbreakingly in *The Girl Who Waited*, and most speedily in the courtship of Sergeant Rory in *The Wedding of River Song*.

So we are always waiting for Amy to have to make her choice: husband and home, or Doctor and the unknown. When the resolution does come, it's pleasingly complicated. Trapped by the Weeping Angels, Rory is zapped back to the 1930s, getting stuck in a time zone which (for plot reasons) the Doctor is unable to visit. So what will Amy choose?

As we've been told multiple times, Amy will always choose to be with Rory – but she doesn't step back into quiet domesticity. Instead, she steps into an unknown world and an uncertain future. Yes, she might be following her husband where he's gone, but not back home. Even more, she's bringing adventure with her. Far from being essential to Amy living life to the full, the Doctor, it turns out, was always an optional extra, a supporting character – a companion, even – in the story of Amy's life.

The Doctor, the husband, the home life, the career, the adventure – Amy Pond gets them all, but, crucially, that adventure doesn't end when the Doctor leaves. Unlike Rose, unlike Donna – we don't see a female companion returned to the domestic space while events carry on without her. Life with Amy Pond – and life as Amy Pond – is an exciting adventure in and of itself. What's a girl to do? Whatever she wants.

References

Russ, J. (1995) "What Can a Heroine Do? or Why Women Can't Write" in *To Write Like a Woman: Essays in Feminism and Science Fiction.* Bloomington: Indiana University Press.

The Ones He Leaves Behind

Foz Meadows is the author of *Solace & Grief* and *The Key to Starveldt*, the first two books of a YA urban fantasy series published by Ford Street. She is a contributing writer for *The Huffington Post* and *Black Gate*, and a contributing reviewer for *A Dribble of Ink* and *Strange Horizons*; her poetry has appeared in *Goblin Fruit*, and she also keeps her own blog, *Shattersnipe*. Foz describes herself as a bipedal mammal with delusions of immortality. Though Australian, she currently lives in the UK with not enough books, her very own philosopher and a Smallrus. Surprisingly, this is a good thing.

"The Doctor likes traveling with an entourage. Sometimes they're human, sometimes they're aliens and sometimes they're tin dogs."

—Sarah Jane Smith, *School Reunion*

"I said I would never leave you
but come on.
What are you, new?"

—*A Softer World*, 264

When I was 11 years old, my father – a man with no interest in science fiction or fantasy, but who nonetheless made an effort to support my love of it – presented me with several *Doctor Who* novelizations he'd picked up at a book sale. It was the first time I'd ever heard of the series and, in all honesty, I was intimidated by it. The books had black covers emblazoned with the faces of various frowning old men; everything about the presentation suggested seriousness and, as my father's only knowledge of the show was that it involved space travel (and hence was something I might like), I set the books aside, unread, and eventually got rid of them – and so missed out on getting into *Doctor Who* as a child. Almost a decade later, using the series reboot as my entry point, I found myself falling in love with the sheer unbridled potential of the Doctor and the TARDIS (to say nothing of David Tennant's gravity-defying hair). But in an ongoing adventure story that's otherwise about the joys of gallivanting madly through the universe, it's the companions who serve as the show's emotional core – not only because they keep the

Doctor company, but because they anchor an otherwise untethered nomad to some semblance of everyday life.

Since 2005, we've seen many companions come and go: women and men whose lives have been fundamentally altered by their relationship with the last of the Time Lords, and whose actions have invariably helped to save the universe (or at least some corner of it) from destruction. Yet for every adventurer who's lived aboard the TARDIS, there are more who never make it that far: the ones who accompany the Doctor only briefly. As much as any companion arc, it's these stories which cut to the heart of what companionship means to the show's creators, and thus to the show itself: the question of who goes on to have adventures with the Doctor, and who he leaves behind.

First, however, we need to establish a few key terms. Though many characters *help* the Doctor in various ways, that's not the same as *traveling* with him, which is here defined as taking at least one trip on the TARDIS away from their home time or planet while in his company. By this definition, neither Jackie Tyler's accidental arrival at Torchwood headquarters in *Army of Ghosts* nor her return home in *Journey's End* count, with Ida Scott in *The Satan Pit* and Adelaide Brooks in *The Waters of Mars* excluded for much the same reasons.

Similarly, it's important to establish what we mean by companionship, as the term applies in varying degrees to different characters. I'll be using the following gradated definitions:

- *Primary companion:* A protagonist who travels with the Doctor for a majority of episodes across one or more seasons.
- *Secondary companion:* A recurring character who travels with the Doctor for a minority of episodes across one or more seasons, and who otherwise spends their time elsewhere.
- *Fleeting companion:* A character who, regardless of any other appearances, only travels with the Doctor once, or whose multiple trips in the TARDIS are only shown or inferred in a single episode.
- *Potential companion:* A character who is either implied to be companion material or openly invited to travel with the Doctor, but who never actually does so.
- *Peripheral companion:* A recurring character who never actually travels with the Doctor in the sense defined above, but who nonetheless plays an active role in his adventures.

Though not absolute, these categories are nonetheless useful for breaking down companion relationships. As such, I've applied them to specific characters as follows:

Character Type: Name (first appearance)
Primary: Rose Tyler (X1.1, *Rose*)
Primary: Martha Jones (X3.1, *Smith and Jones*)
Primary: Donna Noble (X3.0, *The Runaway Bride*)
Primary: Amy Pond (X5.1, *The Eleventh Hour*)
Primary: Rory Williams (X5.1, *The Eleventh Hour*)
Primary: Clara Oswald/Prime (X7.7, *The Bells of Saint John*)
Secondary: Mickey Smith (X1.1, *Rose*)
Secondary: Captain Jack Harkness (X1.9, *The Empty Child*)
Secondary: River Song (X4.8, *Silence in the Library*)
Secondary: Madame Vastra (X6.7, *A Good Man Goes to War*)
Secondary: Jenny Flint (X6.7, *A Good Man Goes to War*)
Secondary: Strax (X6.7, *A Good Man Goes to War*)
Fleeting: Adam Mitchell (X1.6, *Dalek*)
Fleeting: Abigail Pettigrew (X6.0, *A Christmas Carol*)
Fleeting: Kazran (X6.0, *A Christmas Carol*)
Fleeting: Brian Williams (X7.2, *Dinosaurs on a Spaceship*)
Fleeting: John Riddell (X7.2, *Dinosaurs on a Spaceship*)
Fleeting: Nefertiti (X7.2, *Dinosaurs on a Spaceship*)
Fleeting: Angie Maitland (X7.7, *The Bells of Saint John*)
Fleeting: Artie Maitland (X7.7, *The Bells of Saint John*)
Potential: Lynda Moss (X1.12, *Bad Wolf*)
Potential: Reinette, Madame de Pompadour (X2.4, *The Girl in the Fireplace*)
Potential: Astrid Perth (X4.0, *Voyage of the Damned*)
Potential: Jenny (X4.6, *The Doctor's Daughter*)
Potential: Lady Christina de Souza (X4.15, *Planet of the Dead*)
Potential: Rita (X6.11, *The God Complex*)
Potential: Clara Oswin Oswald/Future (X7.1, *Asylum of the Daleks*)
Potential: Clara Oswin Oswald/Victorian (X7.6, *The Snowmen*)
Peripheral: Jackie Tyler (X1.1, *Rose*)
Peripheral: Harriet Jones (X1.4, *Aliens of London*)
Peripheral: Wilfred Mott (X4.0, *Voyage of the Damned*)
Peripheral: Craig Owens (X5.11, *The Lodger*)
Peripheral: Madge Arwell (X7.0, *The Doctor, the Widow and the Wardrobe*)

Peripheral: Lily Arwell (X7.0, *The Doctor, the Widow and the Wardrobe*)

Peripheral: Cyril Arwell (X7.0, *The Doctor, the Widow and the Wardrobe*)

It should be noted, however, that this isn't a complete list of characters. In aid of brevity, I've omitted many who fall into the peripheral category – specifically, most of the family members of primary companions, with the exception of Jackie Tyler and Wilfred Mott, who have the biggest role in events – along with Sarah Jane Smith and K-9, on the grounds that they predate the reboot. Madge Arwell and her children are counted as peripheral rather than fleeting companions, as they never actually travel in the TARDIS, instead leaving Earth by other means. And despite the revelation of Clara's multiple echo-identities in *The Name of the Doctor*, I've elected to treat each of her iterations as a separate character, named according to their origins: not only because each version has a separate birth, background and history, but because none of them realize they're the same person.

Otherwise, I've been as accurate as possible – and in a list that's otherwise close to having gender parity, it's glaring to note that all the potential companions are female: not because there's anything wrong with female characters, but because all but two of them end up dying (and even then, Jenny is only left behind in *The Doctor's Daughter* because the Doctor *thinks* she's dead). Straight away, that raises alarm bells: why so many dead women? What distinguishes them from the fleeting and secondary female companions? The answer is troubling: overwhelmingly, the women who died were either single or romantically linked with the Doctor; the others, with one exception, are not.

Lest this seem like an oversimplification, it's worth examining the issue in greater detail. Of the eight potential companions, the only ones not depicted as flirting with the Doctor are Jenny and Rita; Jenny because she's his daughter, and Rita (one sadly suspects) because she's a woman of color. Of the female fleeting companions, Abigail is spoken for, Angie is a child, and Nefertiti, apart from being portrayed as a sexually aggressive WOC whose advances the Doctor actively rejects, ends up with John Riddell. Of the female secondary companions, Madame Vastra and Jenny Flint are in a committed relationship with each other, while River continues the pattern by being, despite her continued appearances, dead. Lady Christina is the only exception: she flirts with the Doctor (though crucially, he doesn't reciprocate), but though she asks to travel with him, he refuses to take her on.

What this all amounts to, then, is an alarmingly high incidence of women in refrigerators – ladies whose deaths are orchestrated for the specific narrative purpose of developing the emotional arc of male characters. Which isn't to say that these characters represent the only casualties of the reboot; far from it. *Doctor Who* is a show where people die more or less constantly, and being a compassionate, life-saving soul, the Doctor tends to feel badly about it. But with the exception of Lynda Moss, who dies in battle in *The Parting of the Ways*, all these women – including Jenny, who doesn't really die; and River, who returns despite being dead – are subsequently eulogized in a way that other characters, and particularly male characters, rarely (if ever) are.

Just as important, however, are the implications this pattern has for our wider question of who becomes a companion, and why – or why not, as the case may be. Because it's not just the fact that most of the potential companions die that's important – it's the fact that, by implication, *every male character able to become a companion does so.* For instance: though the Doctor takes an initial dislike to (or at least, engages in constant mockery of) Mickey and Rory, their respective relationships with Rose and Amy ensure them a tour of the universe. Both Jackie Tyler and Rory's father Brian end up aboard the TARDIS by accident, but only Brian gets to have a real adventure; Jackie just gets told to stay away from the TARDIS controls. (The fact that Rose, Martha and Donna all have absent fathers and nagging, excoriating mothers who want them home is a different problem in and of itself.) In short, and despite the fact that the majority of companions are female, there's nonetheless a very real sense in which their ultimate fate is determined by gender.

Speaking in a May 2012 interview with *Doctor Who Magazine*[52], Steven Moffat had this to say on the subject of the Doctor's companions:

> "...you are always going to have the same sort of person, just because it's the same man choosing them, and it's the same person being chosen.
>
> I think the function of a companion is pretty simple. I don't think that's very difficult. It's just a question of who credibly is going to agree to go in the TARDIS? Who's going to do it? Is it going to be a mother of 15 children? No. Is it going to be someone in their 60s? No. Is there going to be a particular age range? I mean... who's going to have a crush on the Doctor? You know, come on! It's more than a format. It's evolved from good, dramatic reasons."

52 www.geekosystem.com/steve-moffat-doctor-who-companions-attractive-girls/

This is, to say the least, an extremely limiting notion of companionship. The idea that someone is automatically excluded on the basis of being too old is problematic even before you consider William Hartnell's age while playing the first Doctor in classic *Who*, to say nothing of the fact that Rory Williams is technically (until the very end of Matt Smith's run) older than the Doctor himself. What Moffat really means here, it seems, is that a companion should be *physically* young, regardless of their actual age – and when you tie that to the very strong implication that a companion ought to have a crush on the Doctor, then the overwhelming heteronormativity of popular television means you're pretty much restricting yourself to young women. (Captain Jack's love of the Doctor is a rare exception to the rule.) As a consequence of this mindset, our primary companions thus far have been six young, attractive people, five of them women, who've more or less abandoned their lives, jobs, friends and family to go traveling with the Doctor – and while the totality of space and time is certainly an alluring prospect, it's striking how all of these companions have ties to the world, rather than being either rootless or actively looking to escape their daily lives.

By contrast, however, the opposite is overwhelmingly true of his *potential* companions. Of the eight we've seen, only three have had strong personal ties to home and normalcy – Rita, who was a doctor; Victorian Clara, who was a nanny; and Madame de Pompadour, who was a king's mistress – while the other five were wholly unfettered and ready to travel: Lynda and Astrid Peth both explicitly stated they had no family to keep them anywhere; Jenny (the Doctor's daughter, not Madame Vastra's partner) was newly-created and thus had nothing else to do; while Future Clara and Lady Christina both specifically asked to join the Doctor. Arguably, there's a benign reason for this schism: companions with homes and families have more narrative potential, thereby providing the writers with extra backstory details they can work into the plot. But while that's certainly a relevant consideration, it's not the full story. Above and beyond their differences in personal circumstance, the most crucial distinction between the primary companions and their potential counterparts is *destiny* – or, to put it more bluntly, a contrived specialness above and beyond their value as a person.

Rose is the Bad Wolf, influencing time and space to save humanity. Donna is inextricably bound to the Doctor, becoming part Time Lord herself. Amy and Rory are River Song's parents. Clara is scattered throughout the Doctor's timeline for the express purpose of saving him, over and over, from the predations of the Great Intelligence. Of the primary companions, in fact, only Martha is truly someone he's met at random, which arguably makes her actions in saving the world all the more praiseworthy: unlike the others, her specialness is derived through skill and hard work, not necessitated by the backwards-traveling impetus of her future importance. (Martha, in fact, is the exception in many cases – sometimes positively, sometimes not – and whether that was ultimately an intentional decision or an accident, it's not irrelevant that the only primary companion whose specialness has to be *earned*, rather than being seen as innate, inevitable or a mystery to be solved, is a woman of color.)

Like Martha, then, the potential companions lack a preordained destiny; but whereas Martha is given a chance to prove herself (*prove* being the operative word; the Doctor treats her more brusquely than he does his other primaries, partly because he's resentful of the idea that she might replace Rose, but mostly, I suspect, because of subconscious bias on the part of the writers), the potentials are not. Instead, they die: two in acts of self-sacrifice, one of natural causes and the rest at the hands of monsters. And once again, I'm forced to the inevitable conclusion that there's an awful, inherent gendering to how the Doctor's companions are treated – not just the potentials, but *all* of them. Because not only do we have a situation where *only female companions die*, but with the sole exception of Rory, who ends up living out a happy life with Amy in old New York – which, while a comparatively pleasant fate, is nonetheless billed as a Traumatic Exit – all the men get to live *on their own terms* once they've left the Doctor. Mickey marries Martha. Captain Jack has a separate show's worth of solo adventures. Strax reappears in Victorian England, his death at Demon's Run in *A Good Man Goes to War* evidently having been temporary (though otherwise, it counts as the only male companion death of the lot). Kazran lives a wealthy, powerful life, and lives to see his beloved Abigail again. Adam Mitchell is returned to his family, as are Brian and Wilf. John Riddell shacks up with Nefertiti, Artie and his sister Angie go home again, and Craig (*The Lodger*) gets married and has a child.

But for the women, it's a different story entirely. Which isn't to say that none of them get a happily ever after or a stab at normalcy – some clearly do. It's just that they have to suffer more hardship first, like Rose waiting years in her parallel world before being paired with her human-Doctor, or Donna's entire memory of her travels being wiped clean before she settles down, or Martha's whole family being tortured and traumatised before she marries Mickey, or Amy losing both her daughter and her fertility before finally living with Rory, and do you see the pattern, here? That lasting happiness for the Doctor's female companions seems to be inextricably tied to their being married or in a relationship? Madame Vastra and Jenny Flint are married to each other, true – they're almost my favorite things about the reboot – but that's still two more female characters whose happiness derives from wedded bliss. Madge Arwell derives her strength from marriage and motherhood, for which she's rewarded with her husband's return from the dead. Despite their originally tempestuous relationship, Jackie Tyler happily reunites with the parallel-world version of her husband, Pete, and has another baby. More incongruously still, Nefertiti, a powerful queen of Egypt, has evidently elected to give up her power, prestige and dynasty – whether permanently or temporarily, it's not clear – to go and live with a white imperialist hunter in an era where both her race and sex are guaranteed to make her the subject of oppression and bigotry, while Abigail's impending death (which the Doctor never tries to avert) is glossed over by her supposed joy at getting to spend her last day with a much-aged Kazran. Even River's big moment in her only eponymous episode was marrying the Doctor.

But for everyone else, it's a different story. While Lady Christina and Jenny the pseudo-Time Lord both shanghai futuristic vehicles – a flying bus and a rocket ship, respectively – and go on to have further adventures, as do Madame Vastra and Jenny, the other potential companions all die: Harriet Jones dies, River Song dies, and Abigail is left with only a day to live. Angie and Lily, like Artie and Cyril, only escape on account of their youth, while Clara-Prime's story is yet ongoing; and even then, the implication is that her other various, unseen echoes have all been dying for over a thousand years, each one felled in pursuit of saving the Doctor. This latter revelation in particular sits uncomfortably close to River Song's decision in *Let's Kill Hitler* to give up all her future regenerations, thereby saving the Doctor's life but effectively dooming herself. With precious few exceptions, therefore, we're left with a situation where female companions have a choice between death or marriage once the Doctor's gone, while his male companions go on to do – well, pretty much anything they want.

Obviously, there's nothing wrong with marriage, relationships or romance, and I'm certainly not contending that there's something fundamentally wrong with seeing female companions (or any companions, for that matter) get paired off. It's just that, over and over again, we're being presented with the idea that romance is integral to female happiness in a way that it isn't for men. Which isn't to say that none of the male companions ever get the girl, either – several of them do. But narratively, there's something rather skewed about these relationships. Take Martha and Mickey's marriage, for instance, which we witness in *The End of Time, Part Two*. The last time we saw Martha, she was engaged to a white doctor, Thomas Milligan, whom she originally met in *Last of the Time Lords*. Clearly, marriage to *someone* was always intended as part of her happily ever after – but how she comes to end up with Mickey is neither shown nor explained. Instead, we're left with the abiding impression that it doesn't matter who Martha marries, so long as she has a husband; and given the fact that Mickey lost Rose to the Doctor, I can't help but feel that he's being *rewarded* with Martha, given that she was otherwise set to marry someone else.

And then there's Amy and Rory, whose eventual marriage and commitment to each other is rather severely undermined by the fact that, for the vast majority of Series Five, Amy's love of the Doctor was openly romantic rather than platonic. For all that we come to believe in her relationship with Rory eventually, the early love-triangle is never actually addressed; and is, indeed, actively referenced at the start of *A Good Man Goes to War*, where Amy's speech about Melody's father is deliberately structured to suggest, at least initially, that he might be the Doctor. We see how Amy comes to accept Rory as her one and only, but not how, why or when she stops loving the Doctor; and with the specter of Mickey hanging over the show – that is, with one previous boyfriend of a female primary having already been supplanted by the Doctor – it once more feels as though Amy, on some fundamental level, is Rory's reward, and a sort of cosmic apology for Mickey's original loss. Similarly, and for all the potential of her first appearance, River Song's love of the Doctor, while something we're constantly *told* about, is never really *shown*. When Mels regenerates into River in *Let's Kill Hitler*, from her perspective, it's the first time she's met the Doctor: before then, she's spent her whole life training to kill him. She is, to quote the episode, a *"bespoke psychopath"* – yet somehow, when the Doctor starts calling her River, it's enough to overcome all her vicious conditioning and make her switch sides.

Which makes the chronology of their romance somewhat bizarre: after the events of *Hitler*, River goes off to study archaeology – a period during which she doesn't see the Doctor; or at least, that's the inference, given that her every other appearance seems to come after her arrest and imprisonment – and is then taken directly to Lake Silencio, where

Madame Kovarian forces her to shoot the Doctor. And if that's the case, then we're left with a situation where their marriage in *The Wedding of River Song* actually *predates* their earlier adventures together: meaning, in other words, that River's deep, passionate love for the Doctor comes from little more than their violent encounter in *Let's Kill Hitler*. And that bothers me: not only because it's bad writing, but because it means that, whereas the Doctor marries River in full knowledge of who and what she is, after many tempestuous and passionate meetings, all the events which inform his commitment still lie in her future: she loves him because the story demands that she love him, regardless of what her experiences actually suggest.

Finally, there's Craig, John Riddell and Kazran, all of whom get the girl for seemingly no better reason than that they want her. Craig's relationship is the most realistic of all, not only because he has a long history with his partner, but because she already cares for him, too. By contrast, Abigail's saccharine (and to me, deeply implausible) relationship with Kazran is the product of an idiot plot: despite her yearly adventures in the TARDIS, we're lead to believe that the question of her illness or the number of days she has left doesn't come up *even once*, as a result of which, the Doctor – who has access to all the medical marvels of time and space – makes no effort to cure her; while saintly Abigail, awoken for a final time to find that her youthful, hopeful Kazran has turned into a cruel old man, displays not the slightest trace of either disappointment, bitterness or hesitance. Once again, she loves him because the plot requires her to love him, and so they have their final day together. Which just leaves John Riddell and Queen Nefertiti, and the utter strangeness of her decision to come and live with him in age of rampant imperialism. It would've been just as easy to show them having adventures elsewhere in the universe, or for Riddell to have traveled to ancient Egypt. But instead, Nefertiti comes to his time and place, abandoning her crown to live in an age of racism, sexism and brutal colonialism. In this instance, it's Riddell who gets the girl – not Nefertiti who gets the boy.

So why does the reboot have these problems? Sad to say, I think one of the major reasons is the overwhelming straight-white-cismaleness of the current writing team. In the seven years the reboot has been active, only one of the credited writers has been female: Helen Raynor, who wrote *Daleks in Manhattan* / *The Evolution of the Daleks*, and *The Sontaran Stratagem* / *The Poison Sky* – and *that's it*. In a series that's currently over a hundred episodes long, only four have been written by a woman, and none have been written by a person of color. Throw in Steven Moffat's well-known refusal to countenance even the possibility of problematic elements in the show – though he did admit to the lack of queer characters in Series Five and make some effort to fix it[53], he's remained impervious to the suggestion that his offhand, "cheeky" portrayals of same can be read as disrespectful queerbaiting – and is it any wonder that there are problems?

Eventually, the Doctor leaves everyone behind – not just his potential companions, but all the others whose journeys with him are over. Though his male companions go on to have lives of their own, sometimes being rewarded with female affection, but mostly just continuing their own personal adventures, the women who travel with him tend either to die in furtherance of the Doctor's emotional development, or else to find a very specific happiness in matrimony. And though I (mostly) love the show, it's the characters who break this pattern – the Doctor's daughter, Lady Christina, Jenny Flint and Madame Vastra – who I find myself most wanting to see again. Though classic *Who* has its own set of problems, it nonetheless contained a variety of female companions whose departures were marked by neither death nor marriage, and who didn't pine for the Doctor in the interim. Instead, they simply traveled with him – and it saddens me that, for all its snappy scripting, emotional moments, special effects and memorable adventures, this is one aspect of the new series where our current obsession with unresolved sexual tension and romantic entanglements has lead, not to a reboot of companionship, but its regression.

---

53   www.thebacklot.com/doctor-who-show-runner-steven-moffat-its-the-one-criticism-ive-ever-listened-to/08/2011/

Companion Piece

Science Princess FTW

Mary Robinette Kowal is the author of *Shades of Milk and Honey, Glamour in Glass* and *Without a Summer*. In 2008, she won the Campbell Award for Best New Writer, and in 2011, her short story "For Want of a Nail" won the Hugo Award for Short Story. Her work has been a finalist for the Hugo, Nebula and Locus awards. Stories have appeared in *Strange Horizons, Asimov's, Doctor Who: Destination Prague* and several Year's Best anthologies, as well as in her collection *Scenting the Dark and Other Stories* from Subterranean. A professional puppeteer and voice actor, Mary has performed for LazyTown (CBS), the Center for Puppetry Arts, Jim Henson Pictures and founded Other Hand Productions. Her designs have garnered two UNIMA-USA Citations of Excellence, the highest award an American puppeteer can achieve. She also records fiction for authors such as Seanan McGuire, Cory Doctorow and John Scalzi. Mary lives in Chicago with her husband Rob and over a dozen manual typewriters – visit her at www.maryrobinettekowal.com.

My first doctor was Tom Baker. I adored him, floppy hat and long scarf and all. What I really loved, though, were the companions – and the idea that I could potentially be one someday. Of the people who traveled with him, the one that probably had the strongest connection for me was Nyssa of Traken. Purists will point out that she was an acquaintance of the fourth Doctor and didn't become a companion until he regenerated. Understood... but. But, Nyssa got me through the regeneration and gave me time to fall in love with Peter Davison.

I had been delighted when she was introduced. I went to a Magnet school in North Carolina, and all of my friends were hyperintelligent nerds. Nyssa was a hyperintelligent young woman, like my friends but with one key difference.

Nyssa liked pretty clothes. I know this appears to be a totally superficial reason to like a companion, but the fact that she had those leg o'mutton sleeves and wore them with velvet pants meant a lot to me. It meant that I could like pretty things and also kick ass. Nyssa was a pacifist, so the kicking of ass was almost entirely intellectual. (Other than that one time she blasted a Cyberman with a cybergun. Okay, there was also the time she pointed a gun at the High Council of Time Lords, but she had no intention of killing them. Maybe her pacifism is on a par with the Doctor's...) That wasn't something that was modeled in a lot in other fiction or television at the time. Sure, you had the intellectual beauties like the Bionic Woman, but in the name of empowering her, it was almost as if people were saying that anything that identified a person as feminine weakened her. When she defeated villains, it was with her bionic strength and not her brain. She wore tracksuits.

I'd grown up in a neighborhood where all the kids my age were boys. My friends tended toward the tomboy end of the spectrum. To be fair, I didn't mind that. I loved power tools, and building things, and climbing trees, but I also loved ballroom dancing and dresses with tulle. What I needed, and what Nyssa provided for me, was a role model that showed me that I could have both. It was totally okay to be smart and "girly."

I gravitated to the leg o'mutton sleeve for years because of her. I suspect, in fact, that some of my attraction to steampunk is actually a Pavlovian response to seeing those sleeves again. As I write this, it occurs to me that I could cosplay as Nyssa of Traken and slip straight from a *Doctor Who* convention to a Steampunk one without stopping to change costumes.

Let's take a moment to look at her identifying costume – although she wore others – and examine the symbolism wrapped up in it, shall we?

When we first meet Nyssa in *The Keeper of Traken*, she is the daughter of Tremas and a child of privilege. She's a princess and, in her first appearance, her clothes reflect that. The signature maroon velvet jacket is paired with a diaphanous, iridescent skirt. She has a gold coronet resting on the back of her head that identifies her as someone of status but, and this was key, she was in a garden doing *science*.

Nyssa sciences her way through the story. Always poised and thoughtful, Nyssa moves from caring for the evil Melkur as if she were in *The Secret Garden* to building the servo-shutdown device with Adric that ultimately provides the means of defeating the Master's plan. She is perhaps the first Science Princess on television, allowed to be fashionable and cute while having a fine scientific mind. (Take note, *Adventure Time!*)

Nyssa wasn't a planned companion. Created for a single story, she was brought back for behind-the-scenes reasons as the production team wanted as many familiar faces as possible when they moved to the first new Doctor in quite a long time. This creates a fascinating on-screen introduction as a companion. She doesn't stow away on the TARDIS;

she isn't invited on a whim. Instead, the Doctor realizes at some point that he *needs* her. The Watcher, a ghostly transitional form of the Doctor between two of his incarnations, goes back *to pick her up*.

Many of the Doctor's companions are orphans or have tragic backgrounds. None of them dealt with Nyssa's horrors. Her stepmother turns evil, serves the Master and dies. Not only does the Master kill her beloved father, *he inhabits her father's corpse* and goes on to taunt and hurt her. Finally, Nyssa watches her entire planet blink out of existence due to the Master's plans. She becomes the last of her people, carrying the same terrible weight that the Doctor will later experience in new series incarnations (and it could be argued that Nyssa handled it better, too).

We watch Nyssa grieve, and then she joins the Doctor to save the universe, dedicating her life to helping others. In perfectly practical Science Princess fashion, Nyssa switches to velvet pants and pretty much takes charge of things while the Doctor is out of commission after his troubled regeneration. She possesses the technical knowledge and calm demeanor necessary to bring the Doctor to Castrovalva.

Nyssa was our familiar figure (along with Adric) as we were introduced to Tegan and the fifth Doctor. The difference between her and Adric is that we trust Nyssa more as we go through the fifth Doctor's first season. I was still getting to know this gentler, tetchier, younger Doctor who seemed a million miles away from my beloved Tom Baker. Adric spends much of this season siding with the villains. Tegan complains about pretty much everything that happens to them while she obsesses about getting to Heathrow Airport to be a stewardess. Only Nyssa seems to want to be there, saving the universe and having adventures with the Doctor. She was my gateway to the new Doctor. As she trusted and liked him, so did I.

Nyssa continues to kick ass with her brain throughout the season. She builds the Doctor a zero cabinet to save his life in *Castrovalva*, disables an android with a pencil and sonic screwdriver in *Four to Doomsday* and infamously destroys a glittery android in *The Visitation* with a giant vibrator in her bedroom. She also has a chance to dance in a blue butterfly 1920s fancy dress in *Black Orchid*, along with her identically dressed double Ann Talbot. And yes, it also takes brainpower to learn how to dance from Tegan. (Adric certainly didn't manage it.)

When Adric dies, it is Nyssa's grieving that affects us most. Tegan breaks down, but Nyssa conveys more when she buries her head on Tegan's shoulders. Her grief combines with the weariness of being the last Trakenite, a person who has already lost nearly everything.

After the Doctor "accidentally" leaves Tegan behind in *Time-Flight*, Nyssa finally has an opportunity to be a solo companion. She positively shines in *Arc of Infinity*. She helps the Doctor recover from Omega's attack, holds the High Council at gunpoint in an attempt to save him from dispersal execution, and even destroys Omega's giant chicken henchman. We glimpse how wonderful these two leads could be for future stories. (Big Finish has produced numerous audio dramas with this pairing.) Then Tegan returns to the team, much to the Doctor's obvious chagrin and Nyssa's joy. Prickly though Tegan may be, she is still one of Nyssa's best friends, and Nyssa is glad to have her back.

In *Snakedance*, Nyssa begins a style transformation. Gone are the velvet pants, replaced by an... *interesting* outfit of a blue and white striped blouse, a striped skirt of many colors, red shorts and heels. She has replaced Science Princess with an outfit that is not unlike the color scheme of the future sixth Doctor. Kindness would say this foreshadows her changing role and the Doctor's future incarnation. At the very least, it foreshadows producer John Nathan-Turner's fashion "tastes." When she looks to the Doctor for approval for this external change, she finds disinterest on his part. Again, this was important to me, because it emphasized that what is important to the Doctor about Nyssa is what she does and who she is, not what she wears. She could wear whatever she wanted, even a god-awful skirt, and still be the same wonderful person. It was a sign to me that I could try on different outward appearances as well, without changing the inner self.

Snakedance is a fascinating story for Nyssa. With a possessed Tegan as the antagonist and the Doctor ineffectual and imprisoned for much of the story, Nyssa becomes the protagonist, initiating much of the action. In her third season, Nyssa has grown up. Not only is she a brilliant scientist, she's become a hero, just like her best friend, the Doctor.

Nyssa switches costumes again in the next story, *Mawdryn Undead*, to a more dignified grey and gold skirt and top with cream undergarments. Turlough joins the crew and her role diminishes, leading into her final story, *Terminus*.

In *Terminus*, the last Trakenite contracts Lazar's Disease. She becomes hot, ill, pulled away from her friends. Nyssa feverishly strips away her outfit, and is led to a cure that probably won't work, no longer dressed as a princess or a trendy 80s woman like Tegan. She is alone and dying.

Then she survives the treatment and makes an important choice. Stripped of everything clothing-wise that indicates her status, Nyssa learns what we've known about her all along through the Doctor's eyes: Nyssa remains a scientist and hero. She decides to improve on the cure and save countless lives. It is a sad parting with the Doctor and Tegan, but her friends couldn't be prouder.

She is the Science Princess who loses everything, and yet goes on to save lives with her intellect and compassion. She joins the Doctor in glamorous princess clothing, but leaves in nothing but her shift. Nyssa accepts herself and her competence without need for external markers, and dedicates her scientific knowledge to helping others.

Could a little hyperintelligent nerd girl have a better role model?

Origin Story

Aneira Vaughn is a Welsh historian with a love of sixties and seventies British SFF television. She occasionally writes appalling, cliche-ridden fantasy inspired by *Dungeons and Dragons*. She's not nearly as sorry about this as she should be.

The young woman – usually British, often from London – falls down the rabbit hole into a cracked mirror reflection of her world. Here, death lurks in every statue or shadow, myths become real, and heroes really can save the day in the nick of time. Instead of climbing her way back to reality, she follows the White Rabbit in his frock coat or long scarf or brainy specs deeper into the strangeness, into the blue box, into all of time and space.

There have been many different sorts of companions in *Doctor Who*, but the most pervasive archetype, the figure that we always come back to, is the young human woman discovering the world was so much bigger than she'd ever imagined.

It began in 1966 with Polly. There're elements of Barbara in this archetype, and Dodo might fit if only her introduction and exit from the show weren't such bizarre, ethereal affairs (while her time in the TARDIS is spent jumping from one personality to the next), but it's in Polly, the third woman from modern Earth to step into the TARDIS, that the archetype successfully coalesces, and it's to Polly the show returns again and again to define what it means to be a companion traveling with the Doctor.

In Season Three of *Doctor Who*, companions were being unceremoniously dispatched and the Doctor was about to become a whole new man. With *The War Machines*, the first *Doctor Who* story set wholly in the modern day, we're more grounded in reality than *Who*'s been since the pilot episode. Polly breezes into the narrative all cheery confidence and glamour. She's fun-loving, fashionable and so very sixties. She wears an impressive amount of mascara and her hair's startlingly blonde. Her striking modernity makes a fascinating contrast to the grandfatherly figure of Hartnell's Doctor. It's the last gasp of his tenure in the TARDIS, but he goes into his final stories accompanied by two new companions brimming with youth and energy.

Polly's introduced at her job, working as a secretary in the just completed Post Office Tower. She takes Dodo out to a night club where we meet her friends, Kitty and Ben. Normality has intruded into the fantastic world of the Doctor, but it cannot hold. The Post Office Tower is harbouring an evil pseudo-Internet, intent on a mechanized revolution, and Polly and Ben are irresistibly drawn into the adventure to stop it.

There's a chance to walk away. You don't have to keep running, not when the monsters are defeated. You can turn around, go home. Back in the day, you weren't invited on board the TARDIS. It took an extra leap of curiosity, or determination, to step over the liminal space between the everyday world and the fantastic. In a scene reminiscent of Rose Tyler at the end of her first episode, in the final scene of *The War Machines* Polly runs towards the TARDIS with a smile on her face. She's supposed to be returning a key to the Doctor, but her expression says so much more than that. She might not know what's on the other side of the doors, but with all that she's just experienced, she must suspect it's more than meets the eye.

She accepts the fantastic incrementally. The TARDIS can clearly travel in space, but she questions its ability to time travel. She travels into Earth's past, and mistakes it for modern day Cornwall, before she goes into the future to face aliens invading her world. When the Doctor changes faces, she's the one who believes he's the same man, while Ben still doubts. In *The War Machines*, *The Smugglers* and *The Tenth Planet*, there's a similar set-up to the opening stories of so many of New *Who's* seasons. The new companion is introduced in their natural modern day habitat, and helps save the Earth, before they spend the next two stories taking one trip to the past, and one trip to the future as they come to terms with the new, unlimited nature of their world.

Unlike New *Who*, there's no grand world-saving moment for Polly at the end of the season, but she throws herself into each adventure, her obvious fear at the danger only accentuating how brave she is to go on. The Doctor might want to run back into the TARDIS when a cannonball flies past, but Polly insists they find Ben first. She screams, and screams often, but that's of little consequence next to the fact that whenever her friends are in trouble, her first reaction is to figure out how to rescue them. And if that means throwing stones at soldiers armed with muskets, then so be it.

There's nothing extraordinary about Polly, but, thrown into extraordinary circumstances, she shows very ordinary humanity at its best. Her plans are brilliant in their simplicity: pretend to be a witch, pretend to be a god, melt plastic with nail varnish, catch a soldier in a pit and rob him. Her inclination is to be kind if she can and to help, if it's possible. She'll act as the Doctor's lab assistant or make coffee, if that's what's needed, but she's just as happy to take on her own companion and travel across the Jacobite Highlands on a lengthy rescue mission, armed with guns and knives and oranges. When she finds her own adversary in Lieutenant Algernon Ffinch in *The Highlanders*, by the time he makes his goodbye, despite being robbed and blackmailed by her, he's become a better man.

The coffee making has taken on a significance entirely out of proportion to what it is in context. If there's one scene that's used to show the sexism of early *Doctor Who*, it's the Doctor asking Polly to make some coffee. And if that was all he ever asked Polly to do, and if that was all Polly ever did, there'd be a point, but it's not. There *is* sexism in *Who* – it was there in the sixties and it's there today – but reducing it to that one time Polly made everyone coffee is absurd. It does her character an enormous disservice and reduces a complex, insidious issue down to a sound bite. Polly is in her future, on a moonbase, surrounded by equipment she's not trained to use and a medical problem that's testing the Doctor's scientific skills. She asks what she can do to help, and it's make the coffee. Once. While her fellow companions, Ben and Jamie, are not even managing to contribute that much.

Despite the terrors, and the tedium of making hot drinks for everyone, Polly takes a real joy in her travels in the TARDIS. There's delighted bouncing in the low gravity of the moon, and TARDIS scenes that have a sense of relaxed camaraderie and family that's not really been around since Barbara and Ian went home. Polly is as flirtatious with the Doctor as a companion's ever been by that point, cheerfully complimenting him, calling him wonderful, and praising his appearance after he's been unceremoniously tidied up by the Refreshing Department in *The Macra Terror*. She even borrows his hat at one point.

In the end, of course, Polly leaves, because companions always do, and it's time for another to freewheel amongst the stars. She's not the same person who stepped on board the TARDIS, and the audience who watches her leave isn't the audience who watched her arrive. In the 1960s, no modern companion became trapped in another universe or stuck in an unreachable past. These companions were, at most, one generation removed from the deadliest war in human history: at the end of their adventures in space and time, they got to go home.

Doctor Who goes on, generation after generation, regeneration after regeneration, and Polly's legacy endures with the reiteration of each young human woman curious enough to step inside the blue box. Each time she's different; each time we know who she is. She's us, she's humanity at our best: curious and kind, empathetic and open-minded.

What Has Romana
Ever Done For Us?

Phoebe Taylor is delighted to report that being an adult is turning out to
be a lot more fun than she had anticipated. She shares a flat in London with
an epic DVD collection, a mind-boggling amount of tea, and a number of
Doctor Who action figures... as well as her fangirl flatmates, with whom she
spends entirely too much time discussing fictional characters. By day, she
has a quiet job in the publishing industry protecting other people's intellectual property. By night, she assumes her superhero identity, Purplefringe,
to make vids, watch vids and complain about what a stupid hobby vidding
is. She once told Matt Smith he had a "nice face."

**1978. DOCTOR WHO SEASON 16: The Ribos Operation, episode one,
Scene 3**

> **The Doctor** *(sotto, to K-9)*: That's the new assistant.
> *(Enter ROMANA I looking like the goddess Athena, Princess Leia
> and Galadriel rolled into one. The camera pans slowly up her stately
> figure, from the hem of her flowing white dress to the tip of her tiara.
> In a tone that calmly implies that she is absolutely certain she is better
> than you:)*
> **Romana:** My name is Romanadvoratrelundar. Check your
> records again.

Ok, fine, so that's not *quite* what she says. I may have stolen that last
sentence from another badass female Time Lord with magical hair, who
wouldn't appear on our TV screens for another 30 years. But the point
still stands! Romanadvoratrelundar, AKA Romana AKA "Fred" refuses
to be just an "assistant" to the fourth Doctor – she's a partner, a colleague. She is, much like the Glowy Cube of Destiny that is Season
Sixteen's McGuffin, a complex and powerful being who cannot be
taken merely at face value (though what a beautiful face it is). And
what's more, many of the future ladies of the Whoniverse – particularly
from the Moffat era – owe her a tremendous debt of gratitude. There
would be no River without Romana.

Perhaps that's too bold a claim to make this early on. Shall we go back in time?

I should probably come clean, and confess that I am first and foremost a New *Who* fan. Until March 26, 2005, I knew as much about *Doctor Who* as the Doctor does about fashion.[54] *Rose* sucked 15-year-old me into the show's vortex, where I am still spinning in delight and will probably remain so until I am too old to say "Raxacoricofallapatorius" without my teeth falling out. The Doctors and companions of New *Who* were my first loves, and so it was with some trepidation that I sat down to watch my first complete season of classic *Who* in order to write this essay. Having seen just five classic stories[55] in the past eight years, my knowledge of Ye Olde *Who* was as cobbled together as some of the more dubious monster costumes (seriously, that guy dressed as Kroll? What *is* that?![56]) and – like Romana's knowledge of the universe outside Gallifrey – almost entirely theoretical.

From immersion in fannish speculation over the last few years, I was aware that Romana is seen by many as a key figure in the Doctor's long life. I knew that her second incarnation is generally considered to be more popular and likeable than her first. I knew that Doctor/Romana is a popular ship even now. And I knew that due to her Time Lord background, her close relationship with the Doctor and the contradictory canon surrounding her post-TARDIS life, it has at some point been said of almost every mysterious female character of recent times, "I bet she's Romana!"

Further incursions into LiveJournal and other sources of Whoniversal meta furnished me with a recurring series of adjectives to describe Mary Tamm's Romana: "haughty" came up a lot, as did "arrogant." "Ice queen" was a perennial favorite. "Disdainful," "aristocratic," "intellectual but lacking in experience" – the picture was not overwhelmingly positive. Used to the warmth and emotional depth of the New *Who* companions – not to mention their intricately plotted character arcs and insights into their family backgrounds – I was prepared for disappointment. Or at the very least, boredom.

---

54 Romana: "Well, how do I look?" The Doctor (without looking): "Ravishing." Romana: "That's not what I meant. I mean, will this do?" The Doctor: "Oh yes, very nicely, I should think, except for those shoes." Romana: "Oh, I rather like them." The Doctor: "Well, you please yourself. I'm no fashion expert." Romana (with absolute certainty and no little amusement): "No." —*The Stones of Blood*

55 *An Unearthly Child, Genesis of the Daleks, City of Death, The Five Doctors* and *Battlefield,* if you're interested.

56 KROLL KROLL KROLL KROLL KROLL KROLL KROLL KROLL KROLL KROLL KROLL KROLL KROLL

How wrong I was.

Romanadvoratrelundar is *fabulous*.

From the moment Romana steps into the console room, she has the Doctor on the back foot. Whilst he is sprawled and sullen, resorting to feeble jibes about making *tea*, she is effortlessly graceful and in control of the situation. She exudes a palpable air of superiority. It is the start of *The Ribos Operation*, and for the second time in five minutes the Doctor is unexpectedly confronted by a white-garbed being of supreme confidence and obvious intellect, who knows far more about him than he does about them, and isn't afraid to take him down a peg or five by showing it:

> **Romana:** I may be inexperienced, but I did graduate from the Academy with a triple first.
> **The Doctor:** I suppose you think we should be impressed by that, too?
> **Romana:** Well, it's better than scraping through with 51% at the second attempt.
>
> —*The Ribos Operation*

(Remind you of anyone?)

> **The Doctor:** So where are we now, Dr Song? How's prison?
> **River:** Oh, I was pardoned ages ago. And it's Professor Song to you.
>
> —*The Angels Take Manhattan*

Everything about Romana seems designed to knock the Doctor off-balance. From her perfect, bejewelled coiffure to her pristine dress, every aspect of her being seems at odds with the fourth Doctor's wild mop of hair and hobo-space-pirate attire. (Not entirely unlike a certain future companion whose love of elegant evening gowns and high heels contrasts delightfully with her Doctor's usual tweed-and-bowtie combo...)

Her exaggeratedly refined tones – which quickly slip to something slightly more natural as she settles in – command attention in a completely different way from his booming voice. Romana's movements are subtle while the Doctor flails around – he takes up space in his billowing coat and long scarf, but she manages to silence him with a tiny, challenging tilt of the head. Her world-weary eyerolls and mischievous eyebrow quirks could devastate a lesser man at 30 paces. They are like the mythical Sun and Ice Gods of Ribos, constantly fighting for supremacy (and it's a good thing the TARDIS is dimensionally transcendent; there is just about room for both of their egos in there). The one-upmanship begins:

> **Romana:** I'll look up those coordinates, shall I?
> **The Doctor:** No, there's no need.
> **Romana:** Well, don't you want to know what planet it is?
> **The Doctor:** I know. Cyrrhenis Minima.
> **Romana:** Oh..!

> —*The Ribos Operation*

I mean, really:

> **River:** We're somewhere in the Garn Belt. There's an atmosphere. Early indications suggest that—
> **The Doctor:** We're on Alfava Metraxis, the seventh planet of the Dundra System. Oxygen rich atmosphere, all toxins in the soft band, 11-hour day and chances of rain later.

> —*The Time of Angels*

"Good looks are no substitute for a sound character," the Doctor reminds her. Fortunately for Romana, she has *both* and she knows it. And, as she insolently eats a stolen jelly baby at him, she makes damn sure he knows it too. Her combination of burning intellect and cool self-confidence puts a hole in the Doctor's ego as well as his TARDIS. The TARDIS which, incidentally, she knows how to fly better than he does... and here the parallels become *really* obvious. The scene in *The Pirate Planet* where the Doctor and Romana bicker about the best way to fly his "veteran and vintage capsule" clearly provides the inspiration, some three decades later, for River Song's dexterity in the console room.

> **Romana:** Right. Synchronic feedback.
> **The Doctor:** Won't make a scrap of difference.
> **Romana:** We'll see. Multiloop stabiliser.
> **The Doctor:** Look out, K-9. Hold on.
> **Romana:** Now.
> *(The TARDIS parks herself neatly under an archway.)*
> **Romana:** Well?

> —*The Pirate Planet*

River: Use the stabilisers.
The Doctor: There aren't any stabilisers.
River: The blue switches.
The Doctor: Oh, the blue ones don't do anything, they're just blue.
River: Yes, they're blue. Look, they're the blue stabilisers.
(She presses them and the TARDIS stops shaking.)
River: See?

—*The Time of Angels*

In both cases, the Doctor is pushed rudely off the Biggest Time Traveling Know-It-All podium by someone who has actually taken time to *read the instructions*. The Doctor hates doing that. That's not how he travels. For all that he repeatedly extols the value of books, the Doctor always prefers to learn by *doing* first and foremost, even if it means ending up stuck in a net within 30 seconds of leaving the TARDIS.[57]

There is a lot of discussion in Season Sixteen about "theory" versus "practice" – Newton and Einstein are both mentioned in the context of their ground-breaking theories, and K-9 is often called upon to verify a scientific principle ("The theory is sound, Master") before the Doctor throws himself into the testing of it ("All theories have to be tested sometime"). Binro the Heretic acts as a parallel for Romana in the first story – all his theories come from learning and observation, and although he has not had the opportunity to test them, it transpires that *Binro was right*. Similarly, Romana's book-learning is never derided by the show. Only the Doctor ever mocks her, and one gets the impression that this is probably out of jealousy or insecurity more than anything else. Rather, the overwhelming message of the season seems to be that theoretical knowledge *does* need to be complemented by practical experience (or tested in often unconventional ways), but that it's important to have theories in the first place.[58] It is no coincidence that Romana and *Professor* River Song are both academics as well as adventurers.

And adventurer she is: for someone who has spent her life thus far

---

57 Those who claim that Romana gets captured too often – take note! The first pratfall of Season Sixteen is the Doctor's. And it's his clumsiness that later attracts the Shrivenzale. And he gets captured and nearly sacrificed/ executed/ otherwise tortured almost as often as Romana. And he also loses that bloody tracer.
58 If Romana shares Princess Leia's dressmaker and studied deportment with Galadriel, she *thinks* like Hermione Granger: "According to Bartholomew's Planetary Gazetteer..." Romana has definitely read *Hogwarts: A History*. The Doctor has not. Though he would probably claim that he helped to write it.

on Gallifrey, Romana is a surprisingly good shot, managing to take out a soldier in *The Pirate Planet* in just one blast.[59] She predates both River's scientific knowledge and her love of fast vehicles, as well as a certain disregard for prison guards: "Did you know you could get twice the speed for half the energy?", she remarks to the perplexed soldier arresting her in an air car.

But the similarities go deeper than that. As a result of growing up in the same environment, and possessing an intelligence that outstrips his, Romana is truly allowed to be seen as equal to the Doctor on every level, in a way that few other companions ever have. She is well aware of this fact, and as early as her second scene we already see her begin to literally and metaphorically let her hair down. Having ascertained that the Doctor is capable of the emotional maturity of a toddler ("You're sulking! That's ridiculous in someone as old as you are!"[60]), she is able to relax a little, and let out her characteristic glimmers of humor. She is also able to psychoanalyze the Doctor and, like River, she seems to understand just how his mind works. (River: "Never let him see the damage. And never, ever let him see you age. He doesn't like endings.") Romana's bouts of psychoanalysis come and go, and it is never clear whether she truly believes the psychobabble she is spouting, or whether it is simply a ruse to wind up the Doctor for her entertainment. The knowing glint in her eye and the twitching of her lips as she contemplates using his case in her thesis suggest, to me, that she does not always take herself as seriously as we might think.

Romana I's snarky sense of humor is something that often seems to be forgotten when she's discussed – it's as if she must be seen as even more aristocratic, even more refined than she really is, in order to exaggerate the difference in the more carefree Romana II. This seems unfair. Much of Romana's sense of humor comes across in her body language and facial expressions (those *eyebrows!*), and in her dry tone of voice. Even when she is relegated to the background of a scene (as happens slightly too often...), it is worth watching her infinitely long-suffering facial expressions. When in the foreground, there is a sardonic undercurrent in much of her conversation with the Doctor, which at times borders on flirtation. Despite never fully appreciating the Doctor's levity in near-death situations, she does share his sense of humor (and her smile when she does approve of his jokes is simply *radiant.*)

---

59 Which is considerably better than any of the guards can do...

60 Years later, in *The Snowmen*, Clara discovers the same thing. Clara: "Blimey, you really know how to sulk, don't you?" The Doctor: "I'm not sulking!"

The Doctor: You're being frivolous.
Romana (*eyes sparkling, lips quirking, generally a picture of wounded innocence*): I wouldn't dream of it!

—*The Pirate Planet*

Her humor is dry and ironic, she enjoys wordplay:

The Doctor: Where's your optimism?
Romana: It opted out.

—*The Armageddon Factor*

And has a sense of the ridiculous:

The Doctor: I'll call you Romana.
Romana: I don't like Romana.
The Doctor: It's either Romana or Fred.
Romana (*with a wide smile*): All right, call me Fred!

—*The Ribos Operation*

Perhaps the subtlety of her wit tends to be forgotten over time, eclipsed by stronger visual impressions of the "ice queen" in white with her magic wand. Or perhaps her brand of humor doesn't come across as well to children. Either way, many fans do Romana I a great disservice by failing to comment on her quirks. These set her apart from the vast majority of Time Lords, who seem to be completely devoid of all humor.

The Doctor: Don't jump to conclusions about anyone or anything. It could lead you astray.
Romana: Ah. I'll try and remember that. (*Eyebrows arched, lips suppressing a smile.*)
The Doctor: Good. And don't be sarcastic, either. That can also get you into trouble.

—*The Ribos Operation*

People do jump to conclusions about Romana I, and they are led astray. Just as she initially fixates on the crown as the potential segment of the Key to Time, ignoring the other, less shiny objects, fans often seem to fixate on her tiara as the ultimate symbol of Romana. But as the Doctor says, "the crown has nothing to do with it." The Key turns out to be something rather more mundane – a lump of rock (albeit valuable rock). Rocks and mining are repeated symbols in Season Sixteen, cropping up in almost every story – from the jethrik in *Ribos* and the gemstones and mines in *The Pirate Planet* to the standing stones in *The Stones of Blood* and the sculpted dragon in *The Androids of Tara*. So many underground tunnels are explored that the Doctor has to pre-empt Romana's comment – "Don't say 'another underground passage'." In a form of alchemy, almost all the stones are transformed from mere rocks into something else, or they provide the answer to a mystery. It's a good metaphor for Romana: the persistent themes of metamorphosis, and of exploring hidden depths, tie in very nicely to Romana's own journey (as well as her love of psychoanalysis, of plunging into the labyrinth of another mind). As she learns in *The Pirate Planet*, "never take anything at its face value." Especially not "an open, honest face."

As a Time Lord, her first steps out of the TARDIS on Ribos do not elicit the sense of awe that is the right-of-passage of most companions. This is, however, her first time away from Gallifrey and some of the practicalities initially elude her – but Romana is nothing if not a quick learner. The bitter cold of Ribos teaches her to dress to blend in on her future travels, which is a good deal more than the Doctor ever does, and a poor choice of high heels is only ever made once. The value of a well-timed spot of sleight-of-hand is a skill she picks up almost immediately, despite lacking the Doctor's advantage of having been trained by Maskelyne:

> **The Doctor:** Where did you get those jelly babies?
> **Romana:** Same place you get them.
> **The Doctor:** Where?
> **Romana:** Your pocket.
>
> —*The Ribos Operation*

(And that can't help but bring to mind...)

> **Dorium:** Not cheap, Doctor Song. Have you brought me a pretty toy?
> **River** (*taking off an earring*): This is a Calisto Pulse. It can disarm micro-explosives from up to 20 feet.
> **Dorium:** What kind of micro-explosives?
> **River:** The kind I just put in your wine.
>
> —*The Pandorica Opens*

Romana's first encounter with real danger – when she comes face to face with the ravenous Schrivenzale – does, it must be admitted, leave her paralyzed with fear and screaming for the Doctor's help. In shock, she lets her guard down, clinging to the Doctor and revealing the true extent of her naiveté about the universe. This is the moment she realizes she still has so much to learn. In tones considerably less controlled than usual:

> **Romana:** That thing. What is it?
> **The Doctor:** A Shrivenzale.
> **Romana:** I never imagined. Are there many creatures like that in other worlds?
> **The Doctor:** Millions. Millions! You shouldn't have volunteered if you're scared of a little thing like that.
> **Romana:** I'm not scared, I'm just—

—The Ribos Operation

> **River** (*newly regenerated and in the TARDIS, suddenly scared, overwhelmed and almost childlike*): I seem to be able to fly her. She showed me how. She taught me. The Doctor says I'm the child of the TARDIS. What does he mean?

—Let's Kill Hitler

This is Romana's first vulnerable moment. We see her youth, and in her defensive "I'm not scared," we see that she is, perhaps, slightly impressed by the Doctor after all, and wants to impress him back. She wants him to stop "treating her like a child," as she's nearly 140, don't you know? (In *City of Death*, Romana II gives her age more precisely as 125 – is Romana exaggerating here, in order to appear more mature?) But it's not all bravado – even in her fear, she is desperate to *learn*. When captured in *The Pirate Planet*, she calmly sends K-9 off to fetch the Doctor without raising the guard's suspicions. Although she's taken in by the terrible Kroll costume, she is tied to a pole in the dark at the time, which is hardly conducive to clear thinking. When she encounters the Taran Woodbeast in broad daylight, on the other hand, she is rather less than terrified – in fact, she looks distinctly unimpressed (as do we the viewers, but for somewhat different reasons). By *The Armageddon Factor*, she has undergone the transformation that the Doctor's influence provokes in almost all of his companions, and she is willing to sacrifice herself to save others. Collapsed on the floor of the Shadow's lair, she is dignity personified as she proclaims, "I'm not afraid to die." This time, she means it.

Romana's journey from somewhat naive student to defiant heroine is fairly rapid. She quickly proves herself to be a capable and practical companion (carrying everything in her pockets from medicines to telescopes). She is assertive, and refuses to be patronized even when she has inadvertently displayed her ignorance on a subject. She takes their mission seriously, displaying a touching nervousness when it comes to the momentous task of transforming the first segment of the Key to Time back into its true form. By the time they have recovered the final segment, nervousness has been replaced by righteous anger, as she almost spits at the Doctor, and later actually hits him (who else would dare?):

> **Romana:** We're murderers. First Astra and now Merak.
> **The Doctor:** Romana, it wasn't our idea to use the Royal House of Atrios as carriers, was it?
> **Romana:** No, but what happened to Astra was our fault. We're just pawns here to do the Guardian's dirty work.
> **The Doctor:** I don't like it any more than you do, but it's done. Have you set those coordinates yet?
> **Romana:** Is that all you can say? She was a living being, and now what is she? A component. And Merak thinks she's still alive. No power should have that right, not even the Guardians. We must do something!
>
> —*The Armageddon Factor*

We must do something. The Doctor and Romana are a unit. By *The Ribos Operation* episode two, they are already unconsciously mimicking each other's movements and finishing each other's sentences. This verbal and physical mirroring is apparent in every story. They share plot exposition speeches (often taking half a sentence each), and hit on ideas at the same time:

> **The Doctor:** Come on, quickly. Remember that time loop's stretching.
> **Romana:** Doctor, come on! The time loop's stretching.
>
> —*The Armageddon Factor*

In the audio commentary to *The Ribos Operation*, Mary Tamm describes the Doctor and Romana's relationship as "four hearts beating as two," whilst discussing the flirty undertones to their partnership.

There is, of course, considerably less handholding in *Doctor Who* circa 1978 than in 2014 – less casual hugging, certainly less forehead kissing – but their relationship is still notably tactile. They cling onto each others' arms (and coat tails!) a lot, even when it's not *strictly* necessary. And they bicker like... well:

> **Romana:** You nearly got us killed.
> **The Doctor:** If you call that being nearly killed, you haven't lived yet. Just stay with me, and you'll get a lot nearer. In fact, you're a lot nearer right now.
> **Romana:** You've got an unconscious death wish.
> **Garron:** Don't bicker!
> **The Doctor:** No. No bickering.
> **Romana:** Never bicker.
>
> —*The Ribos Operation*

> **River:** Listen to me. You've lost your friend. You're angry. I understand. But you need to be less emotional, Doctor, right now.
> **The Doctor:** Less emotional? I'm not emotional.
> **River:** There are five people in this room still alive. Focus on that. Dear God, you're hard work young.
> **The Doctor:** Young? Who are you?
> **Lux:** Oh, for heaven's sake! Look at the pair of you. We're all going to die right here, and you're just squabbling like an old married couple.
>
> —*Forest of the Dead*

She may not be the Doctor's wife, but Romana is just as "bespoke" to him as River Song would be later. As one of a very few companions who were handpicked specifically to accompany the Doctor, she's bound to have a lot in common with him. Besides the superficial trappings of their outfits and their various adventures (involving queens, quests, standing stones, implacable justice machines, encounters with android doubles of themselves and nearly being sacrificed to alien gods), they share many more important traits.

However, Romana is wonderful not just for the characters she will later inspire, but for who she is on her own terms. The first time she's captured, the Doctor has to justify going to look for her – "Romana has the tracer, you see" – but by *The Power of Kroll*, things are simpler: "She is important to me." The "negative empathy" between them, remarked upon by Romana early in *Ribos*, soon dissolves and over the course of the season it becomes clear that the Doctor and Romana are in tune in some very fundamental way. They are not mirror images or polar opposites like the Black and White Guardians, but rather they slot together like the jagged segments of the Key to Time.

Romana attempts to rein the Doctor in, whilst at the same time forcing him to up his game to impress her. The Doctor, meanwhile, pushes Romana way beyond the limits of her Gallifreyan comfort zone, showing her just how much more she has to learn whilst also giving her the opportunity to shine. (Who figures out how to fix K-9 in *The Stones of Blood*? Who works out where the Shadow's lair is in *Armageddon*? Who saves Princess Strella?) Season Sixteen is united by a quest to restore "balance" to the universe – and is, in fact, the first season of *Doctor Who* to have a plot arc spanning an entire season – but it ends with the installation of the chaos-courting randomiser in the TARDIS. The fate of the universe at large is left decidedly unclear, but the important thing is that the Doctor and Romana have found their balance together.

The Heroine of Her Own Story

Brittany Harrison writes novels and collects tea arcana. She lives in Baltimore, Maryland. You can find her online at language-and-light.tumblr. com. **Liz Barr** reads novels and drinks tea. She lives in Melbourne, Australia with a cat.

There's a girl.

She's special, but she doesn't know it, and if you told her, she'd laugh at you.

She has no parents – or if she does, they've let her down in ways she can't always articulate. It doesn't matter, because she thinks she doesn't need anyone. She's quick to judge but slow to trust, and the exception, if she makes one, is for another girl, one who needs her.

She's here to survive.

In the 1980s, she was called Alanna. Today, she's known as Katniss Everdeen.

Between 1987 and 1989, she was the Doctor's companion, and her name was Ace.

# # #

For the first few centuries of its existence, published literature was divided into roughly two categories: stories for children, novels for adults. Then came the Baby Boomers and the invention of the teenager, and within a few years, there were novels written with teens in mind. Young adult fiction was born.

Doctor Who came into existence around the same time, a product carefully calculated to appeal to as many demographics as possible – whole families, in fact. The Doctor's first companion was Susan, an adolescent pop music fan who is thoroughly mysterious to her teachers even before they discover she's an alien.

A young woman from another world who desperately wants to experience life on Earth is a compelling hook, but Susan was never intended to be the heroine of this story. That role is filled magnificently by Barbara Wright, very much a grown woman.

And though Susan went on to be replaced by Dodo and Vicki, whose identities as adolescents manifested in the form of Dodo's jaunty mod fashions and Vicki's identification of The Beatles as "classical music," those women were all subjected to the Doctor's loving paternalism. All were fine characters who had heroic moments, but they were never *the heroine*.

Ace was the first teenage girl in the TARDIS since Victoria and Zoe, and the first contemporary teenager since Dodo. And her entrance is, without a doubt, spectacular.

It's usually the Doctor who makes a bewitching first impression on a new companion. But the Doctor's first encounter with Ace in *Dragonfire* reverses this dynamic.

Ace explodes onto the scene – almost literally. She invites herself along on the Doctor's hunt for a legendary dragon, then yells at his associate Glitz for being a "male chauvinist bilge bag." By the time she gets herself fired from her waitressing job by dumping a milkshake over the head of a rude customer, the Doctor has begun to seem mild-mannered in comparison.

And that's before she reveals that she's carrying around a backpack full of homemade explosives.

We've had teens in the TARDIS before, but Ace is the first teen delinquent. (Stop pouting, Adric fans. Sure, he may have sold the Doctor and Romana out to a gang of world-dominating vampires, but Adric was about as delinquent as sour cream.) She got kicked out of school for blowing up the art room ("It was a creative statement!"), burned down a mansion, and her experiments with explosives saw her swept up in a time storm that left her alone, fending for herself on a space station in the future.

Ace is a heavily-armed teenage girl with a social conscience. She could be the scariest, most powerful being in the entire universe.

# # #

Few heroes get to select their mentor. A plot contrivance brought Luke Skywalker to Obi-Wan Kenobi. Albus Dumbledore was at Hogwarts long before Harry Potter turned up. Katniss Everdeen is saddled with the alcoholic and occasionally odiferous Haymitch Abernathy, the last person in the world she would have chosen to be her mentor.

But Ace gets to choose. And she chooses the Doctor.

The Doctor: There are three rules. One, I'm in charge.
Ace: Whatever you say, Professor.
The Doctor: Two, I'm not the Professor, I'm the Doctor.
Ace: Whatever you want.

Ace understands the power of names and re-naming better than most. She confesses to Mel that her real name is Dorothy: "That's how I knew they couldn't be my real mum and dad. My real mum and dad would never have given me a naff name like Dorothy." That's the first and last we ever hear of Ace's father. Ace's mother is a powerful, invisible figure, one who inspires desperate hatred in Ace. We never find out exactly what Ace's mother did – or didn't do – to earn this, but Ace's feelings run so deep, she almost can't function when the topic of her mother is raised. In renaming herself, she claims autonomy over her identity, discarding the "Dorothy" her mother wanted her to be.

And she, in turn, renames the Doctor. You might dismiss it as a joke, but the name is prophetic. The Doctor and Ace's relationship develops into a mentor/student-style collaboration. They are Merlin and the sorcerer's apprentice, Ace the magician-in-training whom the Doctor maneuvers, and manipulates into a series of learning experiences devised by him to make her face her fears and grow stronger.

Ace's re-naming of the Doctor is also a bid for agency as she deals with a man who is impossibly old and powerful compared to her. "The Doctor" is the name that reflects his ambitions, his attempts at self-invention; "Professor" is a name that cuts across those ambitions and re-shapes him in a mould better suited to meet Ace's needs. She isn't a child who wants an adult to fix things and make them better for her, but a young woman who lacks trusted teachers to mentor her passage into adulthood.

# # #

YA genre fiction uses science fiction and fantasy as metaphors for the struggle of growing up. Part of that is learning to question authority. Ace goes through the same process. Not that Ace needs any help in learning to mistrust authority – she learns, instead, to mistrust the Doctor.

This is particularly true of *Ghost Light* and *The Curse of Fenric*, in which the Doctor brings Ace face to face with her greatest fears. The Doctor's curriculum for Ace is stocked with lessons that spring on her like traps, and she is forced to question not only her beliefs about herself, but her faith in the Doctor. His goal is to help Ace come to terms with dark and painful aspects of her own past, to better prepare her for the challenges of adult life. Ace volunteered for this; she wants to learn what the Doctor has to teach. But she doesn't always appreciate his methods.

In *Ghost Light*, we learn that Ace possesses a deeply buried vulnerability, born of trauma and grief: the racially motivated murder of her best friend.

> **Ace:** When I lived in Perivale, me and my best mate, we dossed around together. We'd out-dare each other on things. Skiving off, stupid things. Then they burnt out Manisha's flat. White kids firebombed it. I didn't care anymore.
> **The Doctor:** I think you cared a lot, Ace.
> **Ace:** That's when I came over the walls of the house. This house. I was so mad, and I needed to get away. It was empty, all overgrown and falling down. No one came here. But when I got inside it was even worse. I didn't know then. It was horrible!

The Doctor compels Ace to confront her troubled past by taking her back in time to explore the origins of that terrible house, Gabriel Chase.

The year is 1883. Ace doesn't immediately recognize Gabriel Chase as the house she told the Doctor about. More importantly, the Doctor doesn't volunteer the information. We can't understand what an enormous deception the Doctor has practiced on Ace until the very moment we see her standing on the grand staircase, shouting at the Doctor in anger, fear and betrayal.

Secrecy was necessary for the Doctor's plan to work – Ace would never have returned to Gabriel Chase voluntarily. But his manipulation seems unnecessarily harsh. It's as though he thinks the only way to break through Ace's defences is to expose her to a shock. If not for the fact that Ace trusts the Doctor absolutely, his bringing her to the weird house full of sinister characters would be little more than a cruel joke.

But she does trust him, even if the Doctor uses her confidences in ways she's not prepared for. The only reason the Doctor can force Ace to face her demons is because she's told him what they are. The lessons he crafts for her often come as a brutal surprise, but she stays with him, and keeps learning.

The larger plot of *Ghost Light*, which centers around an alien ship hidden in the cellar, and a Victorian amateur-of-science-turned-serial-killer, seems almost incidental in comparison to Ace's personal drama.

The villain of the piece, Light, is only frightening because he has too much power and too little humanity. This is a common trait among the villains and monsters of this era. He hardly seems capable of disturbing the stalwart Ace to the degree we've seen.

It's clear that Ace's own grief and anger at the murder of her childhood friend is the true ghost that haunts Gabriel Chase. The Doctor's intervention seems to be effective; by the time they leave the house, Ace's equanimity is somewhat restored, as though all that was needed to begin the healing process was to expose the wound.

Ghost Light addresses one side of Ace's trauma. *The Curse of Fenric* addresses another: Ace's relationship with her mother – and the Doctor. Secrets are revealed which force a re-examination, not only of Ace and the Doctor's initial meeting, but of their entire relationship, including the Doctor's motivation in asking Ace to travel with him.

We learn that Ace is one of "the Wolves of Fenric," a descendant of Viking explorers into whose DNA encoded the means of a monstrous alien's escape from imprisonment. Worse, it is stated that all of Ace's experiences to this point are the result of external manipulation – by Fenric, and the Doctor. Fenric takes credit for creating the time-storm that transported Ace to Iceworld, and the Doctor claims that he guessed as much, and selected Ace as his companion for that very reason.

And maybe it's even slightly true, but the extent of what the Doctor knew, guessed, or intended regarding the inevitability of encountering Fenric again is very uncertain. We only have his remarks to Fenric to go on, and much of what he asserts to Fenric he later disavows – primarily his remarks about Ace being "a social misfit" who he would never have chosen to travel with if she had not been destined to play a role in Fenric's destruction.

Rule one, River Song will say one day, "The Doctor lies." He lied when he told Ace he didn't care for her, so he may have lied – or at least stretched the truth – in saying he chose Ace. What about her barging in on his conversations, befriending Mel, going dragon-hunting without him? Are we to believe this was all the Doctor's manipulation, leaving Ace with no agency of her own?

The seventh Doctor is a master manipulator, but he's also an opportunist and a consummate liar. Maybe he was aware of Ace from the beginning, and set up the dragon-hunt as bait. Or maybe he took advantage of an opportunity, just as he takes advantage of the explosives he'd rather Ace didn't carry.

The Doctor casts so much doubt on his own motives during that final confrontation with Fenric, it's easier to start from the other side and consider the things we know to be true: that his affection for Ace is profound and genuine, that he deeply regrets the pain he causes her, and that he's committed to fulfilling the role of Ace's mentor and guardian.

Even if the Doctor was exercising his capacity for accomplishing multiple objectives with a single action, it doesn't negate the trust and friendship between them. It does test it, however, nearly to the breaking point.

The Curse of Fenric also brings Ace into the orbit of Kathleen Dudman and her infant daughter Audrey, whom Ace befriends, not realizing that Kathleen is her grandmother and Audrey her mother. Ace is as shattered by the revelation that baby Audrey, whom she has grown to love, grows up to be the mother she hates, as she is by the Doctor's apparent betrayal of her trust.

Ace's wounds are old and deep, and again the Doctor seems to feel that the defenses she's built up around them can only be penetrated by abrupt, shocking confrontations. But as in *Ghost Light*, the catharsis of sudden exposure appears to do the trick – suggesting that possibly the Doctor knew what he was about all along. By the end of the story, Ace appears to achieve a measure of peace.

> **Ace:** I don't love her! She's my mum, and I don't love her! What's wrong with me? Why can't I stop hating her?
> **The Doctor:** Love and hate, frightening feelings, especially when they're trapped struggling beneath the surface. Don't be frightened of the water.

Having brought Ace face to face with her past, her final story takes her home.

The current trend in young adult fiction is for dystopian futures. With a target audience raised on climate change denial, school shootings and the War on Terror, what other future could be believable?

Ace, though, comes from a grim dystopian recent past: Britain under Thatcher. It's not a coincidence that she shouts abuse at tyrants, befriends Soviet soldiers and thumbs her nose at anything aristocratic or authoritarian. Her accent, appearance and very existence were created as an affront to Thatcherism.

And when, in her final story, she returns to contemporary Perivale, the bleak London suburb where she grew up, the final piece of the puzzle clicks into place. Perivale looks like a bland, lower middle class town, but it seethes with violence – and not just because of the aliens. This is a town where the local youth club runs Darwinian self-defence classes. Where the homes of people of color are firebombed. No wonder Ace wants and needs to change the world.

But if she left Perivale as a disaffected, delinquent youth, she has come back as a young woman. She forms a bond with the alien Karra and fights to protect her childhood friends. And when it seems as if the Doctor is lost forever, she straightens her spine, dons his hat and sets out to finish his work.

Part of the key to the success of YA fiction is that it contains coming of age stories about girls, something all too rare in contemporary media. And this is Ace's Bildungsroman. When the Doctor returns, he and Ace are equals, ready to face the universe and all its threats and wonders together.

"Home," Ace says. "The TARDIS." Perivale is where she comes from, but the TARDIS – the universe – is where she chooses to be. She left Earth for the first time as a kid. She leaves again as a grown woman, ready to save the world once more.

Companion Piece

Sara Kingdom Dies at the End

Tansy Rayner Roberts is the author of fantasy novels such as *Power and Majesty* and *Splashdance Silver*. Her time-traveling short story collection, *Love and Romanpunk*, was published in 2011. She is the co-host of two all-female podcasts: *Galactic Suburbia*, about SF publishing from the feminist perspective; and *Verity!* for all things *Doctor Who*. You can find Tansy's blog at tansyrr.com and follow her on Twitter at @tansyrr.

There has never been another *Doctor Who* companion like Sara Kingdom. She's the Terminator, Xena: Warrior Princess and Avon from *Blake's 7* rolled into one. Her path is a dark one, of violence and vengeance, and she finds redemption by making friends and helping to save the universe.

Played by the incomparable actress Jean Marsh, Sara's stoic and occasionally angsty character journey is told over nine of the 12 episodes of the epic story *The Daleks' Master Plan* (1965-1966). She kills her brother out of blind loyalty to a political leader who has secretly betrayed the whole human race, and spends the rest of the story trying to make amends for that terrible mistake. And oh yes, she dies at the end.

That isn't a spoiler. Well, it is, but when I was growing up with a battered copy of *The Doctor Who Programme Guide* clutched tightly in my hand, it was normal to experience the old stories knowing what the main narrative beats would be: whether a companion joined or left, who died, major plot twists and reveals, along with the cast list and production code.[61]

Sara Kingdom might have only appeared in nine episodes of *The Daleks' Master Plan* (despite the actress's own opinion on the matter, she is regarded as an official companion because she takes several trips in the TARDIS during this time), but only two of these – episode five, "Counter Plot"; and episode ten, "Escape Switch" – still exist in visual form. So how exactly do we "watch" this story?

We have the audio version, with linking narrative by Peter Purves.

---

61 I missed some subtleties by learning about *Doctor Who* this way – it was years, for instance, before I realized that Kamelion never appeared in the stories between *The King's Demons* and *Planet of Fire* – but knowing how the stories ended was part of my overall experience.

No telesnaps, sadly, to add Sara's impassive expressions and dirty looks to the soundtrack of the missing episodes. Two Target novelizations by John Peel (the story was too long for a single book), *Mission to the Unknown* and *The Mutation of Time*, add a great deal of internal narrative to Sara's story in particular, and have been excellently adapted to audio with Peter Purves and Jean Marsh as narrators. For those who struggle with the fan recons or audio-only soundtracks, this may be the best way to get the hang of the story.

Having said that, while the Peel novelizations do a good job of providing a more detailed and emotionally resonant version of the Sara Kingdom story, he also adds a lot of crying and moping, and insists on reminding us at regular intervals how extremely attractive both Sara and Steven are to each other. Your mileage may vary as to whether this improves or detracts from the story.

But wait, there's more! Comics, audio plays and even a pilot spin-off script feature Sara Kingdom before, during and after (yes, really) the events of the TV story. Much of this supplemental material is excellent, but I'm going to stick to the "pure" version of Kingdom as first depicted in the original story.

The Daleks' Master Plan was the first story in which the Doctor's companions became collateral damage. Sure, Barbara and Ian lost two years of their lives, Susan was abandoned in a war-torn future and Vicki was abandoned in a war-torn past. But Ian and Barbara were deliriously happy to have made it home, and both of the younger girls were bought off with boyfriends and in the 1960s that was most definitely considered a Good Way To Go.

But then companions started dying, and nothing was quite the same.

Early *Doctor Who* (and, it has to be said, all *Doctor Who* ever) has a variety of tonal shifts, moving from comedy to drama and back again, sometimes within the same scene. In Season Three, those tonal shifts became especially noticeable because the comedy was so broad, and the tragedy so grim. *The Daleks' Master Plan*, written by (at least) two different screenwriters, is like a condensed time capsule of Season Three tonal shifts – the story flits between being a bleak dystopian political drama, space opera, a planetary horror movie and a cheeky time travel romp. It contains alien delegates, invisible monsters, Christmas merriment, two different types of comedy policemen, spaceships, explosions, betrayal, sacrifice, slapstick, jungle planets, pyramids, interplanetary teleportation, the Meddling Monk and Daleks.

It's basically wall to wall awesome.

Sara Kingdom wasn't the first futuristic companion to join the show, but Steven and Vicki were both isolated from their respective societies when rescued by the Doctor, so we never saw much social context about their background. But Sara's world, with its cutthroat planetary politics, assassinations and galactic alliances, was well established on screen before she walked across it and tried to kill the Doctor.

Excellent world-building, you say? Really? Isn't this the same Terry Nation who phoned in most of his Dalek serials during the 1970s, who infamously wrote a tiny fraction of the number of scripts he was supposed to produce for this story and then went on holiday, leaving script editor Donald Tosh to do the rest without him?

Yes, says I. This is also the Terry Nation who created *Blake's 7*. More than any of Nation's other *Doctor Who* work, it is *The Daleks' Master Plan* which demonstrates clearly how the writer who created the Daleks also created one of the most morally ambiguous and character-rich science fiction TV shows of all time.

Episodes One to Four ("The Nightmare Begins," "Day of Armageddon," "Devil's Planet," "The Traitors"): In which Bret Vyon is betrayed, Katarina reaches the Place of Perfection and Kingdom comes...

The story so far: the first Doctor, Steven and Katarina – a native of ancient Troy – land on the scary jungle planet Kembel and are swept up in a complex political plot largely involving a McGuffin power source that the Daleks desperately need, the Taranium Core. They team up with Space Security agent Bret Vyon (a baby-faced Nicholas Courtney), who becomes an ally of the TARDIS crew provided they help him with his mission, to bring word back to Earth of the horrible betrayal he has uncovered. Mavic Chen, Guardian of the Solar System and Bret's own employer, is working with the Daleks against his own people.

The shared manly awkwardness that falls over the Doctor, Steven and Bret after the gratuitous death of Katarina bonds them eternally, and from that point on, Bret feels like a *Doctor Who* companion even though he never gets to travel in the TARDIS.

When Bret, the Doctor and Steven arrive on Earth, Chen sets his toughest and most loyal Space Security agent, Kingdom, to kill them.

Then this happens:

1) The man Bret is hoping to get help from betrays him, and Bret's response is to shoot him instantly, much to the Doctor's disgust. This is foreshadowing.

2) Kingdom – Sara Kingdom – is revealed to be a girl.

3) Kingdom is super loyal to her boss, and her job right now is terminating traitors and recovering the Taranium Core, despite the fact that she and Bret obviously know each other. She shoots him dead without giving him a chance to explain.

Bret Vyon's death is caused mostly by Chen, and tangentially by the Daleks, but the true responsibility for the deed lies with his actual assassin, Sara. Sure, she was following orders, but we all know how forgivable that is from a historical point of view.

Killing Bret is the moment that will define Sara for the entire story, even though it is rarely mentioned after her first two episodes, and it's also the bit that makes her feel like a *Blake's 7* character rather than someone belonging to the *Doctor Who* universe. More than a decade later, Avon would kill more than one person he cared about in the belief that they had betrayed him... and I think it's fascinating that in this case, that the "anti-hero commits an unforgiveable act of violence and has to live with the consequences" storyline was given to a woman. The gender equality of women in dystopian science fictional futures – or at least, their equality when it comes to ruthlessness, mindless violence and impassive facial expressions – would be a characteristic of Terry Nation's future work, and *Blake's 7* in particular.

But he did it first in *Doctor Who*, with Sara Kingdom.

Episode Five ("Counter Plot"): In which a horrible truth is revealed...

Still playing the role of the Terminator, Kingdom pursues the Doctor and Steven into a mysterious room that turns out to be an experiment in teleportation. Whoops.

All three are teleported to what turns out to be Mira, another jungle planet full of horrible perils. Steven disarms Sara while she is unconscious because teleportation makes ladies faint, despite her physical superiority as proved in every other single episode of this story – though I like the fact that he is *only* able to disarm her because she's unconscious. When Sara awakes, Steven and the Doctor set about trying to convince her that her beloved boss Mavic Chen is the traitor. Funnily enough, she's not keen on the idea that her entire life (and the last hour of it in particular) might be a massive lie.

Think of it from Sara's point of view. She's just killed Bret who was a filthy traitor (a private tragedy she will mourn when she has time), she's stranded on a stupid planet that's actively trying to murder her, and in order to survive, she has to team up with the criminals she was hired to execute.

To top it off, Steven and the Doctor shatter her world when they finally convince her that Bret was a hero, not a traitor. She was in the wrong by shooting him, which sucks entirely because, as she now reveals to them...

Sara Kingdom: "Bret Vyon was my brother!"

Ladies and gentlemen, may I present: family TV by British people. Take a bow, Terry Nation, you're an evil, evil genius.

Episode Six ("Coronas of the Sun"): In which Sara Kingdom has no choice...

From her revelation about Bret Vyon onwards, we see a gradual change in Sara. This could be down to the change of writers, as episode six is the point at which the episodes are mostly credited to Dennis Spooner rather than Nation (or, indeed, Donald Tosh). However, if you take it as read that Sara is inwardly suffering about Bret's death while being outwardly stoic, there is little inconsistency. In particular, while she has stopped trying to kill the Doctor, she is not yet ready to put herself entirely in his hands.

> **Steven:** You must learn to trust him. He's had dealings with the Daleks before.
> **Sara (flatly):** I have no choice.

Sara doesn't have to trust the Doctor to recognize that they can be useful to each other, and for all intents and purposes she does join the team at this point. She helps with the Doctor's plan to fool Mavic Chen with a fake Taranium Core, she displays an actual sense of humor when teasing Steven about his backwards knowledge of technology, and she shows concern about Steven's wellbeing after he zaps himself unconscious with a forcefield.

Sara's not the Terminator anymore, but she's not going to be making cups of tea or spraining her ankle any time soon.

Taken as weekly episodes, Sara's gradual change of attitude works better than when we listen to the whole story at once – and it's important to note that even as Sara softens slightly, she still retains her edge. It doesn't hurt that Jean Marsh brings something extra to the character, often compensating for the limitations of the script.

In "Coronas of the Sun," only a week (in TV time) after the Big Reveal about the traitor Mavic Chen, Sara comes face to face with him.

While the narrative barely slows down long enough to make the most of this moment, Jean Marsh employs a venomous "Traitor!" hiss that reminds us how important this confrontation is to her character arc. Brief though it is, the scene reinforces the fact of Chen's alliance with the Daleks and ensures Sara doesn't look silly for taking the Doctor's word for something so important.

The Doctor has the Taranium Core now, and as long as he can keep it from the Daleks, their "master plan" is doomed. But that's a pretty passive solution for the Space Security agent whose heart is crying out for vengeance... and as she steps onboard the TARDIS, Sara Kingdom has no actual idea that the Doctor can't steer the thing straight.

You'd think that would be something he might mention before letting someone join him, right?

Episode Seven ("The Feast of Steven"): In which we wish a happy Christmas to all of you at home...

"Sara Kingdom awoke with a cry, sitting upright in her bed. For a few seconds she did not recall where she was. Her heart was beating furiously, and she was still shocked from her nightmare. Gradually, as she huddled in the blankets, the room began to make sense to her..."

—*Doctor Who: The Mutation of Time,*
by John Peel

"The Feast of Steven" is notorious as a gleeful parade of comic banter and slapstick, pressed awkwardly between the two "acts" of the more serious space opera. The change of tone in this episode is so drastic that John Peel inserted a time gap of several months before it when novelizing the story, and when the BBC attempted to sell *The Daleks' Master Plan* overseas, "The Feast of Steven" was left out.

I'm ridiculously fond of this episode.

Comic interlude or not, Sara remains thoroughly in character, playing it straight against everyone else's absurdity. While the Doctor and Steven deal with the baffled policemen in the first half of the episode (which makes more sense when you know the original intention was a crossover episode with *Z-Cars*), Sara gets on with fixing the TARDIS scanner.[62]

The TARDIS lands next in 1930s Hollywood (because – why? What

---

62 This is an impressive achievement for a human, especially as she keeps getting interrupted by middle-aged blokes who have opinions about what she's wearing.

was going through your head with this one, TARDIS?) and again, Sara takes it on the chin while surrounded by romps and silliness, remaining above it all though she does express confusion at the end at everyone demanding she takes her clothes off...

Many believe that "The Feast of Steven," including its Christmas toast and the Doctor breaking the fourth wall at the end to wish "A Happy Christmas to All of You At Home," sticks out like a sore thumb in the middle of a more serious story, but I would argue with that because the following episode is also largely humorous and works as yet another distinct set piece...

Inappropriate comic interludes are an essential aspect of *The Daleks' Master Plan* – it's a feature, not a bug!

Episode Eight ("Volcano"): In which Sara Kingdom is Xena: Warrior Princess...

> **Sara:** What do you mean, you don't know?
> **The Doctor:** My dear, this machine can only tell us we're being followed. Not who by.
> **Steven:** It must be the Daleks.
> **The Doctor:** Yes, a hasty conclusion, but possibly right. Although I don't understand how they could have tested that Taranium so quickly.
> **Sara:** We must get back to the planet Kembel.
> **The Doctor:** Oh, nonsense, my dear.
> **Sara:** We must. We've got to destroy the Daleks' invasion fleet.

Sara Kingdom is still the only one taking the story seriously. She does not discuss the death of Bret, but you can certainly read her character as continuing to be haunted by it without overt mention in the text. Not having the visuals makes it harder, but Jean Marsh scrapes her words out as if they hurt her, and we are reminded all over again that it was lucky they put such an excellent actress in the role.

It's this "comedy/action middle" of "The Feast of Steven," "Volcano" and even – to some extent – the Egypt episodes that followed which made me first think about the similarity between Sara and Xena. They are both characters with a dark, damaged past, trying to make amends while never quite forgiving themselves. Xena made new friends, saved a bunch of people and had all manner of comic interludes (many of which she responded to as the blank-faced straight woman while everyone around her was busting their gut with slapstick), but whenever someone called her on the horrible things she had done in the past, she accepted that – even to the point of allowing herself to be imprisoned for murder – because, you know, it was all true.

The darkness of Xena's past and future didn't stop her having some fun along her journey, and the same is true for Sara. Her friendship with the Doctor and Steven opens up a new life to her, and her heart seems to have lifted a little despite her default stony expression. It's clear, though, that defeating the Daleks is the only future she cares about, regardless of the risk. The occasional cheerful bit of banter with the Doctor or Steven doesn't mean she has or ever can forgive herself for murdering her own brother.

It's a shame that a key emotional beat is ignored in this episode – that is, neither the Doctor nor Steven confess to Sara that the chances of them ever returning to her time and place of origin are ridiculously slender. In a later episode, Sara seems to know about the directional problems of the TARDIS, which means either that she was smart enough to figure it out on her own, or that the conversation happened off screen. It's disappointing we didn't get to see her react to it properly, though.

Episode Nine ("Golden Death"): In which Steven Taylor is a feminist...

Three time ships converge on ancient Egypt for a showdown – the Doctor's TARDIS, the Monk's TARDIS and the Dalek time ship featuring Mavic Chen.

After a couple of stories in which Sara's main job has been to a) fix the TARDIS scanner and b) react to people around her being idiots, it's nice to see her given more action here. In particular, the teamwork she and Steven display together is enormously enjoyable, with bonus points for playing against gender stereotypes.

When they are captured, Sara gets hold of a broken piece of pottery, and Steven encourages her to "start sawing." She releases him, allowing him to untie her. Then, as they get into a fight with the Egyptian guards, Steven noticeably struggles against his opponent while Sara finishes hers off with great expertise before coming to his aid.

> **Sara:** Not bad. Remind me to teach you a few tricks some time.
> **Steven** *(breathing hard)*: Remind me not to pick a fight with you!

The lovely thing about their dynamic is the lack of male "chivalry" which characterized every male-female partnership in *Doctor Who* up to this point. Ian, while adorable, was incredibly protective of Barbara. Everyone fussed over or patronized Susan and Vicki because they were so young. Katarina was treated as a child.

But with Sara, Steven finally gets a chance to act like the kind of casually feminist man that should be common in any science fictional future. He accepts her capabilities at face value, and never seems threatened by her competence or combat skills.

It's impressive that Steven would be written this way, in 1965-66. Sara is not only allowed to be strong, but the men around her are allowed to be completely okay with her being strong. This makes for a far more realistic version of the future than we generally get in science fiction of this era. Technology is easy to predict, but social changes far less so – and for once in this regard, 1960s *Doctor Who* got it exactly right.

Episode Ten ("Escape Switch"): In which the Daleks win...

This is the last episode that we get to watch instead of listening to, and it doesn't contain a lot of inspiring material for Sara – but Jean Marsh does her best. Even in a scene where she is required to say nothing, her eyes display the venom and anger she feels towards Mavic Chen. Marsh also saves some class-act dirty looks for the Meddling Monk, which makes me wonder a lot about what we're missing in the audio-only versions. Sara Kingdom can kill you with her eyes!

The Doctor is magnificent in this one. When he turns up, strolling through Egypt with his stick and his panama hat to bellow demands at Chen and the Daleks, who have taken his friends captive, it feels something akin to Matt Smith declaring his intentions to a sky full of aliens. For once, the Doctor has something to hold the Daleks hostage with, and it's clear he likes the power. Sadly, he has to give up the Taranium Core to save Sara and Steven's lives...

> **Sara** (*devastated*): But that means the Daleks have won. There's nothing to stop them now.

Not so fast – the Doctor has stolen the Monk's directional controller! There is a rare moment of delighted laughter breaking the tension between the three travelers as they realize they actually do have a chance now to return to Kembel and finish what they started. It's so strange to see Sara laugh – and of course, it's not comedy policemen or

Hollywood slapstick that made it happen. It's the possibility of destroying the Daleks forever.

Episode Eleven ("The Abandoned Planet"): In which Sara doesn't push Mavic Chen off a cliff...

On Kembel, the Doctor is determined to defeat the Daleks and make up for letting them have the Taranium Core. Separated from him, Sara's commitment to the mission becomes more intense. She is ruthlessly pragmatic, insisting Steven teach her to use the "power impulse compass" he is using, because if something happens to him, she will need that skill. "Oh you're so cheerful, aren't you?", Steven tells her.

Sara pushes ahead, determined to get to the city, while Steven advises caution. It's clear that Dennis Spooner has (finally) remembered that while the Doctor is committed to defeating the Daleks, and Steven is "the action hero," this is Sara's story and she is the one with the greatest emotional stake in the proceedings.

> **Steven:** Just a minute.
> **Sara:** Why? *We've got to defeat the Daleks.*
> **Steven:** *We've got to try to defeat the Daleks.* If you and I just charge in there, what chance do you think we've got against the greatest war force ever assembled?
> **Sara:** Oh, for heaven's sake, we'll go carefully. Look, Steven, just because the Doctor isn't here, don't think that you're the only one who can outwit the Daleks.

Mavic Chen, locked in a cell with the other delegates because the Daleks don't like him anymore, assumes that Kingdom is still loyal to him, having apparently missed all of the dirty looks she had been shooting him on their prior encounters.

Actually, everyone responsible for this story (except possibly Jean Marsh) seems to have forgotten that Sara has a specific grudge against Chen. This, combined with Sara's general stoicism and restraint, means we don't get a whole lot of emotional pay-off in this reunion.

It's Steven who shouts at Chen, while Sara calmly suggests that the delegates should all be released in order that they can mobilize a force against the Daleks. She continues to not speak to Chen even while provoked quite sorely by him, with only the Peter Purves audio narration providing us with her reaction: *"Sara stares at him impassively, unmoved."*

When Chen's ship appears to blow up, Sara's concern is that he now can't inform Earth about the danger of the Daleks. It's good that the fate of the solar system is more important to her than her own personal revenge, but a little frustrating.

When Chen turns up again, having faked his own death, Sara finally displays emotion, her voice shaking with anger and shock on the words "You're alive!" Such is the power of all that prior restraint that this feels like a significant moment, but I remain a bit disappointed that she didn't push him off a cliff or into a carnivorous plant at this point.

Episode Twelve ("The Destruction of Time"): In which Sara Kingdom dies at the end...

So, we have to accept that the confrontation between Sara Kingdom and Mavic Chen is never going to happen. She has written him off as mad, and irrelevant. Sara's focus, and her final path towards redemption, is all about defeating the Daleks.[63]

The Doctor activates the Time Destructor to destroy the Daleks, and sends Steven and Sara back to the TARDIS. Steven knows his place and obeys the Doctor, but Sara can't accept fleeing to safety when she could be of use.

She wants to help the Doctor, but more importantly she doesn't trust him enough to let him make the big decisions for her. This is consistent with Sara's journey so far – she has been willing to travel in the TARDIS and play the part of companion, but when it comes down to it, Sara Kingdom is her own woman.

> **Sara:** Wait! Steven, we can't just leave him.
> **Steven:** The Doctor knows what he's doing. At least, I think he does.
> **Sara:** All we're doing is running to save our own lives. If anything goes wrong and the Daleks recapture the Time Destructor, we'll have failed forever.
> **Steven:** I know what you're saying. Now, I'd go back too if I thought it would help. Whatever he's doing, he's doing because he thinks it's the best way. Now come on!

Steven runs towards the safety of the TARDIS. Sara pretends to agree with him, and runs back to the Doctor at the first opportunity.

As the Time Destructor goes into overdrive, the Doctor and Sara both age impossibly quickly, struggling towards the TARDIS. The Doctor falls

---

63 Mavic Chen's execution by the Daleks, when it finally comes, is a deeply unsatisfying experience on audio – and those listeners who like me are frustrated at the lack of resolution between Chen and Sara would probably enjoy the Big Finish audio *The Guardian of the Solar System* by Simon Guerrier, performed by Jean Marsh.

more than once, and Sara uses her remaining strength to help him until she finally dies.

Steven, watching this on the scanner, runs out to them, and watches Sara's body fall to dust before his eyes. He is also affected by the ageing effects of the Time Destructor, but attempts to smash it, then flicks a switch *which actually as it turns out reverses the process why did the Doctor not do that OMG?*

I feel it worth noting that Steven was only able to save the Doctor here because Sara fixed the scanner back in the Christmas episode. Thank you and goodnight.

> **The Doctor:** Thank you, my friend. Thank you, Steven. By chance you reversed the Time Destructor. Instead of Time rushing forward, it's now racing back.

The Daleks are destroyed by the Time Destructor while the Doctor and Steven stay safe in the TARDIS, their relative youth restored. As they emerge (after the Taranium Core has burned out), the Doctor is inappropriately delighted with their achievement, chuckling to himself at the sight of Daleks destroyed by their own machine. Steven, however, is devastated and has to regularly remind the Doctor to be sad instead of cheerful.

> **Steven:** I wish Sara could have seen the end.
> **The Doctor:** Yes, my boy. So do I. You know, Steven, the one thing that Sara lived for was to see the total destruction of the Daleks. Well, now it's all over. Without her help this could never have been achieved, hmm. (chuckles)
> **Steven:** What is it?
> **The Doctor:** Million of years of progress. Reversed back. That's all that remains of a Dalek! (chuckles again)
> **Steven:** Let's go, Doctor. I've seen enough of this place.
> **The Doctor** *(inappropriately perky)*: Well, my boy, we finally rid this planet of Daleks!
> **Steven** *(utterly miserable)*: Bret! Katarina! Sara...
> **The Doctor** *(finally remembering to be sad too)*: What a waste. What a terrible waste.

Considering the violent nature of the character upon her introduction, and regardless of the slightly shonky logic in the use of the Time Destructor at the end, death feels like a fitting end to Sara Kingdom's storyarc. Her choices in this final episode were different to Steven's and evolved naturally from their characters – he defaulted to obeying the Doctor and she did not. Steven was originally cast, like Ian before him as a "heroic bloke" to balance out the more infirm, elderly character of the Doctor, and to punch things when necessary – but here, it's Sara who gets to be the hero.

Heroes die at the end. The mythological sagas tell us this. It's hard to write death-as-redemption when your hero is a woman, because so many female characters are killed in a "women in refrigerators" way (early in the story, gratuitously, in service to a male narrative), and readers are now cynical and exhausted about the many, many dead women that litter the floor of science fiction.

Katarina was undeniably "fridged" – her death was hasty and unnecessary. It was used for shock value, to emotionally bond the men around her, and was a gratuitous moment far too early in the story. But this is not what happened with Sara.

If she had continued as a companion for another year or so, relaxing and adventuring with Steven and the Doctor, maybe leaving unexpectedly during *The War Machines*, or finding a husband on the planet of *The Savages*, Sara's character would be far less memorable, and it's likely that her violent origin would have been muted or forgotten.

Dying at the end, in service to their own narrative, is something we need to let female heroes do sometimes. Ripley and Buffy both swandived to their doom, choosing it for themselves (regardless of what happened next) and Xena submitted to that final heroic sacrifice when her show came to an end.

Sara Kingdom was there before any of them, stealing the show from the male regulars with a valiant death that brought a satisfying conclusion to the story, and made it clear who had actually been the protagonist of this particular *Doctor Who* story all along.

A Question of Emphasis:
The Doctor as Companion

Amal El-Mohtar is the Nebula-nominated author of *The Honey Month*, a collection of short stories and poems written to the taste of 28 different kinds of honey. She is a three-time winner of the Rhysling Award for Best Short Poem, and edits *Goblin Fruit*, an online quarterly dedicated to fantastical poetry. Her work has appeared in multiple magazines and anthologies, including *Lightspeed*, *Apex*, *Strange Horizons*, *Kaleidoscope: Diverse YA Science Fiction & Fantasy Stories* (Twelfth Planet Press), *Glitter & Mayhem* (Apex Books) and *Steampunk III: Steampunk Revolution* (Tachyon). She currently lives in Ottawa. You can find her online at amalelmohtar.com. Incredibly, despite having also contributed essays to *Chicks Unravel Time* and *Queers Dig Time Lords*, she has yet to run out of things to say about *Doctor Who*.

For roughly the first 14 years of my *Doctor Who* fandom, I had no idea it was a television show. From ages seven to 21, I was under the impression that the stories I'd discovered about a time-traveling gentleman and his interesting friends existed nowhere outside my cousin's bookshelves in a tiny mountain village in Lebanon, nestled between volumes of *Asterix and Obelix* and Enid Blyton's *The Six Bad Boys*.

These characters were words before they were people – and being of a somewhat synaesthetic bent, the words *were* the characters. The Doctor in my head quickly outgrew the cartoonishly rendered Jon Pertwee on the cover of Terrance Dicks' novelizations to become a combination of letters and light, wisdom and activity, an irrepressible narrative force pushing through a trochee – a *DOC*-tor in browns and brilliance, kind and understanding if a bit insufferable at times. Jo Grant was very different: *Jo* was pure bright pale gold with a refreshingly sour tang, the feel of grapefruit peel with something kind of rosy underneath – probably a consequence of having first met her on Spiridon, where she was nursed to health with unfamiliar fruit.

The Brigadier was something else again.

The Brigadier's implacability, his humor, his banter with the Doctor, his sputtering confusion at the insubordination of a police officer utterly indifferent to his military rank – all this was green and gold to me, with the word that is "Brigadier" resolving itself into some kind of Praetorian helmet in my imagination, over light hair and a clean-shaven face that looked nothing at all like Nicholas Courtney (nor Arthur Darvill for that matter – the nose was nothing like).

It makes perfect sense to me that I had him all wrong, though, because I misread the word "Brigadier" for years.

Even now, writing this, I twitch a little and correct myself. The word is pronounced brig-ah-DEER, as anyone who watches the show or has a passing knowledge of British military ranking is aware. I, however, absorbing new vocabulary from three different languages while in single digits, read it for a very long time as bri-GAY-dee-er (completely unaware of the fact that I was foreshadowing years of slash fic). The Brigadier joined the company of such words as "melancholy" (me-LANK-o-lee) and "awry" (AW-ree) that I read frequently without ever hearing pronounced, and so cemented themselves in my head with emPHAses on the wrong sylLABles.

It now occurs to me that my childhood misreading could well serve as a metaphor for the ways in which we have come to perceive the Doctors and their companions. For the last five decades, we've been encouraged to read the Doctor as the constant, the default, while the companions come and go more often than his faces; the companions are good for kicking off a plot, for assisting, for getting into trouble, for not staying put or doing as they're told. But frankly, so is the Doctor; surely he is as much a strange and catalytic appendage to their lives as they are to his? And yet, we have not usually been encouraged to think of the Doctor as *their* companion – though increasingly, from what I've seen, the show's emphasis has been slowly transferred from him to the lives of those around him.

We only ever see the third Doctor's Brigadier in his professional capacity. He is simultaneously assistant and obstacle, always in uniform, always self-assured and patient in the face of the Doctor's contemptuous rages. He is also, in many ways, the anti-companion: utterly uninterested in the mysteries of outer space or the potential for scientific discovery ("just once, I'd like to meet an alien race that isn't immune to bullets"), far too fond of weapons as a first resort ("small arms, grenades, nothing very substantial") and expecting the Doctor to follow where he leads rather than the other way around. But, on the other hand, he is totally unintimidated by the Master ("Nice to see you again!", *punch*) and a character of unimpeachable integrity. He is no starry-eyed traveler, but he is fully as committed to protecting the Earth and its inhabitants as the Doctor. He was not chosen by the Doctor; he was assigned to him. We know very little about his family or life outside UNIT, presuming he even has one; we almost always see him with his troops or with the Doctor. During his character-establishing years of active service within UNIT, the closest we get to seeing his personal life is when he answers his phone from bed in *The Daemons*. It isn't until his very last appearance on *Doctor Who* (in *Battlefield*) that we see him picking cherry trees for his garden with his wife, and it was only after Nicholas Courtney's passing that the Brigadier's daughter, Kate, was introduced to the TV masses in 2013.

Nor is the Brigadier overawed by the Doctor. The Doctor is, variously, a resource, a subordinate, an alien, a scientist and a friend; we almost never see the unflappable Brigadier dazzled or intimidated by the Doctor and his world. Confronted with indestructible winged gargoyles in *The Daemons*, the Brigadier disinterestedly tosses off a "chap with the wings, five rounds rapid" – a line made immortal by the sheer nonchalance of it. In fact, the Brigadier's casual disdain for non-human life leads one to suspect that if the Doctor were not working for UNIT, the Brigadier would just as serenely direct rapid rounds at the chap with the lace cuffs and satin-lined cape.

Indeed, it is fascinating to me that in the show's initial incarnation, the Doctor is its moral compass, showing up humanity's cruelties, follies and inadequacies with his alien superiority. The contrast is particularly stark during Jon Pertwee's time with UNIT, when the Doctor and the Brigadier come to respectively represent the butting heads of pacifism and militarization, intellect and brute strength, individuality and conformity. The various companions' perspectives are valued in relation to their alignment with the Doctor's: thus Captain Yates and the Brigadier, following orders from on high, are far more likely to be wrong about an alien menace, mysterious village or crashed spaceship than Jo Grant, whose loyalty seems given first to the Doctor and then to UNIT.

Compare all this to the companions in New *Who*. Rose, Mickey, Martha and Donna all have families who are important to them, whom they struggle to protect, and who form the emotional core of several episodes: *Father's Day*, *Rise of the Cybermen*, *The Sound of Drums* and *Turn Left* come to mind. Amy changes the universe to get first Rory and then her parents back; Madame Vastra, Jenny, and Strax are a family unto themselves; and Clara, in addition to always being at the center of families through her recurring role as a governess, has a life story that is able to ransom a planet for a symbolic leaf in *The Rings of Akhaten*.

Admittedly, Russell T Davies and Steven Moffat have differed in their approaches to companions: in Davies' run, we get regular people – a shop girl, a medical student, a temp – who rise to the occasion through the Doctor's encouragement; with Moffat, every companion is a mystery to solve. From Amy's affinity with the Crack in Time to the riddle of River Song to Clara's Impossibility, Moffat requires the companions to justify the Doctor's interest in them through their very existence, while under Davies' management the show's premise was that any ordinary person can become a hero. But in both cases, the show's overall focus, the foregrounded arcs, have tended to be about the companions.

Increasingly, the show has been shifting its emphasis away from the Doctor and toward the companions. More and more, we are supposed to identify with the companions first – with that desire to be taken away and shown marvels, whisked and wanted and told that we are important in a cosmic way, that we too can be at the centre of grand things, of history and futurity and the hearts of dying stars. But in the show's new formulation, the Doctor wants these things too; he repeatedly tells his companions that he needs them in order to see the world afresh, to see it through their eyes. He also, crucially, and in a sharp break with tradition, needs their wondering gazes to be able to see him as something that isn't monstrous – something that is, instead, "very very old, and very kind," as Amy says to him in *The Beast Below*. "You need someone to stop you," observes Donna Noble; "you shouldn't travel alone," says Amy. The Doctor, rather than being the moral bedrock of the show, the certainty around which the narrative is organized, is made fluid, subject to the vagaries of circumstance and the mitigating power of his companions' gazes.

Ultimately, this era's companions don't need the Doctor to feel special, to be morally guided, or to improve as people – he needs them. And as the narrative tide turns, as the show's focus centers more and more on the lives of the extraordinary individuals whom the Doctor invites into the TARDIS, we might be forgiven for thinking that it is the Doctor who is, in truth, the companion – the imaginary friend, the misread syllable. The Doctor no longer lends the companions a feeling of greatness: he diagnoses their greatness. He confesses himself drawn to the curious, the inexplicable, the mysterious – all the qualities that originally drew the companions to him.

And, closing the circle, he strives to live up to them.

Chicks Dig Gaming

Edited by Jennifer Brozek, Robert Smith? and Lars Pearson

Out Now...
ISBN: 978-1935234180
Retail Price: $14.95. Also available on Kindle, Nook, Kobo and iTunes.

Companion Piece
Credits

Publisher / Editor-in-Chief
Lars Pearson

Design Manager / Senior Editor
Christa Dickson

Associate Editor
Joshua Wilson

Designer (Companion Piece)
Adam Holt

The publisher wishes to thank...
A huge thank you to Liz and Liz, for doing so much of this book's heavy lifting. Editors are always the starship captains of these endeavors while we Starfleet admirals – while still part of the process – bark out orders from relative positions of safety, and their work is much appreciated. Thanks also to Katy Shuttleworth, for yet-another clever and beguiling cover; all of our essayists, for such intriguing and varied points of view; Christa Dickson; Adam Holt; Shawne Kleckner; Robert Smith?; Lynne M. Thomas; Josh Wilson; and that nice lady who sends me newspaper articles.

mad norwegian press

1150 46th Street
Des Moines, Iowa 50311
madnorwegian@gmail.com
www.madnorwegian.com

And please join the Mad Norwegian Press group on Facebook!